ALFA ROMEO GIULIA

TECHNICAL MANUAL FOR 1969 AND ONWARDS SPICA FUEL INJECTED MODELS

© 2019 Veloce Enterprises Inc., San Antonio, Texas USA
All rights reserved. This work may not be reproduced or transmitted in any form without the express consent of the publisher

Introduction

Welcome to the world of digital publishing ~ the book you now hold in your hand, was printed using the latest state of the art digital technology. The advent of print-on-demand has forever changed the publishing process, never has information been so accessible and it is our hope that this book serves your informational needs for years to come. If this is your first exposure to digital publishing, we hope that you are pleased with the results. Many more titles of interest to the classic automobile and motorcycle enthusiast, collector and restorer are available via our website at www.VelocePress.com. We hope that you find this title as interesting as we do.

Note from the Publisher

The information presented is true and complete to the best of our knowledge. All recommendations are made without any guarantees on the part of the author or the publisher, who also disclaim all liability incurred with the use of this information.

Trademarks

We recognize that some words, model names and designations, for example, mentioned herein are the property of the trademark holder. We use them for identification purposes only. This is not an official publication.

Information on the use of this Publication

This manual is an invaluable resource for those interested in performing their own maintenance. However, in today's information age we are constantly subject to changes in common practice, new technology, availability of improved materials and increased awareness of chemical toxicity. As such, it is advised that the user consult with an experienced professional prior to undertaking any procedure described herein. While every care has been taken to ensure correctness of information, it is obviously not possible to guarantee complete freedom from errors or omissions or to accept liability arising from such errors or omissions. Therefore, any individual that uses the information contained within, or elects to perform or participate in do-it-yourself repairs or modifications acknowledges that there is a risk factor involved and that the publisher or its associates cannot be held responsible for personal injury or property damage resulting from the use of the information or the outcome of such procedures.

Warning!

One final word of advice, this publication is intended to be used as a reference guide, and when in doubt the reader should consult with a qualified technician.

NOTES ON THE USE OF THIS MANUAL

Page Numbering

As each of the individual publications in this manual have their own index, the page numbers corresponding to that index are printed to the top corner of each page. The number printed to the center bottom of the page is the page number within the book.

Contents

SPICA Fuel Injection: It should be noted that Alfa Romeo never published an 'all inclusive' manual for cars fitted with the SPICA Fuel injection system. The six separate publications included in this manual are the only documents that were ever issued by the factory that contain the appropriate maintenance, repair, service, adjustment and trouble shooting information for the SPICA Fuel Injection system.

While these publications were issued under a variety of different titles, they would be considered to be predominately 'Technical Maintenance & Specifications Manuals'. They were also intended to be used in conjunction with the individual factory 'Mechanical Repair' publications as they provide model specific technical information and specifications. This manual is a compilation of the factory 'Technical' publications listed below and, while the list is not inclusive, the publications were selected as being representative for the 1750cc and 2000cc series of SPICA fuel injected Alfa Romeo Giulia models.

Title / Models	Publication date / Number		Book Pages
Technical Characteristics and Principal Inspection Specifications: 1750 Berlina, 1750 GT Veloce, 1750 Spider Veloce	April 1969	1502	Pages 1 - 34
Instruction and Maintenance Manual for Fuel Injection Models USA: 1750 All Models USA	October 1969	1470	Pages 35 - 78
Instruction and Maintenance Manual for Fuel Injection Models USA: 1750 All Models USA	February 1971	1671	Pages 79 - 124
Instruction and Maintenance Manual for Fuel Injection Models USA: 2000 All Models USA	1972		Pages 125 - 174
Technical Characteristics and Principal Inspection Specifications: 2000 Berlina, 2000 GT Veloce, 2000 Spider Veloce	May 1973	2106	Pages 175 - 214
Instruction and Maintenance Manual for Fuel Injection Models USA: 2000 All models USA Alfetta	July 1975	2374	Pages 215 – 265

NOTE: The reader is encouraged to review the entire manual as the level of detail on a particular subject varies throughout the individual publications.

Measurements & Values

The metric system is the primary measurement method used in both the manufacture of these vehicles and in the production of the factory 'Mechanical Repair' and 'Technical' publications. As such, the reader is urged to verify that the conversion of those metric measurements to other forms of measurement is correct. All measurements and values contained within this compilation of the factory publications are made without any guarantees on behalf of the publisher, who also disclaims any and all liability incurred with the use of this manual.

The importance of using the Alfa Romeo 'Mechanical Repair' publications in conjunction with this Manual

As noted previously, Alfa Romeo also issued 'Mechanical Repair' publications that that were focused on the overhaul and service of various mechanical and electrical components. As these 'Mechanical Repair' publications were meant to be used in conjunction with the 'Technical' publications, we feel it is important that the reader is made aware of the associated Workshop Manual that compliments this Technical Manual.

Alfa Romeo Giulia Workshop Manual 1962-1975 All Models 1300cc, 1600cc, 1750cc & 2000cc
ISBN 9781588502254

This 338 page manual was compiled using data from seven of those individual factory 'Mechanical Repair' publications plus a number of additional pages of maintenance, repair, overhaul and wiring diagrams that were not included in the original factory publications. Consequently, it provides a generic 'Workshop Manual' for the repair and overhaul of the 1965-1971 Giulia series of automobiles. However, as the 1962-1975 series of Alfa models shared many of the same mechanical components, these 'Mechanical Repair' publications are also of use to owners of both the earlier and later models. For example, even though the engines were of four different capacities they are sufficiently alike for a single set of instructions to suffice for their maintenance and overhaul. The combination of the manual above, when used in conjunction with this Technical Manual, will provide a comprehensive 'Workshop Manual' for the SPICA fuel injected series of Alfa Giulia.

The additional pages in this manual include maintenance and repair information on:

Drum brakes, hydraulic braking system, Dunlop disc brakes and additional information on ATE disc brakes. Front hubs, shock absorbers and stabilizer rod, ZF steering box, Burman steering box, steering linkage and steering adjustments. Electrical components including control box, regulator, generator, starter motor, windscreen wiper motor (both Bosch & Marelli), lamps and lighting and wiring diagrams for 14 different models.

The factory 'Mechanical Repair' publications included in this compilation are:

(1) **Engine, Clutch & Gearbox Manual for the 1600 Giulia TI, Sprint GT & TI Super.**
(First printed October 1964 this is the third printing dated December 1968 Publication No. 1008-R2).

(2) **Propeller Shaft, Rear Axle & Suspension for the Giulia 1300, 1300TI the Giulia 1600 TI Super, Sprint GT, GTC, TI, Super, Sprint GT Veloce & Spider 1600.**
(First printed October 1966 this is the fourth printing dated April 1971 Publication No. 1222-R3).

(3) **ATE Disc Brakes all Models, as appropriate.**
(First printed July 1966 this is the second printing dated November 1969 Publication No. 1202-R1).

(4) **Wheel, Suspension & Front End Geometry, for all Giulia and 1750 Models plus 2000 models amendment.**
(This May 1970 Publication No.1507 includes the October 1977 printing of the December 1971 amendment No. 1838-R2 for the 2000 models - Only sections that are 'owner appropriate' are included).

(5) **Electrical for the 1600 Giulia Super, 1750 Berlina, 1750 GT Veloce & 1750 Spider Veloce.**
(September 1969 Publication No. 1384 - Only sections that are 'owner appropriate' are included).

(6) **Air Conditioning all Models, as appropriate.**
(October 1972 Publication No.1969).

(7) **Body, for all Giulia and 1750 Models** - Only sections that are 'owner appropriate' are included.
(September 1970 Publication No.1570).

Alfa Romeo Giulia Technical Manual for 1962 and onwards Carbureted Models
ISBN 9781588502261

Owners of the carbureted equipped cars are directed to the above publication which combines a selection of the appropriate factory 'Technical' publications into a single manual for the 1300cc, 1600cc and 1750cc series of carbureted Giulia models.

NOTES

1750 Berlina
1750 GT Veloce
1750 Spider Veloce

FUEL INJECTION MODELS

U.S.A. VERSION

technical characteristics and principal inspection specifications

CONTENTS

TECHNICAL CHARACTERISTICS

PRINCIPAL CHARACTERISTIC DATA	Page	1
Performance	"	1
Tires	"	2
Fuel, oil and coolant	"	2
Lubricants	"	2
Injection system	"	3
Valve timing	"	6
Ignition	"	6
Spark plugs	"	6
Cooling system	"	7
Electrical equipment	"	10
Bulb's wattage	"	10
Tightening torque specifications	"	11

MAJOR INSPECTION SPECIFICATIONS

Camshafts	Page	13
Valves and valve guides	"	13
Valve seats	"	13
Valve cups	"	14
Valve springs	"	14
Connecting rods	"	14
Piston pins	"	14
Piston pin holes	"	14
Pistons and piston rings	"	15
Cylinder barrels	"	15
Crankshaft	"	16
Clutch	"	17
Transmission	"	18
Rear axle and suspension	"	19
Front suspension	"	20
Brakes	"	21

WHEEL ALIGNMENT

Checking of wheel angles and car "trim" under static load	Page	23

1750 GT VELOCE and 1750 SPIDER VELOCE VARIANTS .... Page 27

TECHNICAL CHARACTERISTICS

PRINCIPAL CHARACTERISTIC DATA

Number of cylinders	4
Bore	80 mm. (3.15")
Stroke	88.5 mm. (3.48")
Total cylinder displacement	1779 cc.
Max. power at 5,500 rpm	SAE 132 HP
Front track	1324 mm. (52.1")
Rear track	1274 mm. (50.1")
Wheelbase	2570 mm. (101.1")
Min. turning circle	11100 mm. (437")
Overall length	4390 mm. (172.7")
Overall width	1565 mm. (61.6")
Overall height (unladen)	1430 mm. (56.3")
Curb weight	1110 Kg. (2442 lbs)
Number of seats	4
Tires 165 x 14	PIRELLI cinturato SR / KLEBER COLOMBES V 10 / MICHELIN ZX

PERFORMANCE

With 41 : 9 final drive

Gear	After breaking in mph
1st	28
2nd	46
3rd	68
4th	91
5th	112
Rev.	30

Oil pressures with hot engine - psi
- Engine running fast .... minimum 50, maximum 65-70
- Engine idling .... minimum 7-14

W A R N I N G: Check that alternator warning light goes off as soon as the engine exceeds idling.

Tires

Recommended tire pressure (cold) in psi at a maximum-loaded vehicle weight of 3340 lbs

Make	Front	Rear
Pirelli	22	23
Michelin	26	26
Kleber Colombes	24	29

Note: For sustained speeds exceeding the limits specified by Federal regulations, inflate to the following pressures:

Michelin	28	31
Kleber Colombes	27	31

Fuel, oil and coolant

Cooling system:

Alfa Romeo coolant mixture . . . . abt. 2.5 gals

Fuel . . . . " 12 gals
(For best engine performance the use of premium grade fuel is advised)

Fuel reserve . . . . " 1.6-1.8 gals

Oil
- Engine (pan and filter) when full * . . . . " 7.1 qts
- danger level . . . . " 4.75 qts
- Transmission . . . . " 3.8 pts
- Differential . . . . " 3.0 pts
- Steering box . . . . " .6 pt

* This quantity is that needed for regular changing. The total amount of oil in the circuit (pan, filter and passages) is . . . . 7.8 qts

It is recommended to top up with the same type of oil as that in the engine.

Recommended lubricants

Part	Classification	Commercial equivalents AGIP	SHELL	ESSO
Engine	SAE 20 W/40 API MS	AGIP F.1 Supermotoroil Multigrade 20 W/40	SHELL Super Motor Oil 10 W/30	UNIFLO Motor Oil 10 W - 20 W - 40
Transmission Steering box and differential	SAE 90 API EP	AGIP F.1 Rotra Hypoid SAE 90	SHELL Spirax 90 EP	ESSO Gear Oil GX 90
Drive shaft universal joints and slip yoke	NLGI 1	AGIP F.1 Grease 15	SHELL Retinax G	
Front wheel bearings (see maintenance schedule)	NLGI 2/3	AGIP F.1 Grease 33 FD	SHELL Retinax AX	

API - American Petroleum Institute
NLGI - National Lubricating Grease Institute
SAE - Society of Automotive Engineers

Fuel injection

Fuel is supplied to the engine by injection into the intake port of each cylinder in quantities exactly metered in accordance with the opening of throttles and RPM range.

The metering device, or "control unit", consists mainly of a barrel-shaped cam which slides automatically lengthwise as the RPM varies and rotates about its axis exactly timed with the opening of throttles.

The lift of a follower, moving closely against the cam contour, controls the delivery of the injection pump, without any lag in respect to the demand of power.

On deceleration, the fuel delivery is automatically cut off thus permitting not only to eliminate the unburned gases in a condition remarkably critical for the exhaust emission levels, but also to affect favorably the fuel consumption.

The control unit also includes suitable compensating devices which gives proper corrections for atmospheric pressure, engine and room temperature, cold starting and initial running.

For more detailed directions on the use, maintenance, testing and adjustment of the injection system, refer to the "Instructions and Maintenance manual".

Inspection specifications

Injection pump:

SPICA AIBB 4 C.S. 75

Injector rating:

new : 360-400 psi
used : > 260 psi

Timing the injection pump with the engine

At 70° BTDC of the induction stroke, the timing marks on the injection pump must be aligned.

Air induction system

The filtered air enters the engine thru four intake ports each with a throttle valve.

The idling air (throttle valves closed) is fed thru a separate circuit which, starting from the air cleaner connects to the intake ports downstream of the throttle valves and includes the idle equalizers "12".

The accelerator pedal is mechanically linked thru the rods "9", "10" and the relay crank "8" to both the throttle valve lever and the control unit lever. Therefore, any position of the accelerator pedal corresponds to an exact position of throttle valve and control unit levers.

Fuel feed system

Inserting the key in the ignition switch "16" and rotating clockwise to the first click will operate the electric pump "3". The gasoline flows from the tank "1" thru tank filter "2" and main filter "4" and feeds the injection pump "5".

The excess fuel, acting also as a coolant for the injection pump, before returning to the tank, passes thru a calibrated orifice which regulates the fuel pressure within the injection pump. A pressure switch "17" inserted in the delivery pipe will switch on the warning light "18" on dashboard if a pressure drop occurs in fuel lines.

A pressure relief valve in the main filter limits the fuel pump outlet pressure bypassing fuel to the recovery pipe.

Crankcase ventilating system

The exhaust gases and the oil vapors developed during engine operation collect in the camshaft cover; from here they are sucked in the combustion chambers and burned.

The crankcase ventilating system controls gases both at high engine RPMs and at idling speed when the throttles are closed.

When the throttles are fully opened the vapors flow thru the hoses to the oil separator "14" and to the manifold chamber communicating with the intake ports.

When the throttles are partially closed, the secondary circuit comes into operation; such a circuit starts from the oil separator "14" and conveys unburned gases and vapors directly into the intake ports downstream of the throttles by means of the equalizers "12" provided with calibrated orifices. The oil collected in the separator returns to the pan via a suitable hose.

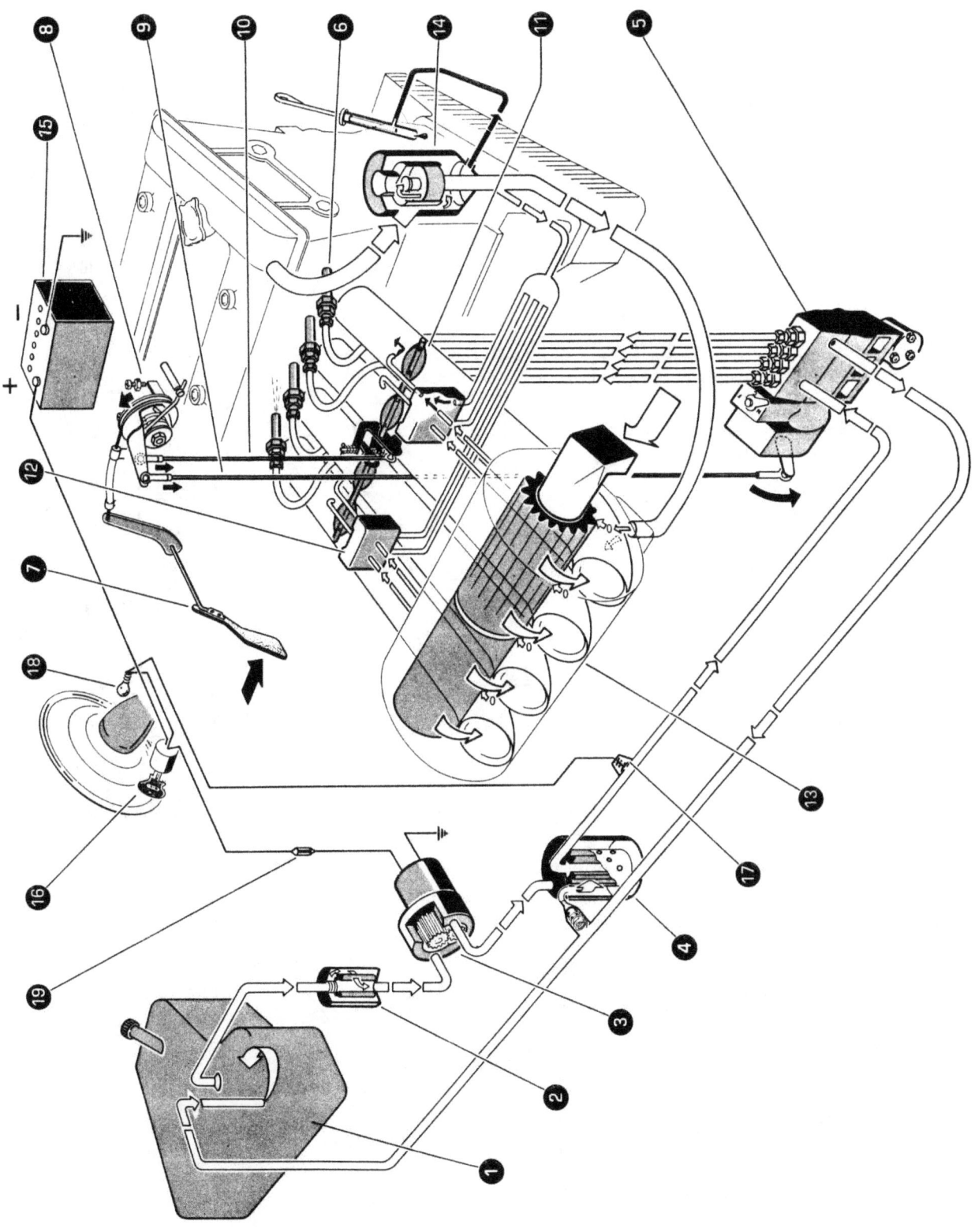

Checking of valve opening and closing angles

Clearance (with cold engine) between the unlobed profile of cam and the valve cup ceiling
- intake ...... .475 to .500 mm (.0187 to .0197")
- exhaust ...... .525 to .550 mm (.0206 to .0216")

Opening of intake valve
- lift of cup .... .20 mm (.008")
- corresponding to an angle (before TDC) ...... 18° 30' ± 1° 30'

Closing of intake valve
- lift of cup .... .20 mm (.008")
- corresponding to an angle (after BDC) ...... 42° 30' ± 1° 30'

Opening of exhaust valve
- lift of cup .... .15 mm (.006")
- corresponding to an angle (before BDC) ...... 42° 30' ± 1° 30'

Closing of exhaust valve
- lift of cup .... .15 mm (.006")
- corresponding to an angle (after TDC) ...... 18° 30' ± 1° 30'

ANGLE VALUES OF THE ACTUAL DIAGRAM OF VALVE TIMING SYSTEM WITH COLD ENGINE
(clockwise rotation direction of the crankshaft as seen from the front end)

- opening of intake valve (before TDC) .... 36° 50'
- closing of intake valve (after BDC) .... 60° 50'
- opening of exhaust valve (before BDC) .... 54° 10'
- closing of exhaust valve (after TDC) .... 30° 10'
- induction stroke .... 277° 40'
- exhaust stroke .... 264° 20'

IGNITION

Firing order: 1 - 3 - 4 - 2 (no. 1 cylinder is that at the fan side)

IGNITION DISTRIBUTOR TIMING

Opening of contact points of ignition distributor S = .43 to .48 mm (.017 to .019")
The distributor is correctly fitted when the oiler is toward the engine.

Idle ignition	Maximum advance M Before T D C
1° / 3° A T D C	31° / 37° at 5000 rpm

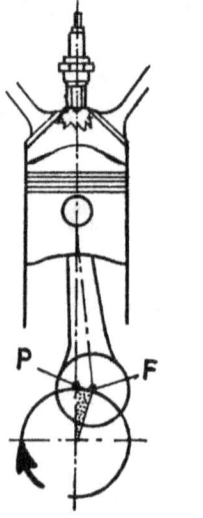
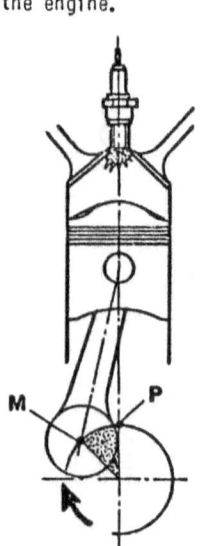

P = T.D.C.
F = Idle ignition
M = Maximum advance

SPARK PLUGS

Lodge HL

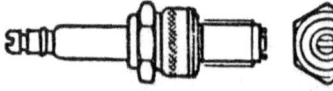

COOLING SYSTEM

The cooling circuit is provided with a compensating reservoir containing a special ALFA ROMEO Coolant Mixture which gives full protection against freezing down to -22°F.

TO ENSURE THE EFFICIENT OPERATION OF THE COOLING SYSTEM
THE FOLLOWING PROCEDURE SHOULD BE OBSERVED.

Occasionally, check level of coolant in the reservoir: this should be done exclusively with a cold engine as with a hot engine the level may increase remarkably, even after stopping the engine.

The level of mixture in the reservoir should never fall below the "Min" or exceed the "Max".

To top up the reservoir use the specified Coolant Mixture.

If too frequent a topping up is required, check the cooling system for damage.

Should sudden and excessive leaks be experienced from the system, the use of fresh water is provisionally allowed. To replenish the circuit follow the directions given on next page.

WARNING

Never remove radiator plug unless absolutely necessary; in any case, to avoid severe injuries, wait that the liquid is cooled down to ambient temperature.

Changing the coolant mixture

Every 18,000 mi - 30,000 Kms (or once a year whichever comes first) flush the circuit and renew the coolant mixture. (See page 8).

IMPORTANT NOTE

In places where the temperature falls below -22°F the antifreeze mixture can be made stronger by varying its concentration.

To this end, a certain amount of mixture shall be drained off the circuit and replaced by the same quantity of "ALFA ROMEO Antifreeze" drawn from suitable containers.

The quantities of antifreeze to be added to radiator and reservoir depending on the lowest anticipated temperature are the following:

Temperature	Quantity of ALFA ROMEO coolant Mixture to be replaced with an equal quantity of "ALFA ROMEO Antifreeze"		
	Radiator	Reservoir	Total
-24°F	400 cc	100 cc	500 cc
-33°F	800 cc	200 cc	1000 cc
-38°F	1200 cc	300 cc	1500 cc

Draining and replenishing the system

Proceed as follows:

Draining

- Remove radiator filler plug "1".
- Unscrew the drain plug "3" and the bleed screw "7" on manifold.
- Turn on the heater cock "6".
- Turn on the drain plug "5" on crankcase; let liquid drain off and empty the reservoir "8" by detaching pipe "9". Then reinstall drain plugs "3" and "5" and reconnect the pipe "9" to the reservoir.

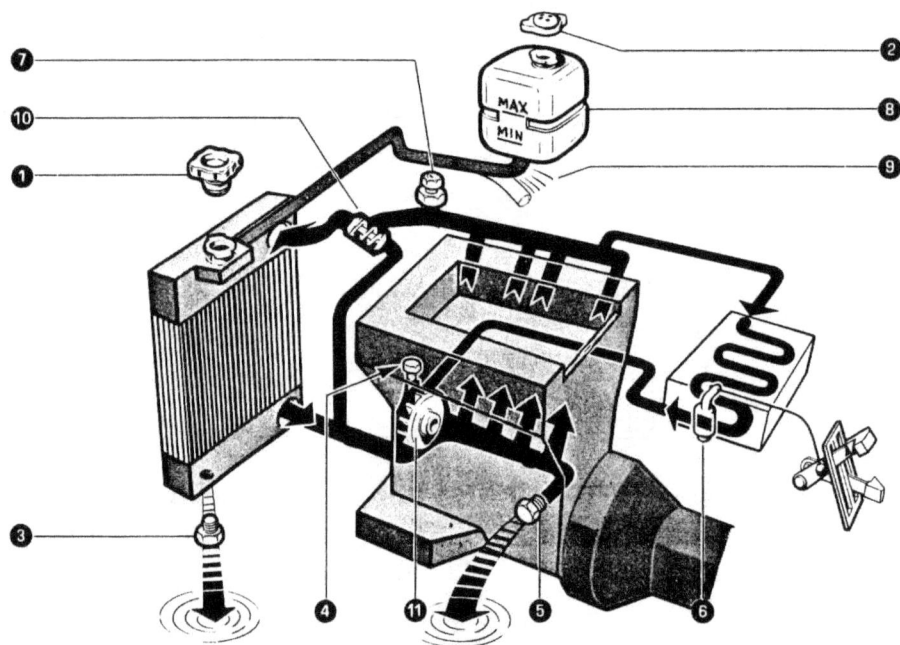

1 Radiator filler plug
2 Reservoir filler plug
3 Radiator drain plug
4 Bleed screw on pump
5 Drain plug on crankcase
6 Heater cock
7 Bleed screw on manifold
8 Reservoir
9 Supply line from reservoir to radiator
10 Thermostat
11 Centrifugal pump

Replenishing

- Remove radiator and reservoir filler plug and turn on the heater cock.
- Open the bleed screw "7" on manifold and "4" on pump.
- Pour coolant mixture through radiator filler port until coolant escapes from bleed screw "4"; then screw in the latter. Go on in adding mixture until it appears at the bleed screw "7" on manifold.
- With the bleed screw on manifold opened and no plug on filler port of radiator, start the engine and keep it idling for a few seconds in order to bleed air completely.
- Close the bleed screw on manifold.
- Add mixture to radiator filler port until full.
- Add mixture also to reservoir until "Max" level is reached.
- Put the filler plugs on reservoir and radiator.

Checking cooling system for proper operation after topping up

After the system has been fully replenished or even topped up owing to drainings for mixture change or for repair, it is advisable to check the system for proper operation as follows:

a) with the circuit closed and the heater cock opened, run the engine until the coolant mixture has reached a temperature of about 80-85°C and keep on idling the engine; in this condition the thermostat opens thus allowing possible air bubbles trapped in the circuit to pass in the radiator and then in the reservoir.

b) let the engine cool down to room temperature in order to allow the mixture in the reservoir to compensate for the air bled off as said above.

c) remove the filler plug and check that radiator is full.

d) fill the reservoir up to "Max" mark.

N.B. - If, when opening the filler plug as in c) above, the radiator is not full, repeat the procedure, keeping the engine running for a longer time at operating temperature (thermostat opened) to bleed all the air from the circuit.
Should the trouble persist, air instead of coolant from reservoir is likely to enter the circuit through some leaking component (radiator filler plug included) in this case, inspect the circuit accordingly, then again repeat the checking procedure.

Electrical equipment

Voltage .... 12 Volts
Battery .... 60 Amp.h

	MARELLI	BOSCH
Alternator		K1 (R,L) 14 V 35 A 20
Voltage regulator		AD 1/14 V
Starting motor		EF (R) 12 V 0,7 PS
Coil		K 12 V
Ignition distributor	S 103 B	
Windshield wiper (2-speed)		WS 4902 AR 5 A (0)

Bulb's wattage

Headlights	sealed beam
Fog lamps	sealed beam
Tail lights - parking & stop	5/21
Front direction indicators and road hazard flashers	21
Tail direction indicators and road hazard flashers	21
Back-up light	21
Front parking lights	5 globular
License plate light	5 globular
Engine compartment light	5 cylindrical
Courtesy light	5 cylindrical
Light in luggage compartment	5 cylindrical
Side marker lights	4 tubular
Lighting on instruments	3 tubular
Blower warning light	3 tubular
Alternator warning light	3 tubular
Parking light warning	3 tubular
High beam warning lights	3 tubular
Fuel reserve warning light	3 tubular
Low fuel pressure warning light	1.2 tubular
Direction indicators and road hazard flashers warning light	1.2 tubular
Low oil pressure warning light	1.2 tubular
Service brake warning light	1.2 tubular

Tightening torque specifications

ENGINE - TRANSMISSION UNIT		Kgm.	lb. ft	Manner of tightening
Cylinder head nuts *	Inspection — when cold	7.2 to 7.4	52.1 to 53.5	Slacken in proper sequence, the nuts by one and one half turn and lubetorque
	Inspection — when hot	7.6 to 7.7	55.0 to 55.7	Warm up the engine and when hot retighten without unscrewing
	After repairing — when cold	7.2 to 7.4	52.1 to 53.5	Retighten with lube
	After repairing — when hot	7.6 to 7.7	55.0 to 55.7	Warm up the engine by actually driving the car and when hot retighten without unscrewing
	After repairing — when cold	7.2 to 7.4	52.1 to 53.5	After tested the car, slacken, when cold and in proper sequence, the nuts by one and one half turn and lubetorque
Spark plugs		2.5 to 3.5	18.1 to 25.3	With graphite grease, when cold
Nuts of the camshaft caps		2 to 2.25	14.5 to 16.3	in oil
Nuts of the connecting rod caps		5 to 5.3	36.2 to 38.3	" "
Nuts of main bearing caps		4.7 to 5	33.9 to 36.1	" "
Screws of flywheel on crankshaft		4.2 to 4.5	30.4 to 32.5	" "
Nut of alternator pulley		3 to 3.5	21.7 to 25.3	dry
Nut of transmission main shaft yoke		11.9 to 12	86 to 86.8	"
Nut of transmission layshaft		4.5 to 5.5	32.6 to 39.7	"
Nut of transmission half-casing		1.8	13	"
Bolts joining transmission output shaft yoke to drive shaft yoke		4 to 4.5	29 to 32.5	"
Nut of transmission inner swivel		3.25 to 3.65	23.6 to 26.4	"
Oil drain plug on pan bottom		7 to 8	50.6 to 57.8	"
Injectors on intake manifold		2.8 to 3.2	20.3 to 23.1	"
REAR FRAME				
Screws securing ring gear to differential case		4.5 to 5	32.6 to 36.1	"
Ringnut securing yoke on final drive pinion shaft		8 to 14	50 to 101.2	"
Nuts securing bearing housing to real axle tubes		4.8 to 5.5	34.8 to 39.7	"
Nuts securing trailing arms to body		10 to 11.5	72.4 to 83	"
Nuts securing trailing arms to rear axle tubes		11.5 to 13	83 to 94	"
Nut securing T-arm to body		4.8 to 5.5	34.8 to 39.7	"
Nut securing T-arm to rear axle		11 to 15	79.6 to 108.5	"
Nut securing link to trailing arm bolt		5.2 to 5.9	37.6 to 42.6	"
Screws securing rear brake caliper to support (ATE brakes)		2.3 to 2.8	16.7 to 20.2	"
Nuts securing wheels		6 to 8	43.4 to 57.8	"
Bolts joining differential yoke to drive shaft yoke		3.5 to 4	25.3 to 28.9	"
Bolts for rebound strap butt joints		.5	3.6	"
Nuts securing rear axle tubes to differential carrier		2.4	17.4	"

* Warning: in case of any repair work involving the removal of cylinder head, the gasket must be renewed at all times.

FRONT FRAME

	Kgm.	lb. ft	Manner of tightening
Nut securing steering wheel to column	5 to 5.5	36.1 to 39.7	dry
Screws securing Burman steering box cover	2.3 to 2.5	16.7 to 18	"
Screws securing steering box & bellcrank bracket to body	4.8 to 5.5	34.8 to 39.7	"
Nuts of steering linkage ball joints	4.8 to 5.5	34.8 to 39.7	"
Nut securing steering arm to box	12.5 to 14	90.5 to 101.2	"
Nut securing shock absorber to suspension arms	8.2 to 9.2	59.3 to 66.5	"
Screws securing suspension upper front arm to body	2.3 to 2.8	16.7 to 20.2	"
Nut securing suspension upper front arm to rear arm	4 to 4.5	29 to 32.5	"
Nut securing suspension upper rear arm to body	12.5 to 14	83 to 94	"
Nuts securing lower arm shaft to cross-member	5.6 to 5.9	40.5 to 42.6	"
(To tighten these nuts use tool A.5.0161 and torque to 5.2 - 5.5 / 37.6 - 39.7)			
Nuts securing steering arm to steering knuckle	4 to 4.5	29 to 32.5	"
Nut securing suspension upper rear arm to steering knuckle	7.5 to 8.5	54.3 to 61.4	"
Nut securing lower ball joint to arm	8.2 to 9.2	59.3 to 66.5	"
Nut securing lower ball joint to steering knuckle	7.5 to 8.5	54.3 to 61.4	"
Nuts securing caliper to steering knuckle	7.5 to 8.5	54.3 to 61.4	"
Screws securing brake splash shields	.8 to 1	5.8 to 7.2	"
Nuts securing wheels & brake discs	6 to 8	43.4 to 57.8	"

ATE BRAKES

	Kgm.	lb. ft	Manner of tightening
Bleed screw	.2 to .35	1.5 to 2.5	"
Caliper joining bolt	2.9 to 3.4	21 to 24.6	"
Inlet fitting to caliper { with gasket	.8 to 1.1	6 to 8	"
{ without gasket	1 to 1.5	7.2 to 10.8	"

MAJOR INSPECTION SPECIFICATIONS

Camshafts

Diameter of journals . . . . A = 26.959 to 26.980 mm (1.0614 to 1.0622")
Diameter of journal bearings . . . . B = 27.000 to 27.033 mm (1.0630 to 1.0642")
Clearance between journals and bearings . . . . B-A = .020 to .074 mm (.0008 to .0028")
End play of camshaft in thrust bearing . . . . C = .065 to .182 mm (.0026 to .0071")

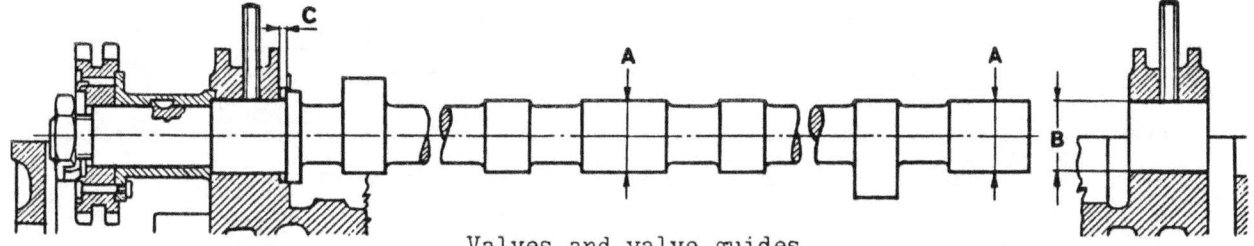

Valves and valve guides

		I N T A K E			E X H A U S T (sodium cooled)
		LIVIA H	ATE	GARRONE	LIVIA C
Valves	Diameter of valve poppet O	41.000 to 41.150 mm (1.614 to 1.620")	41.000 to 41.200 mm (1.614 to 1.622")	41.000 to 41.150 mm (1.614 to 1.620")	37.000 to 37.150 mm (1.4567 to 1.4625")
	Diameter of valve stem M		8.972 to 8.987 mm (.3532 to .3538")		8.935 to 8.960 mm (.3518 to .3527")
	Total length L	106.900 to 107.150 mm (4.2087 to 4.2186")	106.800 mm (4.2047")	107.000 mm (4.2126")	106.300 mm (4.1850")

N.B.: ATE - LIVIA - GARRONE intake valves are alternate supply.

Valve guide { Outside diameter with guide removed . . . . E = 14.033 to 14.044 mm (.5528 to .5529")
              Inside diameter with guide assembled in cylinder head . . . . D = 9.000 to 9.015 mm (.3544 to .3549")

Projection of intake valve guides from their recesses in cylinder head . . . . 13.800 to 14.000 mm (.543 to .551")

Projection of exhaust valve guides from their recesses in cylinder head . . . . 16.800 to 17.000 mm (.662 to .669")

Clearance between guide assembled in { intake . . . . .013 to .043 mm (.0005 to .0031")
cylinder head and valve stem   { exhaust . . . . .040 to .080 mm (.0016 to .0031")

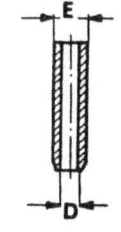

Valve seats

Diameter of valve guide seat in cylinder head F = 13.990 to 14.018 mm (.5508 to .5519")
Interference between seat and valve guide E-F = .015 to .054 mm (.0006 to .0021")

		Intake	Exhaust
Outer diameter of the valve seat intert H	standard	42.597 to 42.632 mm (1.6771 to 1.6784")	38.597 to 38.632 mm (1.5196 to 1.5209")
	oversized	42.897 to 42.932 mm (1.6889 to 1.6902")	38.897 to 38.932 mm (1.5314 to 1.5327")
Diameter of recess in the cylinder head for valve seat insert G	standard	42.532 to 42.557 mm (1.6744 to 1.6754")	38.532 to 38.557 mm (1.5169 to 1.5179")
	oversized	42.832 to 42.857 mm (1.6862 to 1.6872")	38.832 to 38.857 mm (1.5288 to 1.5298")

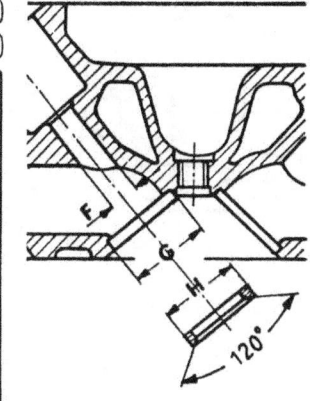

Interference between valve seat insert and recess in cylinder head . . . H-G .100 to .040 mm (.0039 to .0010")

Valve cups

Diameter of cup . . . . . . A { standard 34.973 to 34.989 mm (1.3769 to 1.3775")
oversized 35.173 to 35.189 mm (1.3848 to 1.3854")

Diameter of cup seat in cylinder head . . . . B̄ { standard 35.000 to 35.025 mm (1.3780 to 1.3789")
oversized 35.200 to 35.225 mm (1.3859 to 1.3868")

Clearance between seat and cup . . . . .011 to .052 mm (.0005 to .0020")

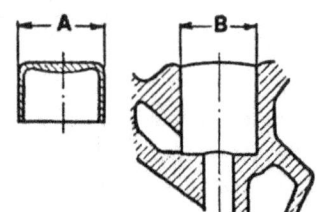

Valve springs

	Free length	Length under test load	Test load
Inner spring l	46.50 mm (1.83") 47.35 mm (1.88") 47.00 mm (1.85")	l1 = 26 mm (1.02")	22.3 to 23.1 Kg. 49.9 to 51.1 lbs
Outer spring L	51.30 mm (2.02") 52.80 mm (2.08") 52.00 mm (2.05")	L1 = 27.5 mm (1.08")	35.67 to 37.13 Kg. 78.6 to 81.8 lbs 35.87 to 37.33 Kg. 79.1 to 82.3 lbs

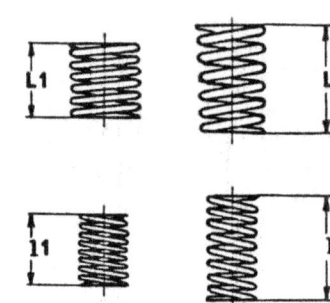

Connecting rods

Length between ₵ of big end and ₵ of small end of connecting rod . D = 156.950 to 157.050 mm (6.1792 to 6.1830")
Inner diameter of the big end of connecting rod . . . . E = 53.695 to 53.708 mm (2.1140 to 2.1144")
Inner diameter of bushing in the small end of rod . . . . C = 22.005 to 22.015 mm (.8664 to .8867")

Thickness of connecting rod bearings F { standard . . . . 1.829 to 1.835 mm (.0720 to .0722")
1st oversize . . . . 1.956 to 1.962 mm (.0770 to .0772")
2nd oversize . . . . 2.083 to 2.089 mm (.0820 to .0824")

Radial clearance between crankpins and bearings for big end of connecting rod . . . . .025 to .063 mm (.0010 to .0024")

Maximum out of parallelism between ₵ of big end hole and ₵ of small end hole . . . . .078 mm (.0031")

Piston pins

O.D. of pin I { black . . . . 21.994 to 21.997 mm (.86590 to .86602")
white . . . . 21.997 to 22.000 mm (.86605 to .86614")

Clearance between con. rod small end bore and piston pin { black . . .008 to .021 mm (.0003 to .0008")
white . . .005 to .018 mm (.0002 to .0007")

Piston pin holes

BORGO piston H { black . . . . 22.000 to 22.002 mm (.86614 to .86621")
white . . . . 22.003 to 22.005 mm (.86626 to .86633")

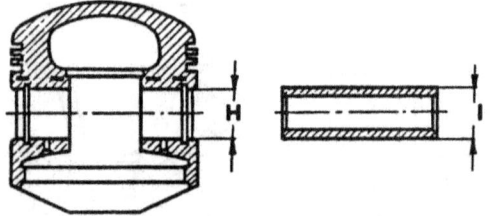

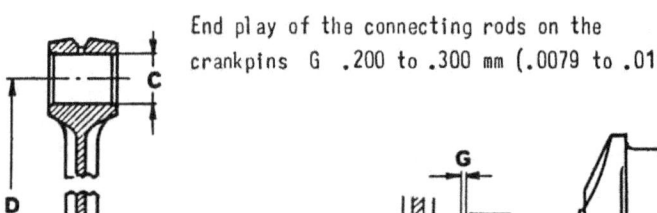

End play of the connecting rods on the crankpins G .200 to .300 mm (.0079 to .0118")

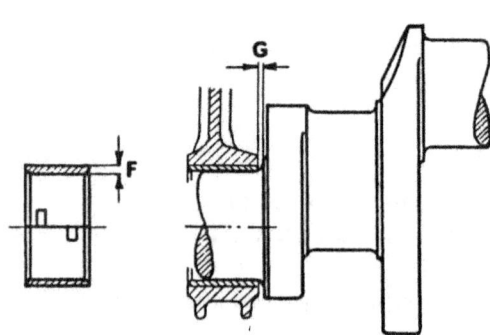

Pistons and piston rings

Diameter of pistons to be measured to square with the hole for piston pin and at a distance of L = 15 mm (.591") from the lower border of skirt.

	Class A (Blue)	Class B (Pink)	Class C (Green)
BORGO piston diameter	79.945 to 79.955 mm (3.1476 to 3.1479")	79.955 to 79.965 mm (3.1479 to 3.1483")	79.965 to 79.975 mm (3.1483 to 3.1487")

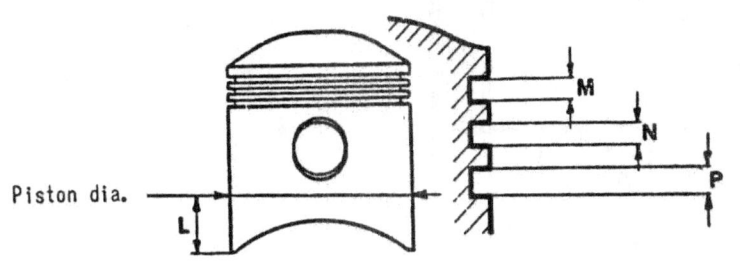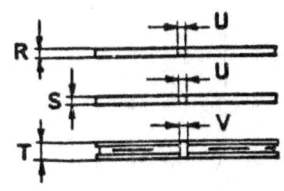

Height of groove in piston for chromium-plated compression ring ...... M = 1.525 to 1.545 mm (.0601 to .0609")
Height of groove in piston for oil scraper ring .... N = 1.775 to 1.795 mm (.0699 to .0706")
Height of groove in piston for oil control ring .... P = 4.015 to 4.035 mm (.1581 to .1588")
Thickness of chromium-plated compression ring .... R = 1.478 to 1.490 mm (.0582 to .0586")
Thickness of oil scraper ring .... S = 1.728 to 1.740 mm (.0681 to .0685")
Thickness of oil control ring .... T = 3.978 to 3.990 mm (.1567 to .1571")
End play of rings in grooves:
   chromium-plated compression rings ...... .035 to .067 mm (.0014 to .0026")
   oil scraper ring .... .035 to .067 mm (.0014 to .0026")
   oil control ring .... .025 to .057 mm (.0010 to .0022")
Gap of compression ring to be inspected in ring gauge or in cylinder barrels . U = .300 to .450 mm (.0118 to .0177")
Gap of oil rings to be inspected in ring gauge or in cylinder barrels .. V = .250 to .400 mm (.0100 to .0157")

Cylinder barrels

	Blue	Pink	Green
Cylinder barrel bore	79.985 to 79.994 mm (3.1490 to 3.1493")	79.995 to 80.004 mm (3.1494 to 3.1497")	80.005 to 80.014 mm (3.1498 to 3.1501")

Clearance between cylinder barrel and piston .... .030 to .049 mm (.0012 to .0019")

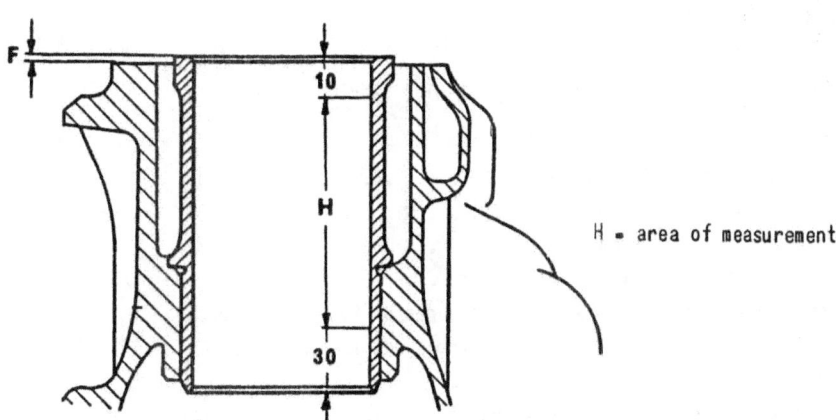

H = area of measurement

Projection of barrels from cylinder block .... F .001 to .060 mm (.00004 to .0024")
Surface roughness of barrel bore .... 20 to 40 microinches RMS

Crankshaft

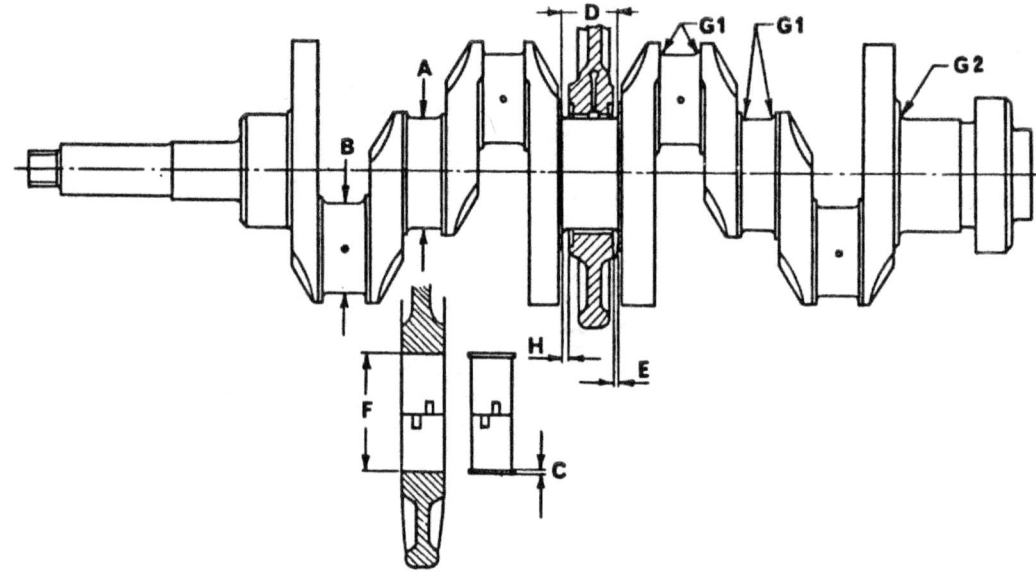

Diameter of main journals A	standard		59.960 to 59.973 mm (2.3606 to 2.3611")
	1st undersize		59.706 to 59.719 mm (2.3506 to 2.3511")
	2nd undersize		59.452 to 59.465 mm (2.3407 to 2.3411")
Diameter of crankpins B	standard		49.987 to 50.000 mm (1.9680 to 1.9685")
	1st undersize		49.733 to 49.746 mm (1.9581 to 1.9585")
	2nd undersize		49.479 to 49.492 mm (1.9480 to 1.9485")
Thickness of main bearings C	standard		1.829 to 1.835 mm (.0720 to .0722")
	1st oversize		1.956 to 1.962 mm (.0770 to .0772")
	2nd oversize		2.083 to 2.089 mm (.0820 to .0822")
Diameter of seat for main bearings in crankcase		F =	63.657 to 63.676 mm (2.5062 to 2.5069")
Length of central journal D	standard		30.000 to 30.035 mm (1.1811 to 1.1824")
	1st oversize		30.127 to 30.162 mm (1.1861 to 1.1874")
	2nd oversize		30.254 to 30.289 mm (1.1911 to 1.1924")
Thickness of thrust rings for central journal E	standard		2.311 to 2.362 mm (.0910 to .0929")
	1st oversize		2.374 to 2.425 mm (.0935 to .0954")
	2nd oversize		2.438 to 2.489 mm (.0960 to .0980")
End play of crankshaft		H =	.076 to .263 mm (.003 to .010")
Radial clearance between journals and main bearings			.014 to .058 mm (.0005 to .0022")

N o t e - Radial clearance = main bearing ID - (twice bearing thickness + journal OD)

Fillet radii	main journals & crankpins	G1	1.7 to 2.1 mm (.07 to .08")
	pin on flywheel side	G2	3.7 to 4.1 mm (.15 to .16")
Main journals & crankpins surface roughness			63 microinches RMS
Maximum elongation of main journals and crankpins			.007 mm (.00027")
Maximum taper of main journals and crankpins measured on their full length			.01 mm (.00039")
Maximum error of parallelism of main journals and crankpins measured on their full length			.015 mm (.00059")
Maximum misalignment allowed between main journals			.01 mm (.00039")
Maximum misalignment allowed between ℄ of the two pairs of crankpins and ℄ of main journals			.300 mm (.0118")

CLUTCH

The clutch is of the hydraulically-operated single plate dry type. The clutch pedal acts on a master cylinder supplied with the same type of fluid as the brake system.

When the clutch pedal is depressed, the fluid under pressure actuates the piston in the cylinder "4" connected to the clutch disengagement lever "5".

The pressure plate is controlled by means of diaphragm spring "6".

The clutch pedal free travel "A" should be about 1 1/4" (30-32 mm). When owing to wear on the clutch disc facing, the pedal free travel is reduced to 3/4" (17-19 mm) the free travel must be restored.

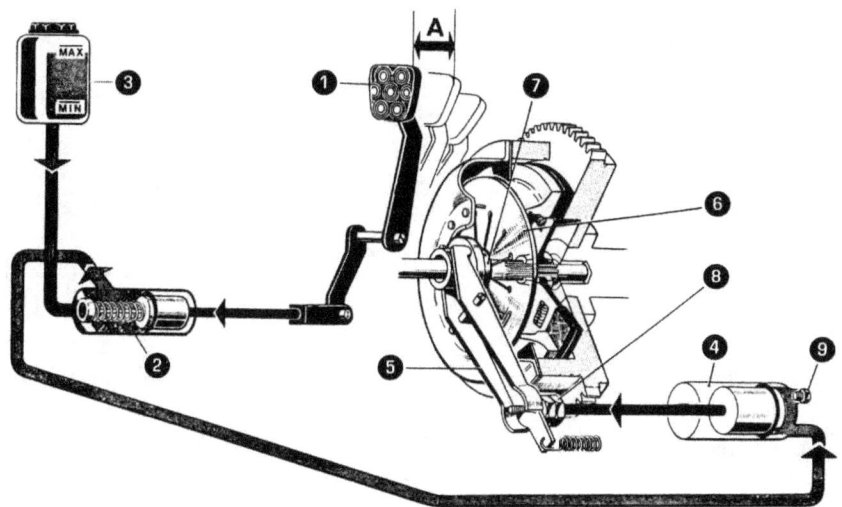

A   Pedal free travel
B   Disengagement lever free travel

1   Pedal
2   Master cylinder
3   Clutch & brake fluid reservoir
4   Slave cylinder
5   Disengagement lever
6   Diaphragm spring
7   Throwout bearing
8   Adjusting nuts
9   Air bleed screw

Adjustment

Measure with a rule the free travel "B" at the end of push rod of cylinder "4" depressing the clutch pedal until the throwout bearing "7" contacts the spring "6"; the travel "B" should be about .08-.10" (2-2.5 mm).

If the travel is shorter, act on the adjusting nut "8".

At the same time make sure that, by pressing the pedal as far as it will go, the push rod can move through a total travel of .53 - .56" (13.5-14.2 mm). If any component of the system has been removed, thoroughly bleed the circuit. To check as specified use special tool no. C.6.0146 (see Tool Bulletin no. 135).

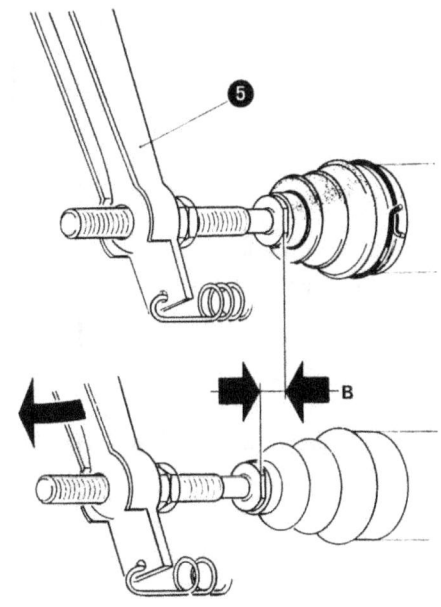

Inspection specifications

Wear limit of driven plate thickness . . . .   6.5 mm
Squareness of driven plate as mounted on gearbox output
    shaft . . . .   0.50 mm

TRANSMISSION

Transmission ratios	1st gear	3.30 : 1
	2nd gear	1.99 : 1
	3rd gear	1.35 : 1
	4th gear	1.00 : 1
	5th gear	.79 : 1
	Rev.	3.01 : 1

Maximum eccentricity of main shaft .... .050 mm (.020")

End play between forks and sleeves
- assembly .... .150 to .340 mm (.006 to .013")
- wear limit .... .850 mm (.033")

Calibration of striking rod ball spring (1st, 2nd, 3rd, 4th, 5th & Rev.)
- free length .... 35.8 mm (1.41")
- length under test load ... 17.2 mm (.69")
- test load .... 7.680 to 8.320 mm (16.97 to 18.3 lbs)

Maximum end play of mainshaft gears
- 1st speed gear .... .170 to .245 mm (.0067 to .0096")
- 2nd & 3rd speed gears ..... .130 to .205 mm (.0052 to .0081")
- 5th speed gear & Rev. ..... .160 to .220 mm (.0063 to .0087")

Radial clearance between gear bushings and mainshaft
- 1st speed gear .... .125 to .170 mm (.0049 to .0067")
- 2nd & 3rd speed gears .... .095 to .140 mm (.0038 to .0055")
- 5th speed gear .... .065 to .107 mm (.0026 to .0041")

Distance between outer planes of the engaging teeth of 3rd and 4th gears . 42.000 to 42.200 mm (1.65 to 1.66")

Distance, in neutral, of the rear band (drive shaft side) of 5th speed sleeve from the <u>r e a r</u> edge of gear engaging teeth .... 12.9 mm (.508")

REAR AXLE AND SUSPENSION

Transmission-axle overall ratios-with 41 : 9 final drive
- 1st gear — 15.049 : 1
- 2nd gear — 9.055 : 1
- 3rd gear — 6.172 : 1
- 4th gear — 4.555 : 1
- 5th gear — 3.603 : 1
- Rev. — 13.710 : 1

Maximum eccentricity of axle shafts	.10 mm (.004")
Play between teeth of planetary gears	.05 mm (.002")
Play between teeth of final drive	.05 to .10 mm (.002 to .004")
Reference dimension on tool C.6.0101 for pinion-to-ring gear fitting	70 ± .0025 mm (2.7559 ± .0001")
Maximum end play between T-arm and attachment to body	1 mm (.04")
Pre-load on pinion bearing	11.5 to 15.5 Kgcm (10 to 13.5 in. lbs)
Total pre-load on final drive bearings	16.5 to 24.5 Kgcm (14.4 to 21.3 in. lbs)

Checking of shock absorbers on test bench - Calibration data (when cold)

	BIANCHI	
	Extension	Compression
High speed	135 to 190 Kgs (298 to 418 lbs)	50 to 80 Kgs (111 to 176 lbs)
Low speed	19 to 55 Kgs (42 to 121 lbs)	9 to 22 Kgs (20 to 48 lbs)

Checking of suspension springs

Free length	467 mm (18.4")
Length under test load	252 mm (10")
Test load	349 to 371 Kgs (770 to 815 lbs)

FRONT SUSPENSION

Adjustment of clearance in wheel bearings

When performing regular servicing or whenever the removal of wheel hubs is required, adjust the bearing clearance as follows:

1) Screw in the castellated nut and lock it to a torque of 2.5 Kgm (18 ft-lbs) while at the same time revolving the wheel hub to set the bearings properly in their seats;
2) Unscrew the nut half a turn or more;
3) Lightly tap on the stub axle end with a mallet in order to return the outboard bearing in its proper position even in the case a slight interference between bearing cone and stub axle exists;
4) Lock the nut in place to 1.5 Kgm (10.8 ft-lbs);
5) Unscrew the nut of a quarter turn;
6) If the hole in the axle is aligned with a slot in the castellated nut insert the cotter pin; if not, screw in the nut by the minumum angle needed to line up the hole and the next slot;
7) Again tap lightly on stub axle end to restore the same condition as under step 3;
8) The end play so obtained on stub axle should fall between .02 - .12 mm (.0008 - .0047").

Wheel bearing lubricating instructions

The quantity of lubricating grease should be about 65 grammes (2½ ozs) for each hub; do not exceed such a quantity to avoid bearing overheating, grease leakage, etc.
The grease should be well distributed inside the bearings and into side recesses.
Subsequently, at the regular schedule, remove the hub cover and pack the outboard bearing.

Ball joints

End play of lower ball joint in its socket . . . . 1 mm (.04")

N o t e - Ball joints require no regular lubrication being provided with special grease seals which retain the grease packed in by factory on assembly - Only if strictly needed (joints squealing) grease with SHELL Retinax A or AGIP F.1 Grease 30 (See I.S. 1.05.097/1).

Checking of suspension springs

	R.H. side	L.H. side
Free length	345 mm (13.6")	355 mm (14")
Length under test load	214 mm (7.9")	214 mm (7.9")
Test load	902 to 958 Kgs (1986 to 2110 lbs)	970 to 1030 Kgs (2138 to 2271 lbs)

Checking of shock absorbers on test bench

Calibration data (when cold)

	ALLINQUANT	
	Extension	Compression
High speed	150 to 190 Kgs (331 to 418 lbs)	55 to 80 Kgs (121 to 176 lbs)
Low speed	25 to 55 Kgs (56 to 121 lbs)	9 to 22 Kgs (20 to 48 lbs)

BRAKES

The brake system consists of four disc brakes operated by a dual hydraylic system.
Each one of the separate circuits, front and rear, is servo assisted by a vacuum booster. The boosters are controlled by a tandem master cylinder, with one cylinder operating the front brakes and the other cylinder the rear brakes.
The friction pads of the front and rear brakes are directly actuated by the cylinders integral with the calipers.
The brakes are self-adjusting.
A modulating valve, inserted in the rear brake circuit, regulates the pressure between front and rear brakes to provide balanced braking action.

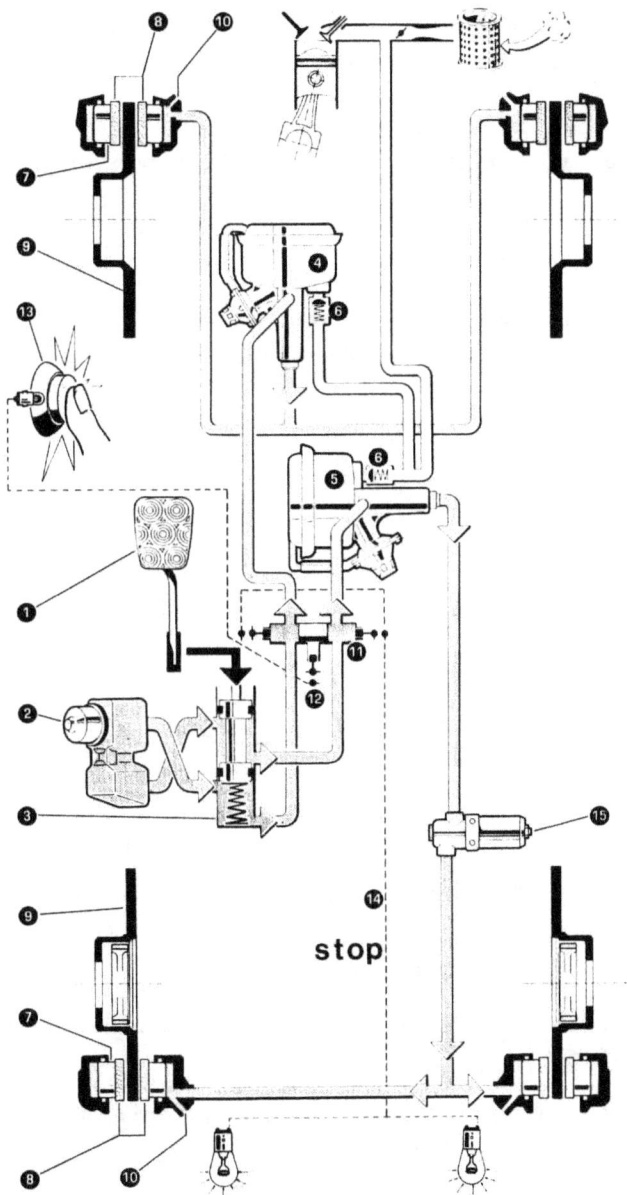

1 Brake pedal
2 Fluid reservoir
3 Master cylinder
4 Front brakes booster
5 Rear brakes booster
6 Suction port
7 Plungers
8 Friction Pads
9 Discs
10 Bleed screws
11 Pressure switch cluster
12 Pressure switch for brake warning light
13 Brake warning light
14 Stop light cable
15 Modulating valve

ATE BRAKES

Disc

When a brake disc is replaced it is necessary to check it for run-out after installation:

- use a dial indicator and the special tool A.2.0151 which is mounted to the caliper by means of the pad retaining pins.

Maximum permissible run out as measured at the swept surface should not exceed .22 mm (.0086").

N o t e - run-out readings can be misleading if bearing clearance is not as specified; therefore, check and adjust if necessary, according to factory instructions.

If the disc is scored, see I.S. 0.00.055/3; the grinding of the surfaces is allowed providing not to exceed an under size of 1 mm (.0394"), equalized on both faces, i.e. .5 mm (.0197") each face; disc wear limit: front 11.5 mm (.452") rear 8.5 mm (.335") thick.

Inspection specifications after regrinding of disc surfaces:

- Max. out of parallelism with disc mounting plane: .05 mm (.0020");
- Max. out of flat: .025 mm (.0010") and max. difference in thickness: .038 mm (.0015") as measured along any radial line;
- Max. out of flat: .025 mm (.0010") and max. difference in thickness: .015 mm (.0006") as measured along any circular line;
- The surface should show no sign of scoring or porosity.

The surface roughness should be:

- 26 microinches as measured circularly;
- 36 microinches as measured radially.

Friction pads

	Front	Rear
Thickness when new	15 mm (.590")	
Wear limit	7 mm (.275")	

Calipers

On replacement of disc or caliper, measure the running clearance between caliper and disc on each side; the difference should not exceed .5 mm (.0197")

To centralize the caliper about the disc, insert shims between caliper and mounting flange as required.

Parking brake

It is mechanically operated and acts on the rear wheels through suitable shoes which spread apart against a drum machined in the disc casting.

For a brief description and repair and maintenance instructions refer to:

ATE DISC BRAKES (Publication no. 1202)

N o t e - When reassembling the operating levers, a slight quantity of grease AGIP F1 Gr SM or SHELL Retinax AM is to be applied to the pivot points and rubbing surfaces of levers.

WHEEL ALIGNMENT

Checking of wheel angles and car "trim" under static load

Put the car under static load, with shock absorbers and stabilizer rods disconnected, with full tank or equivalent with spare wheel, tool kit and the tires inflated as specified.

Before checking, slightly move the car up and down so as to settle the suspensions.

Front seats { 1 weight of 45 Kgs on each seat
2 weights of 25 Kgs on flooring where feet rest

Rear seats { 2 weights of 45 Kgs on seat
2 weights of 25 Kgs on flooring where feet rest

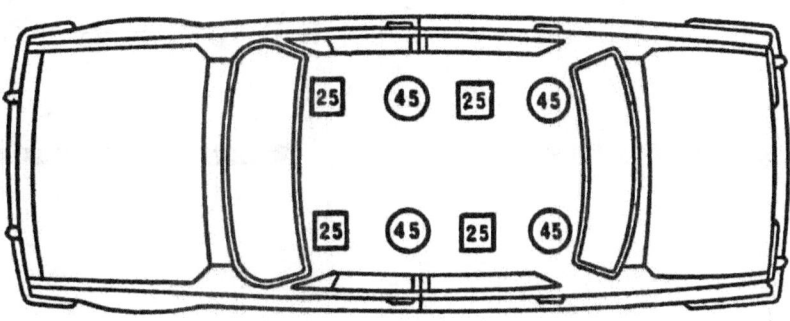

Distance of lower arms of front suspension from a reference level

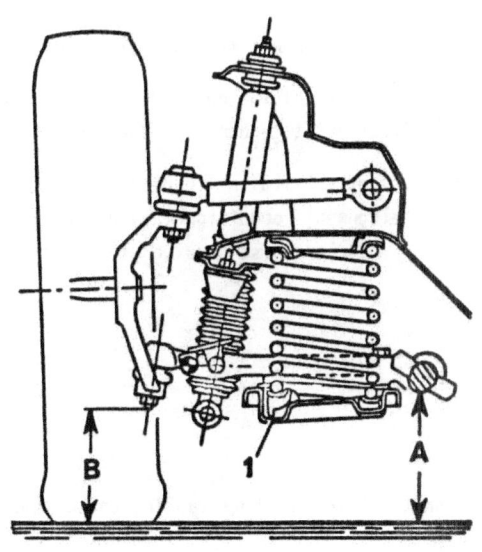

A - B = 34 ± 5 mm (1.34 ± .20")

Dimension "A" must be measured in correspondence of the lower line of shaft as shown.

To adjust add shims in "1".

Shims are available in the following thicknesses:
3.5 mm (.14") - 7 mm (.28") - 10.5 mm (.42")

Distance of rear axle from rubber buffers

$$C = 36 \pm 5 \text{ mm } (1.42 \pm .20")$$

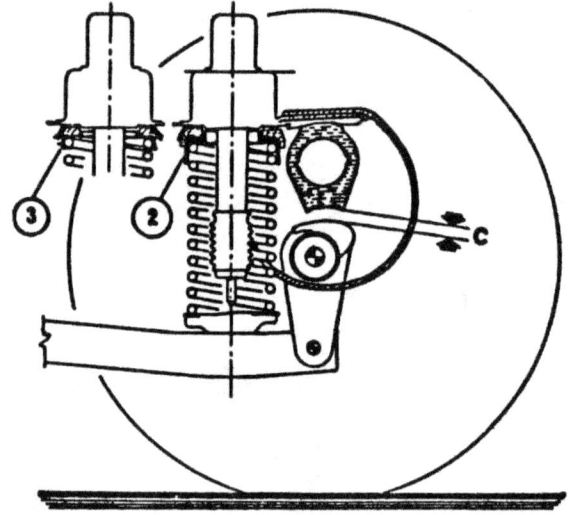

N o t e - To adjust, remove the seat 3 and add shims in 2 as shown.

Shims are available in the following ticknesses:

6.5 mm (.26")
11.5 mm (.45")
16.5 mm (.65")
21.5 mm (.85")

In the conditions as specified check the wheel angles.

Caster angle: $\alpha = 1° 30' \pm 30'$

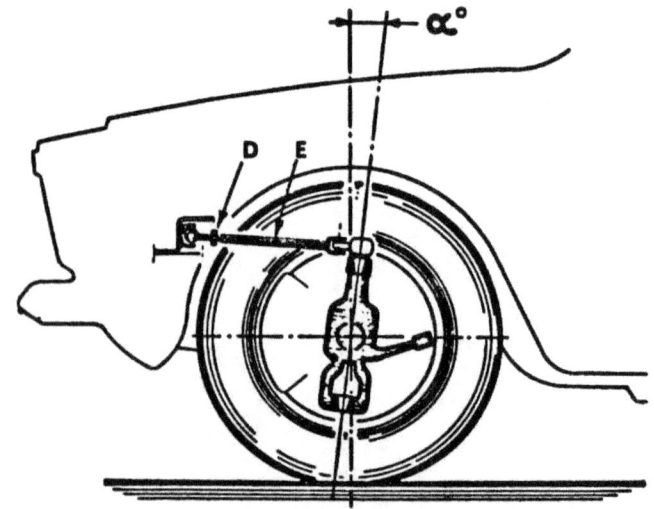

The difference in caster angle between R.H. and L.H. wheel must not exceed 0° 20'.

To adjust, loosen jam nut "D" and rotate rod "E".

Small adjustments of the caster angle allow to correct slight drift tendency of the car.

The caster angle should be checked under static load and alignment conditions as specified and with shock absorbers disconnected at an end.

N.B. - Before checking the caster angle shake the front end of car in order to allow the rubber bushing on the front slanting arm to set properly.

Front wheel camber

Difference in camber angle between R.H. and L.H. wheel = 0° 40'

[Diagram showing front wheel camber: 0° 20' ± 30', H, H + 5 mm (.20"), -1 mm (.04")]

<u>N o t e</u> - Not adjustable. Check the chassis and suspension arms if necessary.

FRONT WHEEL TOE-IN

Lock steering wheel in the central position i.e. with the spokes symmetrically disposed in relation to the vertical. Starting with the rod "1" on the steering box side, place the corresponding wheel so that the toe-in is .06" (1.5 mm). Measure the length thus obtained of the rod and adjust the rod "2" on the other side to a length .20" (5 mm) shorter. Bring the first wheel to a .06" toe-in by adjusting the center track rod "3".

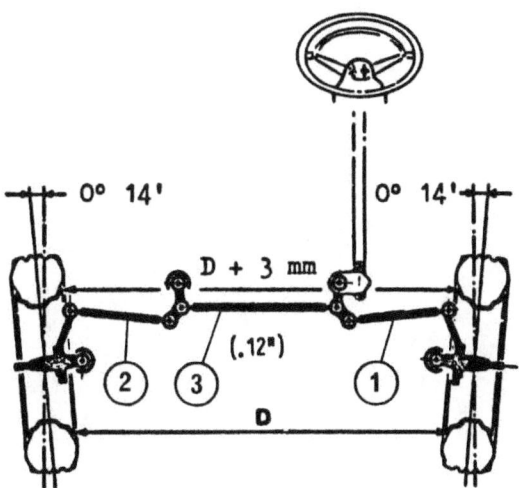

Rod length:

    side . . . . 264 to 280 mm (10.4 to 11")
    track . . . . 530 to 550 mm (20.86 to 21.65")

With the toe-in as specified, the length of rods as measured between ball joint centers should fall within the limits shown. If these values cannot be restored, the cause will probably be attributable to distortion of the body resulting from a collision.

NOTES

"1750 GT Veloce and 1750 Spider Veloce" VARIANTS

PRINCIPAL CHARACTERISTIC DATA

Number of cylinders	4
Bore	80 mm. (3.15")
Stroke	88.5 mm. (3.48")
Total cylinder displacement	1779 cc
Max. power at 5,500 giri/min.	SAE 132 HP
Front track	1324 mm. (52.1")
Rear track	1274 mm. (50.1")
Wheel base — GT Veloce	2350 mm. (92.7")
Wheel base — Spider Veloce	2250 mm. (88.6")
Min. turning circle — GT Veloce	10700 mm. (420.1")
Min. turning circle — Spider Veloce	10500 mm. (413.4")
Overall length — GT Veloce	4080 mm. (161")
Overall length — Spider Veloce	4250 mm. (167.3")
Overall width — GT Veloce	1580 mm. (62.2")
Overall width — Spider Veloce	1630 mm. (64.2")
Overall height (unladen) — GT veloce	1315 mm. (51.8")
Overall height (unladen) — Spider Veloce (with top)	1290 mm. (50.8")
Curb weight (full tank)	1040 Kg. (2293 lbs)
Number of seats — GT Veloce	2
Number of seats — Spider Veloce	2
Tires 165 x 14	PIRELLI cinturato HR / KLEBER COLOMBES V 10 GT / MICHELIN X A S

PERFORMANCE

With 41 : 9 final drive

Gear	After breaking in mph
1st	29
2nd	48
3rd	71
4th	99
5th	118
Rev.	32

Tires

Recommended tire pressure (cold) in psi at a maximum-loaded vehicle weight of 3000 lbs GT Veloce and 2760 lbs Spider Veloce

Make	Front	Rear
Pirelli	24	26
Michelin	20	24
Kleber Colombes	24	26

Electrical equipment

	BOSCH	
	1750 GT Veloce	1750 Spider Veloce
Two-speed windshield wiper	WS 4903 AR 2 A (0)	WS 4904 AR 2 A (0)

Bulb's wattage

1750 GT Veloce

Headlights	sealed beam
Fog lamps	sealed beam
Tail lights - parking & stop	5/21
Front direction indicators and road hazard flashers	21
Tail direction indicators and road hazard flashers	21
Back-up light	21
Front parking lights	5 globular
License plate light	5 globular
Engine compartment light	5 cylindrical
Courtesy light	5 cylindrical
Side marker lights	4 tubular
Lighting on instruments	3 tubular
Blower warning light	3 tubular
Alternator warning light	3 tubular
Fuel reserve warning light	3 tubular
Low oil pressure warning light	3 tubular
Direction indicators and road hazard flashers warning light	1.2 tubular
Parking light warning	1.2 tubular
High beam warning light	1.2 tubular
Low fuel pressure warning light	1.2 tubular
Service brake warning light	1.2 tubular

1750 Spider Veloce

Headlights	sealed beam
Tail lights - parking & stop	5/21
Front direction indicators and road hazard flashers	21
Tail direction indicators and road hazard flashers	21
Back-up light	21
Front parking light	5 globular
Side marker lights	4 tubular
License plate light	5 globular
Engine compartment light	5 cylindrical
Courtesy light (in rearview mirror)	5 cylindrical
Glove box light	5 cylindrical
Ash tray light	3 cylindrical
Lighting on instruments	3 tubular
Alternator warning light	3 tubular
Blower warning light	3 tubular
Fuel reserve warning light	3 tubular
Direction indicators and road hazard flashers warning light	1.2 tubular
Low oil pressure warning light	1.2 tubular
Parking light warning	1.2 tubular
High beam warning light	1.2 tubular
Low fuel pressure warning light	1.2 tubular
Service brake warning light	1.2 tubular

Checking of shock absorbers on test bench – Calibration data (when cold)

	BIANCHI	
	Extension	Compression
High speed	135 to 190 Kgs (298 to 418 lbs)	50 to 80 Kgs (111 to 176 lbs)
Low speed	19 to 55 Kgs (42 to 121 lbs)	9 to 22 Kgs (20 to 48 lbs)

Checking of suspension springs

	1750 GT Veloce	1750 Spider Veloce
Free length	437 mm (17.2")	429 mm (16.9")
Length under test load .	252 mm (10")	252 mm (10")
Test load	268.7 to 285.3 Kgs (592.5 to 645 lbs)	257 to 273 Kgs (566 to 600 lbs)
Colored marks	Blue-Blue Blue-White	White-White White-Blue

FRONT SUSPENSION

Checking of shock absorbers on test bench

Calibration data (when cold)

	ALLINQUANT	
	Extension	Compression
High speed	150 to 190 Kgs (330 to 420 lbs)	55 to 80 Kgs (121 to 175 lbs)
Low speed	25 to 55 Kgs (55 to 121 lbs)	9 to 22 Kgs (20 to 48 lbs)

Checking of suspension springs

	1750 GT Veloce	1750 Spider Veloce
Free length	313.5 mm (12.3")	317 mm (12.5")
Length under test load .	200 mm (7.8")	200 mm (7.8")
Test load	858 to 911.5 Kgs (1988 to 2005 lbs)	820.6 to 871.4 Kgs (1809.4 to 1920.5 lbs)
Colored marks	White-White White-Blue	White-Blue Blue-Blue

WHEEL ALIGNMENT

Checking of wheel angles and car "trim" under static load

Put the car under static load, with shock absorbers and stabilizer rods disconnected, with full tank or equivalent, with spare wheel, tool kit and the tires inflated as specified.

Before checking, slightly move the car up and down so as to settle the suspensions.

Static load
{ 2 weights of 45 Kgs (100 lbs) on front seats
2 weights of 25 Kgs (55 lbs) on flooring where feet rest

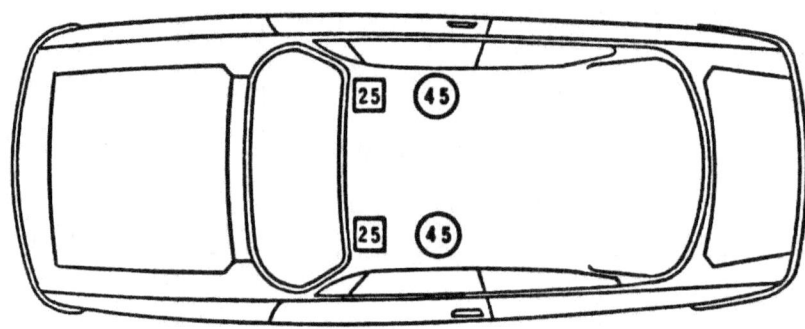

Distance of lower arms of front suspension from a reference level

GT Veloce   : A - B = 34 ± 5 mm (1.34 ± .2") ⎫
Spider Veloce: A - B = 24 ± 5 mm (.94 ± .2")   ⎬ See figure on page 22

Distance of rear axle from rubber buffers

GT Veloce   : C = 41 ± 5 mm (1.62 ± .2") ⎫
Spider Veloce: C = 33 ± 5 mm (1.30 ± .2") ⎬ See figure on page 23

Direzione Assistenza

INSTRUCTION AND MAINTENANCE MANUAL

FOR ALFA ROMEO 1750

FUEL INJECTION MODELS

U.S.A. VERSION

This publication deletes and supersedes the publication no. 1388 dated 9/1968

This manual contains the specifications and the instructions covering the fuel injection system installed on Alfa Romeo 1750 models.

Special care should be given to the regular servicing and maintenance directions, particularly as far as the efficiency of the system is concerned.

It is important that any maintenance and repair work be entrusted only to an authorized Alfa Romeo Dealer as such Dealers are equipped with the proper tools and staffed by specially trained mechanics.

ALFA ROMEO

Direzione Assistenza

CONTENTS

Important note	Page	1
Description of fuel injection system	"	2
Recommendations on the use	"	9
Regular servicing	"	11
Specific adjustments	"	25
Trouble shooting	"	36

IMPORTANT NOTE

The fuel injection system for the 1750 model has been designed not only to attain high performance and low fuel consumption but also to keep the exhaust emissions below the levels permitted by U.S.A. regulations.

The low exhaust emission levels have therefore been obtained by improving the distribution and the combustion. No devices to burn the unburned gases downstream of the exhaust valves are required.

Of course, even with the fuel injection system fitted to the Alfa 1750, the exhaust emissions of cars sold to Customers will not continue to meet U.S. specification unless the owner himself provides to have the prescribed servicing outlined on page 11 regularly carried out by authorized workshops and provided that, when remedying troubles or performing any maintenance work on the engine or fuel feed system, the workshops strictly follow the factory prescribed procedure.

DESCRIPTION OF FUEL INJECTION SYSTEM

GENERAL

Fuel is supplied to the engine by injection into the intake port of each cylinder by means of four pumping elements (one per cylinder) whose delivery is controlled by a "control unit". A cam in the control unit provides a "base" delivery according to the opening of throttles and to RPM range; the "base" delivery is varied by compensating devices giving proper corrections for atmospheric pressure, engine temperature, cold starting, initial running and fuel cut off on deceleration.

FUEL FEED SYSTEM

Operating diagram

Inserting the key in the ignition switch (1) and rotating clockwise to the first click will operate the electric pump (2). The gasoline flows from the tank (3) thru tank filter (4) and main filter (5) and feeds the injection pump (6).

The excess fuel, acting also as a coolant for the injection pump (6), before returning to the tank, passes thru a calibrated orifice (7) which regulates the fuel pressure within the injection pump. A pressure switch (8) inserted in the delivery pipe will switch on the warning light (10) on dashboard if a pressure drop occurs in fuel lines; the pressure should never be lower than 7.1 psi - 0.5 Kg/cm^2.

A pressure relief valve (9) on filter (5) limits the fuel pump outlet pressure bypassing fuel to the recovery pipe at 16 - 18 psi (1.1 - 1.3 Kg/cm^2).

GENERAL ARRANGEMENT OF FUEL SYSTEM

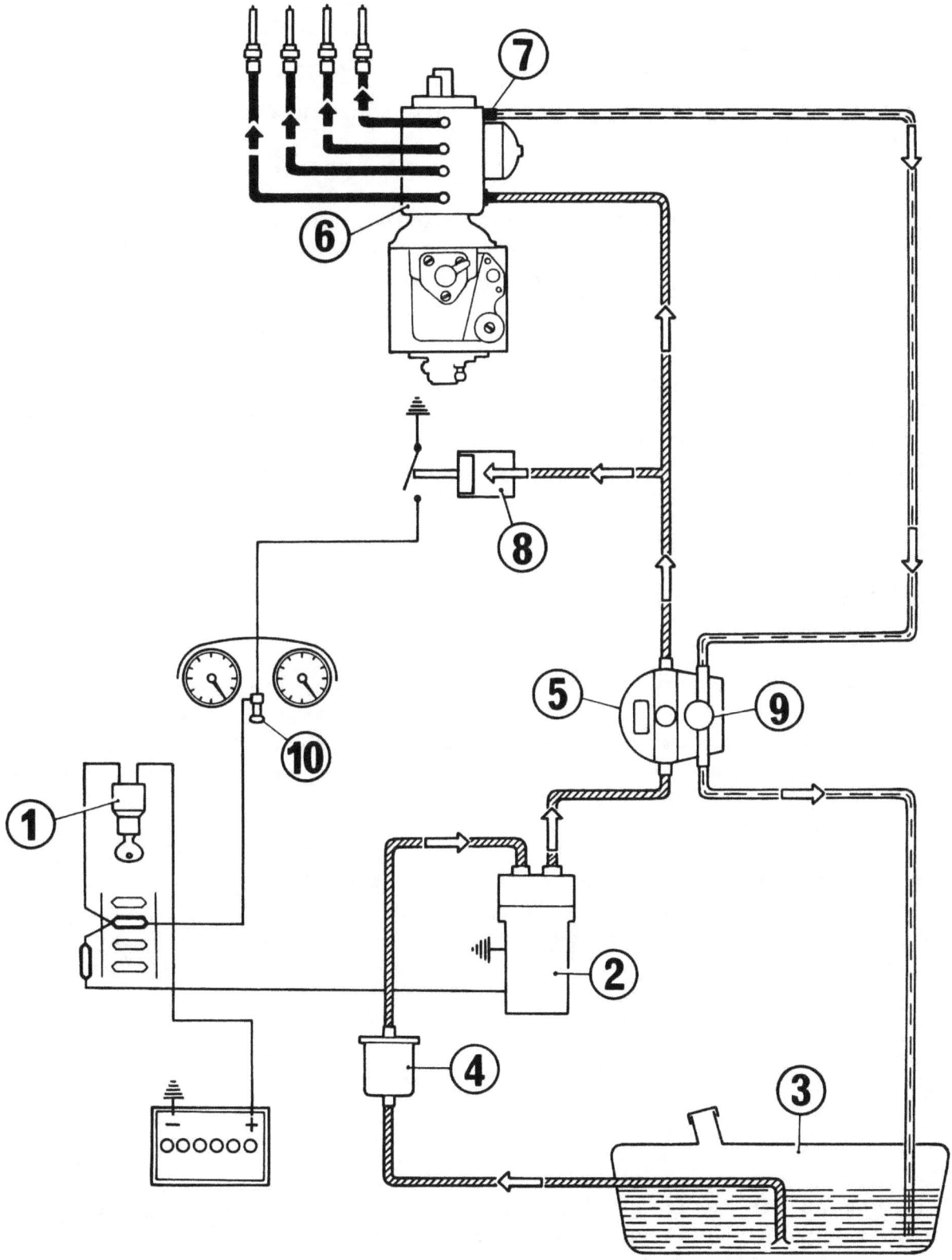

Fig. 1

AIR INDUCTION SYSTEM

The air induction system consists of a silencer (1), incorporating an air cleaner (2), directly connected to the throttle valve throats (3).

The filtered air enters the engine thru four intake ports each with a throttle valve.

The idling air (throttle valves closed) is fed thru a separate circuit which, starting from the air cleaner connects to the intake ports downstream of the throttle valves and includes the idle equalizers (9) (see fig. 2).

The accelerator pedal (5) is mechanically linked thru a relay crank to both the throttle valve lever (4) and the control unit lever (6). Therefore, any position of accelerator pedal corresponds to an exact position of throttle valve and control unit levers.

INJECTION PUMP

The injection pump, SPICA AIBB 4C.S.75, has four variable displacement plungers controlled by the control unit thru a rack. The plungers are actuated by conn.rods driven by a crankshaft revolving at half engine speed. The pump is lubricated with the engine oil drawn from the main gallery just after the main filter.

The lubricating oil, filtered further by a filter in the injection pump mount, seeps past the plungers, lubricates the various moving parts then returns to the pan thru a suitable port in the pump mount itself.

COLD START DEVICE

The cold start device incorporates a solenoid which, energized when the engine is started, enriches the mixture by increasing the injection pump delivery thru an additional movement of control unit rack. The cold start device cuts off when the ignition key is released from cranking position.

AIR INDUCTION SYSTEM AND THROTTLE/CONTROL UNIT LINKAGE

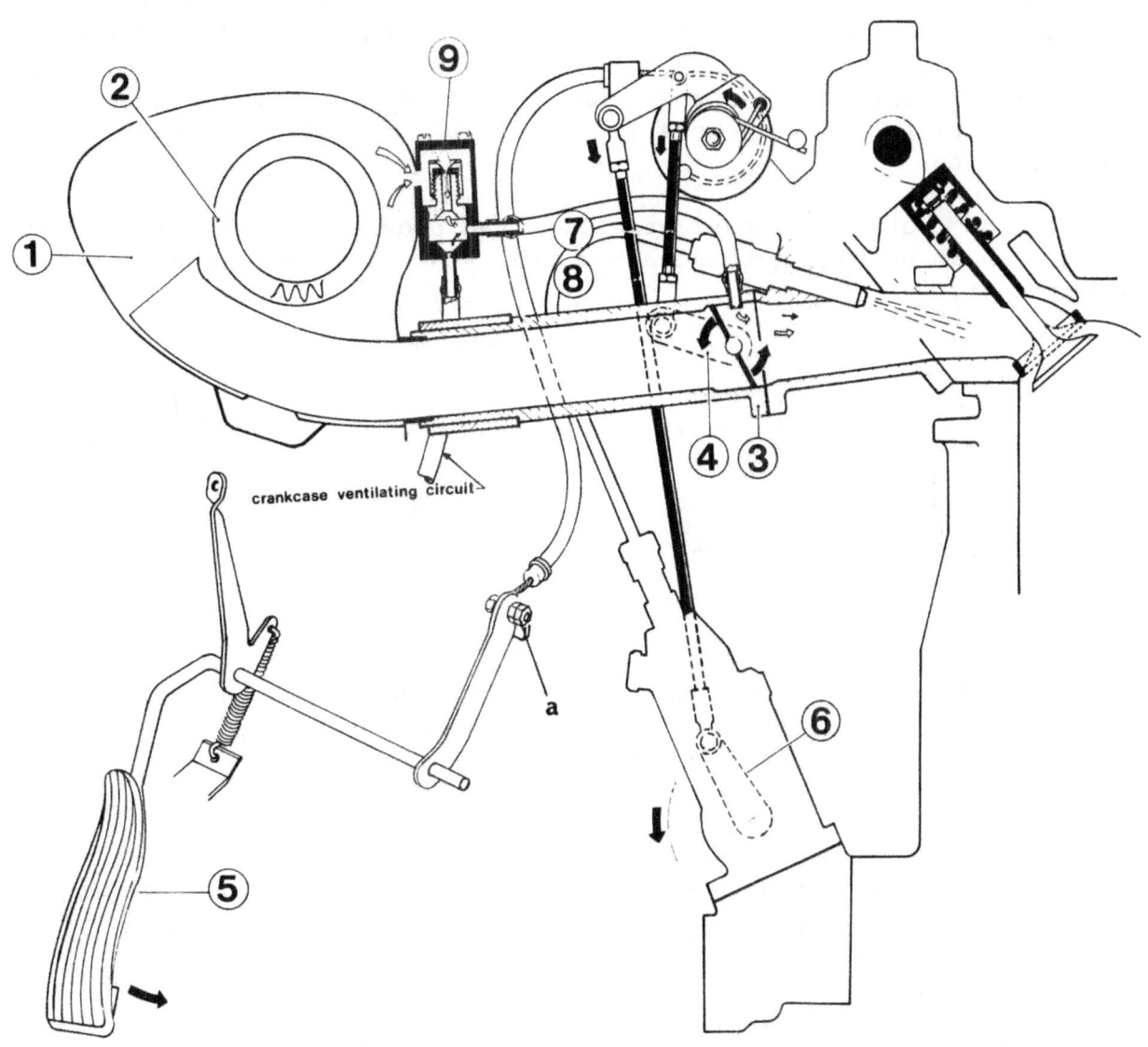

Fig. 2

INITIAL RUNNING DEVICE

This device provides for a smooth operation of the engine soon after a cold start; it consists of a thermostat which, sensing engine coolant temperatures, acts thru a linkage on the control unit rack so as to increase the injection pump delivery in accord with the decrease in temperature and at the same time, thru rods 7 and 8 outside the control unit, opens the throttles so that the engine can be properly fed.

The device cuts off automatically and progressively as the engine warms up to operating temperature thus restoring the standard idling conditions.

CRANKCASE VENTILATING SYSTEM

The exhaust gases and the oil vapors developed during engine operation collect in the camshaft cover; from here they are sucked in the combustion chambers and burned.

The crankcase ventilating system controls gases both at high engine RPMs and at idling speed when the throttles are closed.

When the throttles are fully opened the vapors flow thru the hose (1) to the oil separator (2) and thru hose (3) into the manifold chamber (4) communicating with the intake ports (5).

When the throttles are partially closed, the secondary circuit (9) comes into operation; such a circuit starts from the oil separator and conveys unburned gases and vapors directly into the intake ports dowstream of the throttles (7) by means of the equalizers (6) provided with calibrated orifices to which the hoses (10) are connected for proper distribution among cylinders. The oil collected in the separator returns to the pan via the hose (8).

CRANKCASE VENTILATING CIRCUIT

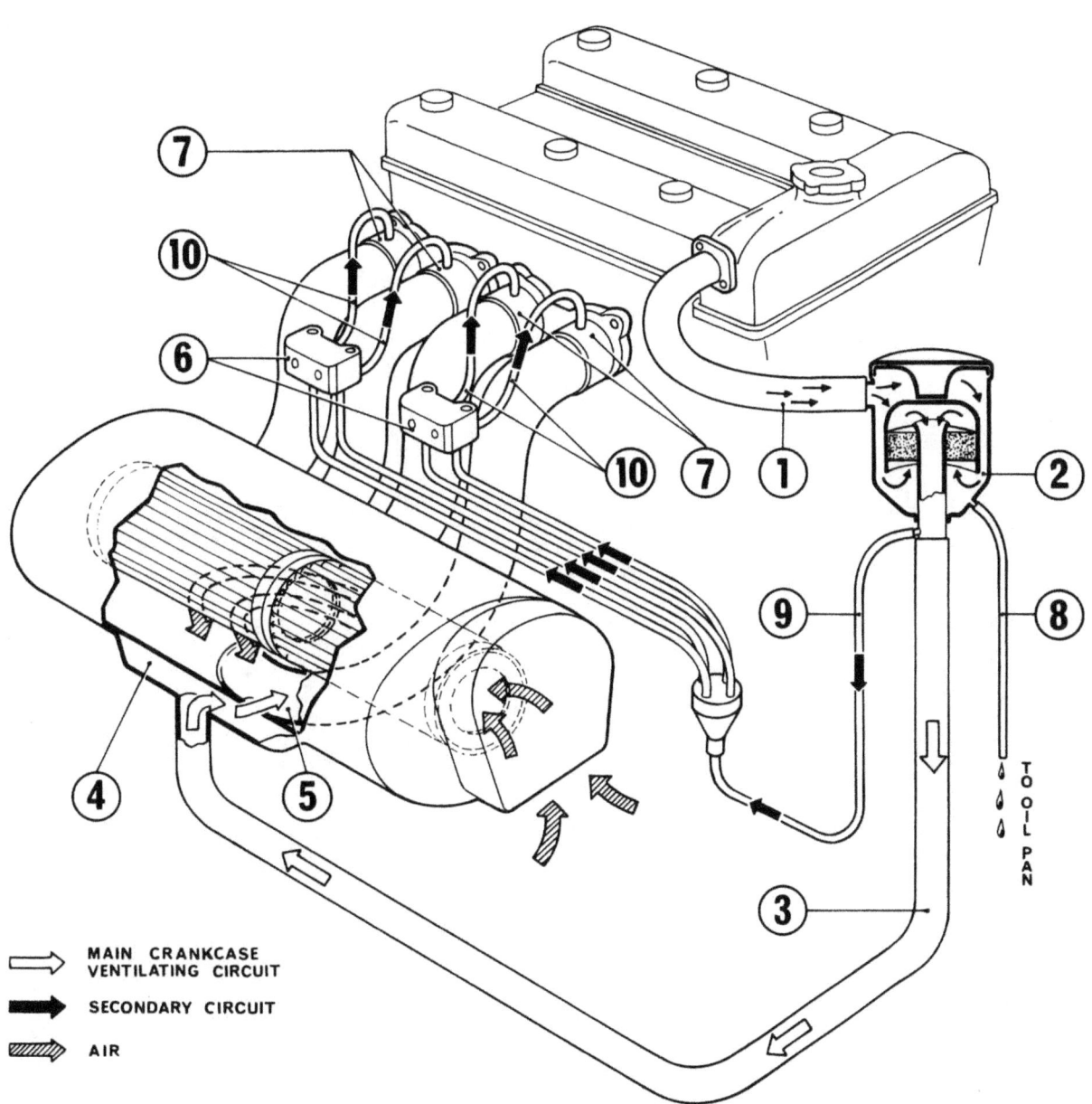

Fig. 3

NOTES

RECOMMENDATIONS ON THE USE

STARTING THE ENGINE

Insert the key in the ignition switch and turn it clockwise to the first click; wait a few seconds to make sure the low fuel pressure warning light goes off.

WARNING: if the warning light does not flash on or stays on, this is an indication of failure of the indicating device or fuel feed system; therefore have them checked as soon as possible.

Turn the ignition key further clockwise to operate the starter. As soon as the engine fires release the key.

Automatic devices act as a standard choke usually does, namely, facilitate the initial running of engine after a cold start until the proper operating temperature is reached.

As an aid in starting from cold, partially depress the accelerator pedal slowly. After a cold start and particularly when the ambient temperature is below freezing point, wait a fairly long time before getting away so as to warm up properly all engine parts and allow the oil to reach all points requiring lubrication.

Top performance must never be demanded of the car until coolant temperature is about 158°F (70°C).

When the engine is already hot or with very high ambient temperatures (above 77°F-25°C) slowly depress the accelerator pedal to facilitate starting.

CAUTION: owing to the special construction of the injection pump, the pump plungers must on no account be operated directly with a lever or any other tool.

UTILIZATION DIRECTIONS

The fuel injection system allows the engine to be used in the widest RPM range; however, in gears higher then the second, the best performance and emission control as well, can only be attained by exceeding 2200 RPM. It is recommended that all driving be done above 2200 RPM, shifting to a lower gear when below this engine speed.

TEMPERATURE SETTING

To keep a constant fuel/air ratio even when the ambient temperature varies as the seasons change, the temperature compensator lever on the control unit shall be shifted to:

- N (normal) for ambient temperatures exceeding 59°F (15°C).

- C (cold) for temperatures between 59°F (15°C) and 32°F (0°C).

- F (freezing) for temperatures below 32°F (0°C).

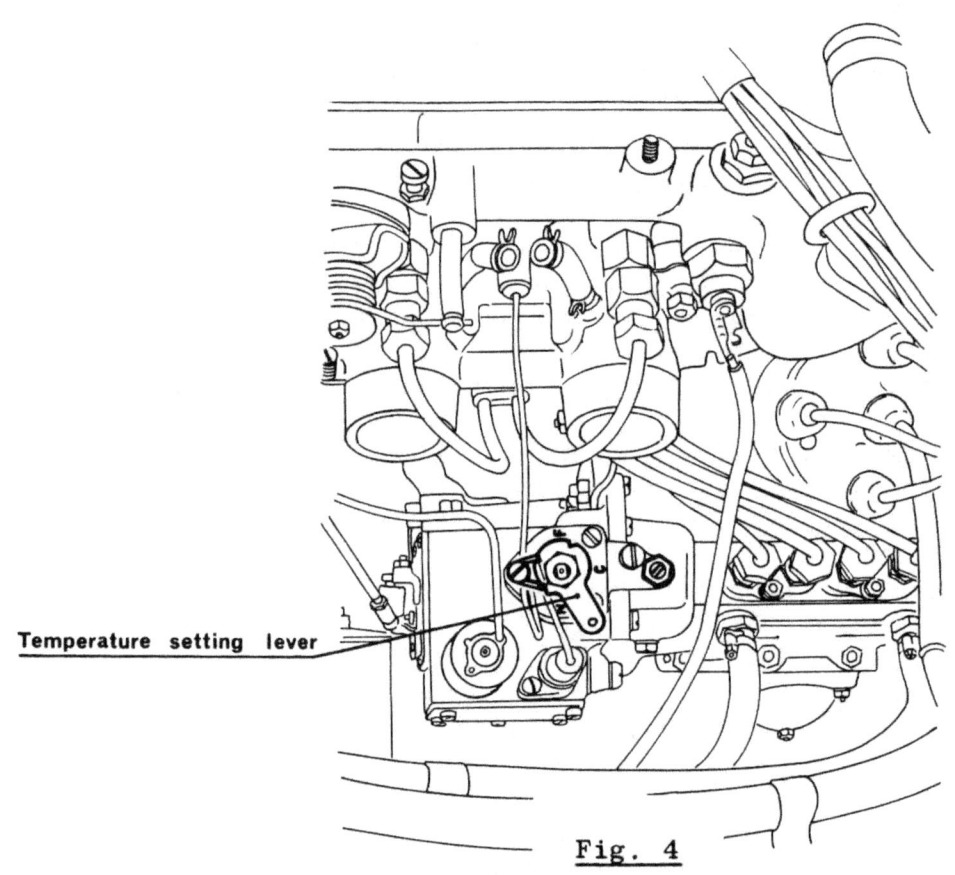

Fig. 4

DECELERATION

On deceleration, the injection pump delivery is automatically cut off this not only eliminates the unburned gases in a condition which is critical for the emission levels, but also favorably affects the fuel consumption.

As this occurs only when the accelerator pedal is released fully, the driver should pay special attention to avoid depressing the pedal even slightly on deceleration, thus preventing detonations from taking place in the exhaust pipes.

REGULAR SERVICING

SCHEDULE OF REGULAR SERVICING REQUIRED TO KEEP THE EXHAUST EMISSION LEVEL WITHIN LIMITS PRESCRIBED BY U.S. REGULATIONS

In order to maintain the fuel injection system in good operating conditions and the exhaust emissions below the limits specified by Federal regulations, the servicing items listed below must be performed at the prescribed period; each item will be set out in details on the following pages.

Every 6,000 miles

Replace air cleaner elements	page 12
Replace main fuel filter element	" 12

Every 12,000 miles (or once a year whichever comes first)

Check spark plugs and replace, if necessary	" 13
Check the alternator and fan driving belt	" 14
Check valve timing chain tension	" 14
Check the distributor and the ignition timing	" 15
Check valve clearance and adjust, if necessary	" 17
Replace air cleaner elements	" 12
Replace main fuel filter element	" 12
Replace tank fuel filter (throw away type)	" 17
Clean throttle valve throats	" 17
Check positioning of throttle/control unit linkage	" 18
Check positioning and alignment of throttles	" 20
Check idle equalizer alignment and idle RPMs	" 21
Road test.	" 23

REPLACE THE AIR CLEANER ELEMENTS

To provide room for subsequent operations, the air cleaner shall be removed as a whole; to do so, detach the two upper anchoring straps at manifold side (see fig. 3); loosen at the engine side the four clamps on the intake hoses; free the crankcase ventilation hoses (3) and (9) from the oil separator; disconnect the four idle hoses (10) from equalizers (6) on cleaner body.

Then the cover of cleaner housing can be removed and the elements replaced after having cleaned the inside of air cleaner housing. Do not reinstall the air cleaner on engine at this point.

REPLACE THE MAIN FUEL FILTER ELEMENT

Perform this operation after that mentioned above and proceed as follows:

- disconnect the battery negative terminal;

- disconnect the starter positive cable if necessary

- CAUTION: first of all clean carefully the outside of filter body to make sure no foreign matter could enter the filter on reassembly;

- slacken the bolt securing the filter to its bracket and remove the filter;

- withdraw the filter element;

- get rid of foreign matter that may have collected in the housing and fit a new element; also replace the housing gasket and the bolt washer, if damaged.

WARNING: extreme cleanliness is required in the area of the fuel filter.

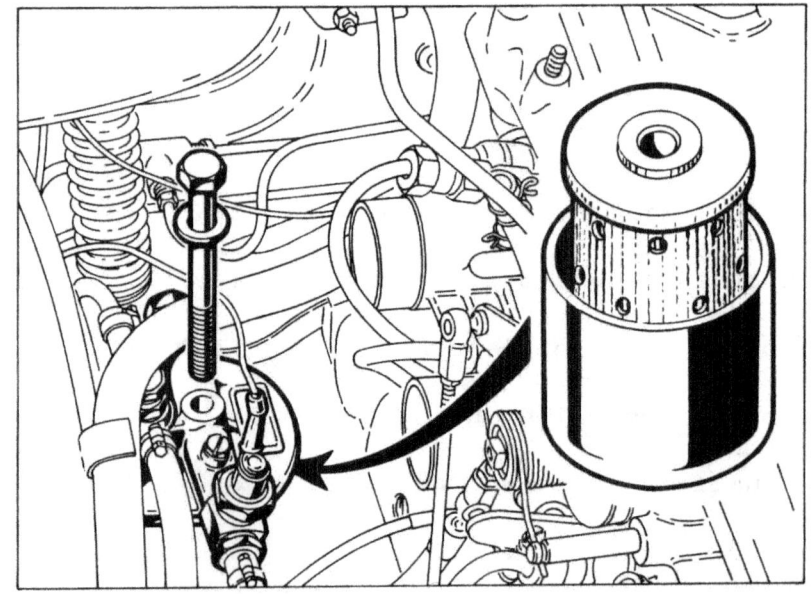

Fig. 5

CHECK SPARK PLUGS (LODGE HL) AND REPLACE, IF NECESSARY

The spark plugs are of the surface gap type with four points and a central electrode. The only maintenance required is occasional cleaning with a brush of the central electrode and points. No routine adjustment is necessary of the gap between the electrode and points.

If the ceramic insulator is cracked or the electrodes are excessively worn away, the spark plugs must be replaced.

The spark plugs should be tightened when cold to a torque of 18-25.3 lb-ft (2.5-3.5 kgm); lubricate the threads with graphite grease before fitting.

The standard plugs fitted to the engine are LODGE HL. A decal, giving the specifications for these plugs, is attached under the hood; here below, the text of the decal is repeated.

> In order to comply with the Federal rule regarding the control of air pollution the engine is fitted with LODGE-HL spark plugs.
>
> These plugs are completely adequate when the automobile is driven at speeds not exceeding the speed limiting regulations. If the automobile is driven at sustained speeds higher than the said speed limits, LODGE-2HL spark plugs must be used.

Under no condition can substitute spark plugs be used, unless they are specifically advised and approved by Alfa Romeo. Use of other plugs can promote serious engine damage, as well as alter emission levels.

CHECK THE ALTERNATOR AND FAN DRIVING BELT

The belt should be tightened enough to drive the fan and alternator pulley without slipping and without overloading the bearings.

The tension is correct when, on pressing the belt down, the sag is about 1/2" (10-15 mm).

To tighten the belt unscrew the nut on the adjusting arm and move the alternator outwards.

CHECK VALVE TIMING CHAIN TENSION

Unscrew the camshaft cover retaining nuts and remove the cover; slacken the chain tensioner setscrew and check that the tensioner spring is working properly; crank the engine for a few seconds to allow the tensioner to tighten the chain and then lock the tensioner setscrew firmly.

On refitting the camshaft cover, make sure the gasket is in sound conditions or replace, if necessary. Moderately tighten the cover retaining nuts in diagonal order.

CHECK THE DISTRIBUTOR (Marelli S 103 B) AND THE IGNITION TIMING

Dwell meter should read between 57 and 63 degrees, with new points closed, corresponding to .017 to .019" (.43 to .48 mm) gap.

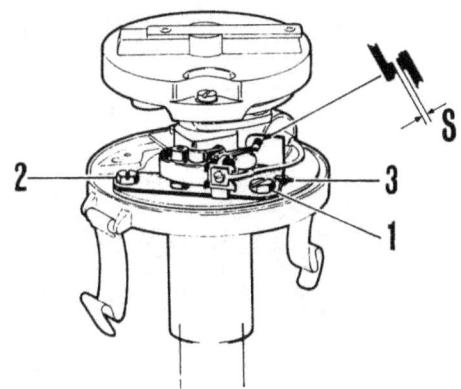

To adjust, loosen the screws 1 and 2, insert a screwdriver in the adjustment slot 3 and pry the stationary-point plate.

S = .017-.019 in.

Smear the distributor cam with grease. Check the inside of distributor cap for any sign of moisture, carbon deposits or cracks and the central power electrode for free movement in its seat and for effective spring action. Finally, check cap terminals for good conditions.

The ignition timing should be checked <u>when the engine is warmed up</u> to operating temperature (coolant exceeding 149°F - 65°C) and running at idle speed by using a timing light.

The timing should be retarded by <u>one to three degrees ATDC</u> (mark F cut in the pulley in line with the pointer) see fig. 6.

With the engine running with no load at <u>5,000 RPM</u>, the ignition advance should be <u>31 to 37 degrees</u>, that is the mark <u>M</u> on the pulley should be in line with the pointer or .12" (3 mm) apart either side.

Timing at idle speed must be adjusted with special care as it affects more greatly the emission levels.

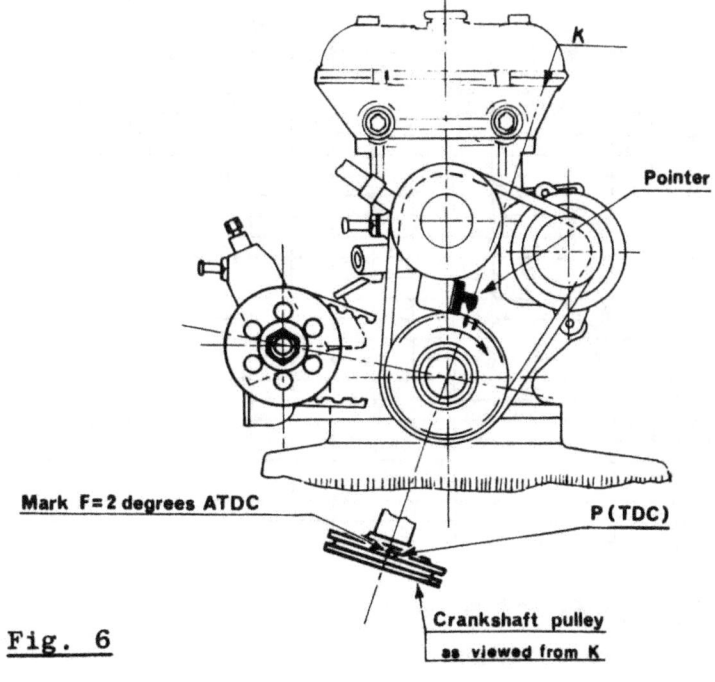

Fig. 6

16

Timing adjustment (maximum accuracy required)

If the timing requires adjustment, preceed as follows:

1 - unscrew the distributor securing nut 1 on the stud so as to allow the distributor to be rotated together with its supporting clamp;
2 - rotate the distributor body counterclockwise or clockwise according to whether it is necessary to respectively advance (A) or retard (R) the ignition setting;
3 - retighten the nut, taking care not to move the distributor body;
4 - recheck timing.

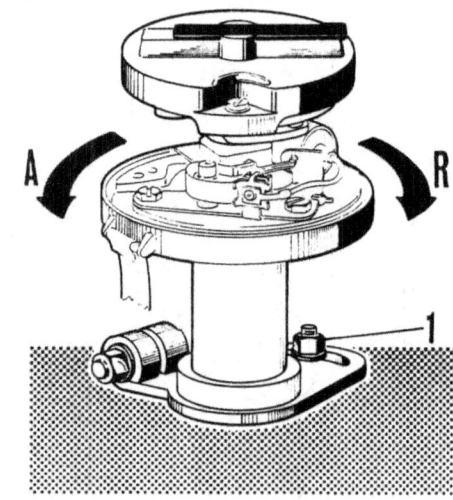

In the event of reinstallation or renewal of the distributor, refer to the directions given on page 25.

Automatic advance graph and specifications of Marelli S 103 B distributor

Contact gap . . . . .017 - .019"
Contact opening angle . . . . 30° $\pm$ 3°
Dwell angle . . . . 70° $\pm$ 3°
Contact pressure . . . . 18 - 21 oz

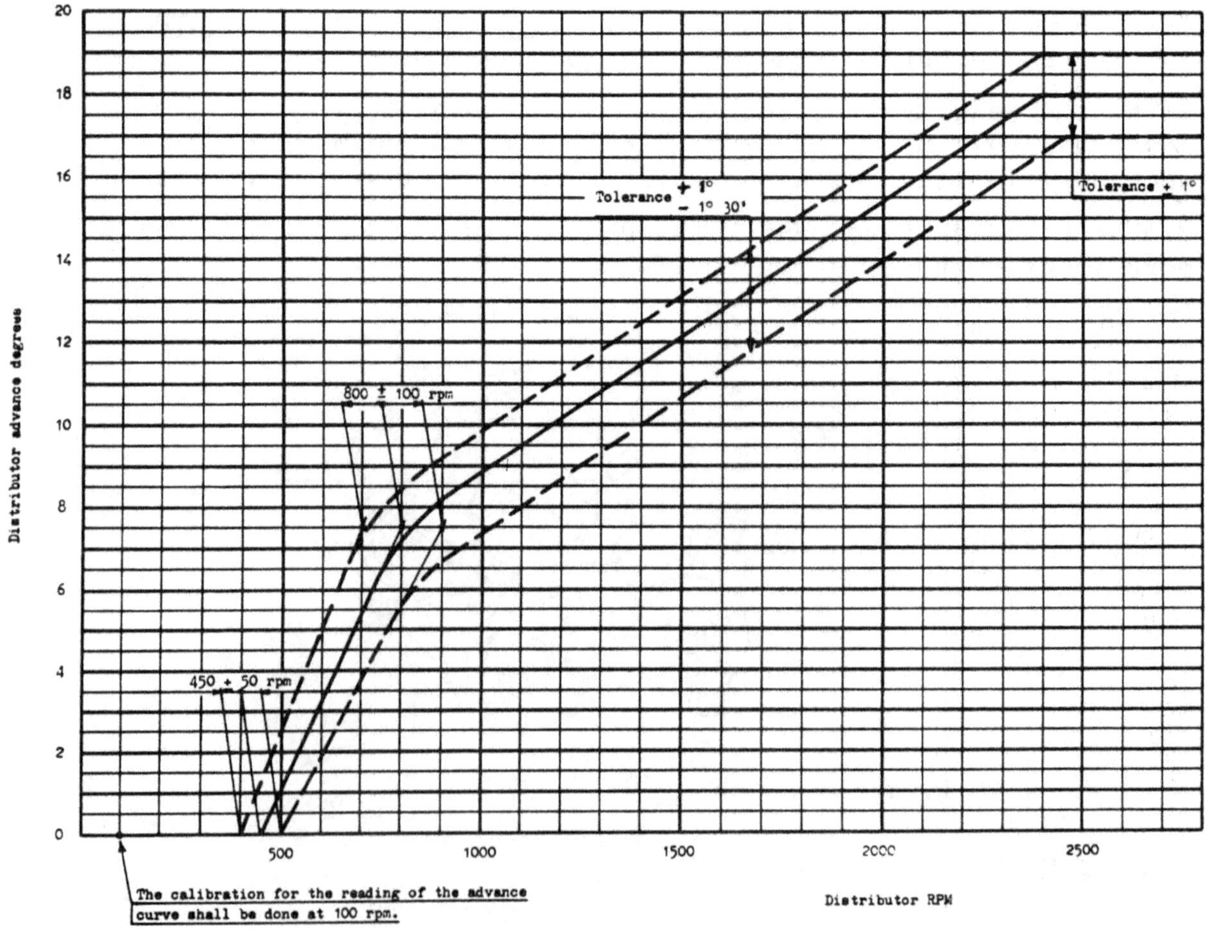

The calibration for the reading of the advance curve shall be done at 100 rpm.

Distributor RPM

17

VALVE CLEARANCE CHECKING AND ADJUSTMENT

The V-mounted overhead valves are directly operated by two camshafts acting thru oil bath cups.

When the engine is cold, carefully measure the clearance "G" with a feeler gage. If the clearance is not as specified, remove camshafts and valve cups; measure the thickness "S" of the adjusting pad on each valve stem and replace it with another of proper thickness so that the clearance is the correct one shown in the diagram.

To facilitate this adjustment the pads are made available in a series of thicknesses ranging from .05 to .014" (1.3 to 3.5 mm) in increments of .001" (.025 mm).

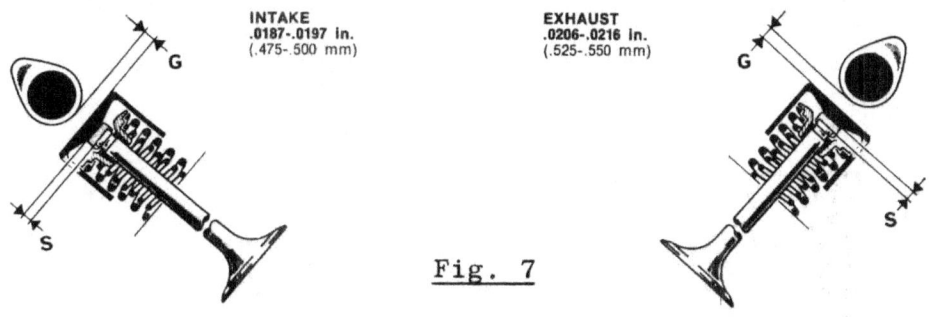

Fig. 7

REPLACE THE TANK FUEL FILTER

To replace the tank fuel filter (throw-away type).(see 4,fig. 1), located on the rear underbody of car, proceed as follows:

- slacken the bolt on the clamp securing the filter to the underbody.
- loosen the clamps securing the hoses to the filter inlet and outlet adapters; it is advisable to stop the pipe from fuel tank provision ally.

Remove the filter and replace it with a new one by proceeding in reverse order of removal. Make sure the hoses are properly positioned.

CLEAN THE THROTTLE VALVE THROATS

Clean the valve throats especially at the areas of contact of throttle valve edges and throat by holding the throttles in full open position and using a brush soaked in gasoline; the cleaning can be completed by rubbing repeatedly the affected areas with a lint-free cloth.

Then, clean in a similar way the throttle valve edges taking care not to strain the spindles.

CHECK THE POSITIONING OF THROTTLE/CONTROL UNIT LINKAGE

This check has to be performed with the air cleaner taken off the engine (see paragraph "Replace the air cleaner elements").
With hot engine (over 158°F - 70°C) and the standard thermostat fitted, check with a feeler gauge that clearance between the control unit input lever and its reference screw is .012 to .024" (.3 to .6 mm) (the nearer to .019" the better) when the relay crank is resting against the idle limit stop; if this is not the case, let the engine cool down then proceed as follows: first disconnect the push-pull rods (7) and (8) (see fig. 2), the cable from the relay crank sheave and the battery negative terminal; remove the cable clamps and fit the tool no. A.4.0121 (fig. 8) onto the studs. Adjust the idle stop screw until the ball joint just touches the reference plane of the tool and lock in this position.

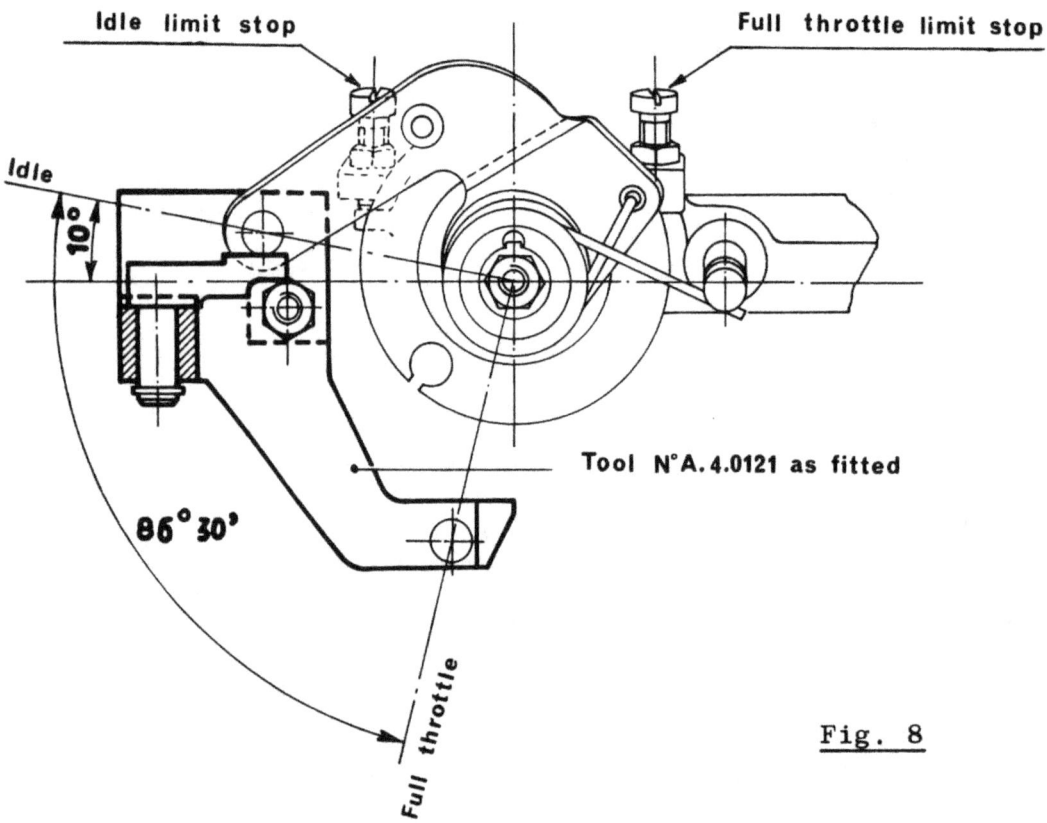

Fig. 8

CAUTION - If the linkage assembly has been removed or if doubts of distortion or straining exist, it is advisable to check also the "full throttle" setting as follows: with the above mentioned tool fitted, rotate the relay crank to bring the ball joint in contact with the "full throttle" reference plane and lock in place the respective limit stop screw.

Now the "actuator" section of the thermostatic control can be removed from the control unit; to do so, remove the two screws retaining the actuator mounting flange and the two screws clamping the actuator pipe anchoring grommet (do not remove the thermostat bulb); then withdraw the actuator taking care not to distort excessively the pipe.

Fit the "dummy actuator" (tool no. A.4.0120 - fig. 9) in place of the standard one just removed. At this point, refit the relay crank/control unit lever rod (8) and, if necessary, adjust the rod length so that the linkage is at rest against the idle limit stop, when, between control unit lever and its reference screw, there is a <u>clearance of .035 - .051" (0.9 - 1.3 mm)</u>.

```
WARNING
Never disturb the reference screw
of control unit input lever.
```

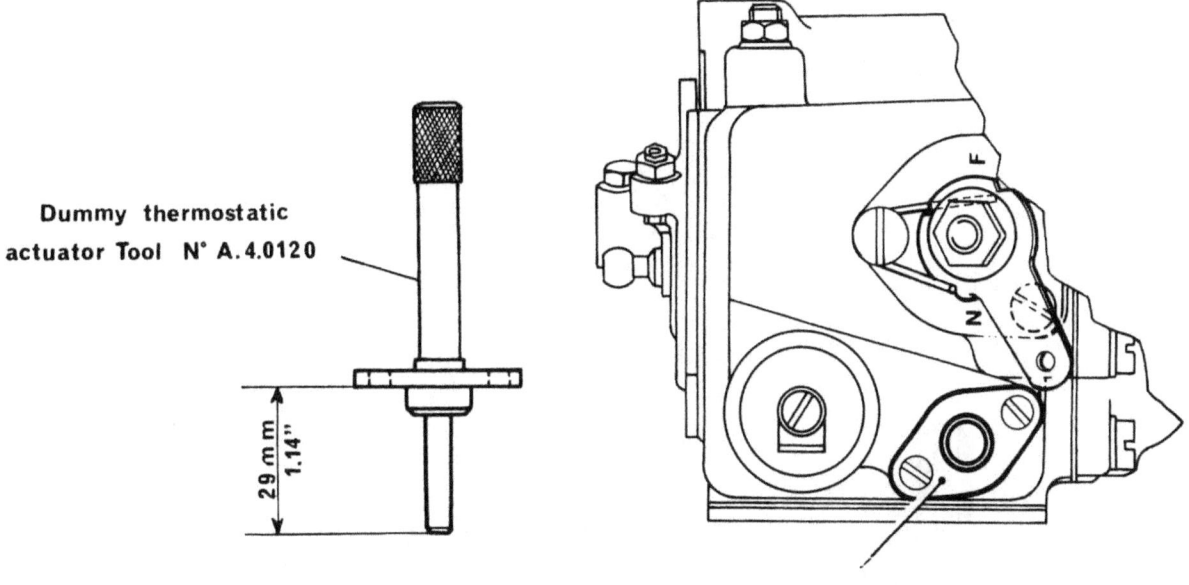

Dummy thermostatic actuator Tool N° A.4.0120

29 mm 1.14"

Dummy thermostatic actuator as fitted

<u>Fig. 9</u>

When the above adjustment is over, reconnect the relay crank-to-throttle rod (7) and, if necessary, adjust the rod length so that the throttle valves are just closed when the linkage rest against the idle limit stop ("just closed" means such a position that, when slightly opening the throttle valves and then releasing them, a definite hit of the linkage against the idle limit stop is felt).

Remove the dummy actuator, reinstall the standard one carefully and tighten it in place.

Again check that - <u>with hot engine</u>- the clearance between the control unit input lever and its reference screw is <u>.012 to .024"</u> (the nearer to .019" the better).

If the injection pump has been removed from engine or any doubt exists that the system setting has been disturbed or any component distorted for a collision, etc., an additional adjustment of throttle angles in relation to control unit lever angles, described on page 25, should be performed.

<u>NOTE</u>: to obtain the specified clearance, a twisting within $\pm 30°$ from the in-line-position of the plastic sockets of each rod is allowed.

CHECK THE POSITIONING AND ALIGNMENT OF THROTTLES

To perform this check, the air cleaner body and hoses shall be removed from the engine and the four adapters of tool no. C.2.0012 connected to the idle fittings on the throttle valve throats; the other end of these adapters shall be connected to the four columns of mercury gage (tool no. C.2.0011) see fig. 10.

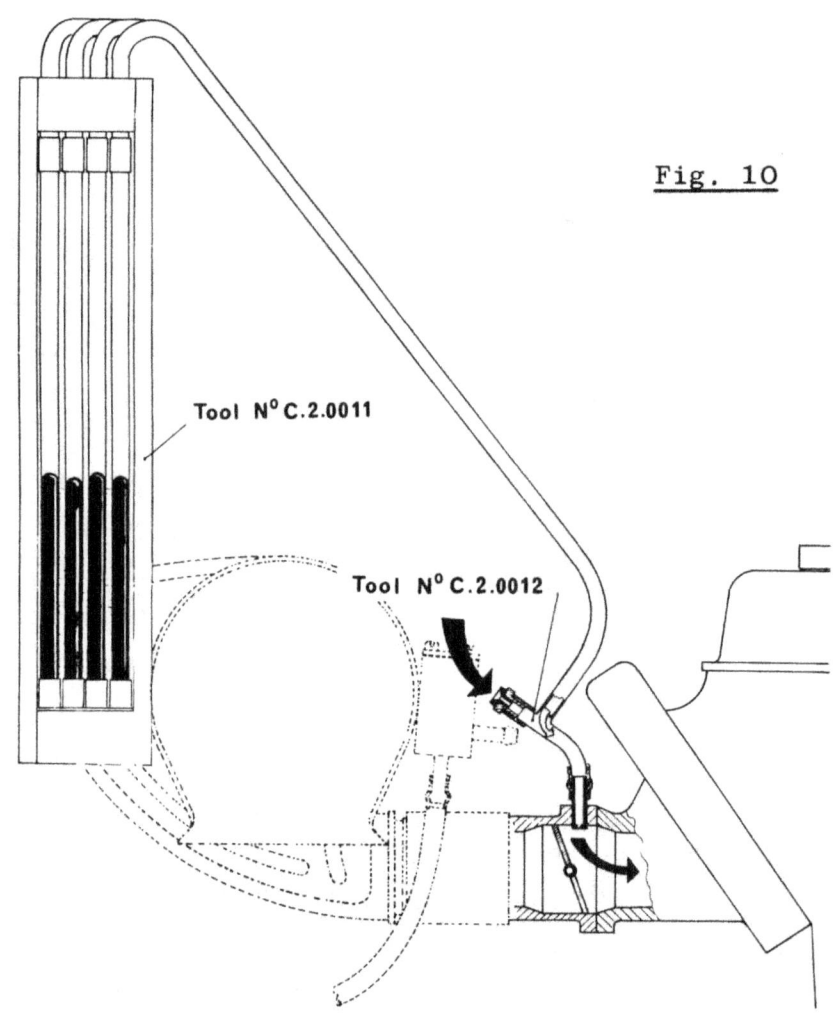

Fig. 10

Start the engine and warm it up until the coolant temperature is at least 158°F (70°C); first check that the clearance between control unit lever and its reference screw is .012 to .024" (the nearer to .019" the better) with hot engine and thermostat actuator fitted.

Now, check that readings on mercury gage columns are much the same (maximum difference: .4"-10 mm); if this is not the case, proceed as follows:

- if readings show that vacuum in front pair of cylinders is higher than in the rear, unscrew the throttle coupling adjusting screw so as to close the rear pair of throttles;

- if vacuum in front pair of cylinders is lower than that in rear pair, disconnect the relay crank-to-throttle rod and set the throttle coupling adjusting screw in such a way as to close the front pair of throttles (screw in the adjusting screw); then, reconnect the relay crank-to-throttle rod and adjust its length so that the throttle valves are in the "just closed" condition as outlined in the paragraph: "Check the positioning of throttle/control unit linkage".

If, before commencing the above adjustments, the engine would run unevenly (lean mixture), make sure the throttle valves are in the "just closed" position; if not the relay crank-to-throttle rod must be shortened.

CAUTION: avoid sudden revving up of the engine or too great a vacuum could take place and the mercury might be sucked out of gage columns.

CHECK IDLE EQUALIZER ALIGNMENT AND IDLE RPMS

Reinstall the air cleaner, clamping in place the hoses and attaching the two upper anchoring straps; also reconnect the crankcase ventilation hoses.
Remove the calibrated restrictors from the adapters (tool no. C.2.0012) and connect the ways from mercury gage columns to the fittings of idle equalizers on air cleaner and to idle fittings on throttle valve throats.

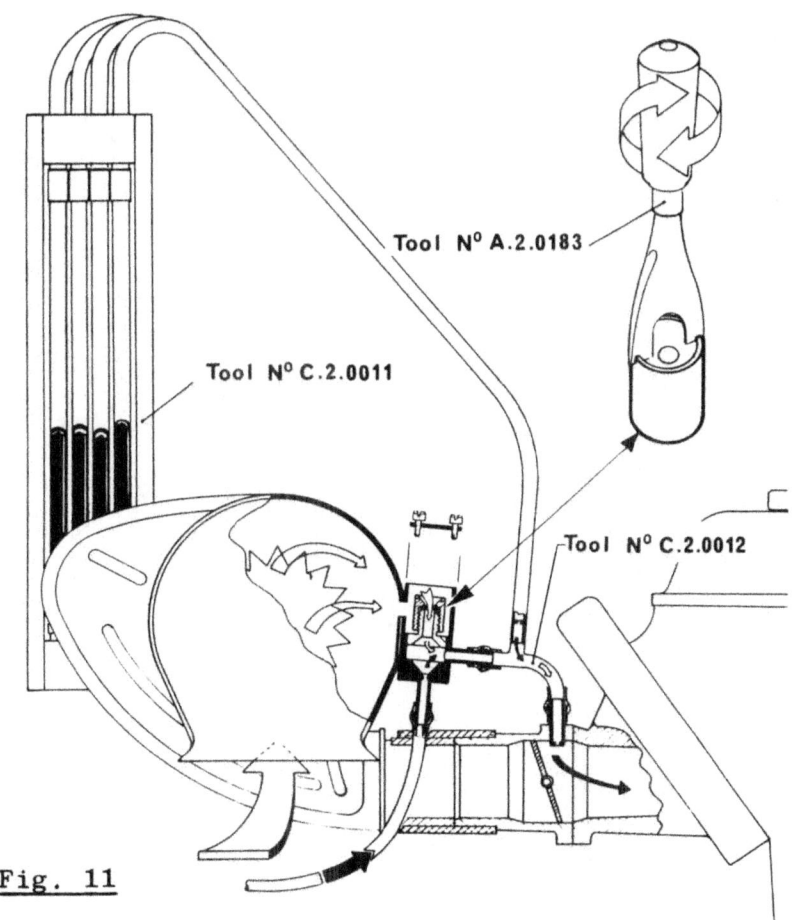

Fig. 11

Start the engine and, when coolant temperature is at 158°F (70°C) as specified, check vacuum in all cylinders for the same reading; if not, bring them to the same level by acting with a screwdriver on the adjusters which, inside the equalizers, calibrate the flow of air; after each adjustment, <u>take care to refit the cover plates to the equalizers before taking readings</u>.

While leveling the readings on mercury gage columns, check at the same time that the engine is running smoothly at an idle speed of at least 720 RPM using an electronic tachometer of proven accuracy.
If too lean a mixture takes place because of increasing the adjuster orifice and the engine thus begins to hunt, screw in at the same time the injection pump delivery adjusting screw, located on control unit (see fig. 12). Repeat the procedure until the engine is idling at the said RPM. (The same "Caution" as given on page 21 applies).

ROAD TEST

With a hot engine drive the car hard for a few miles, using high revs and low gears in order to burn off any deposit from the spark plugs; then drive the car at a constant speed of 30 mph in third gear to see whether the engine operates smoothly, without any hesitation; otherwise, screw in the injection pump delivery adjusting screw by half a turn and repeat the test. If, after that, possible malfunctions are not yet remedied, screw in the injection pump delivery adjusting screw by a further half turn (see fig. 12).

NOTE: to act on the adjusting screw, first loosen the locknut with the wrench tool no. A.5.0168 then turn the screw with the screwdriver tool no. A.2.0185.

This screw is not to be adjusted before all previous steps are completed. It will not correct for inaccurate ignition timing or maladjusted throttles.

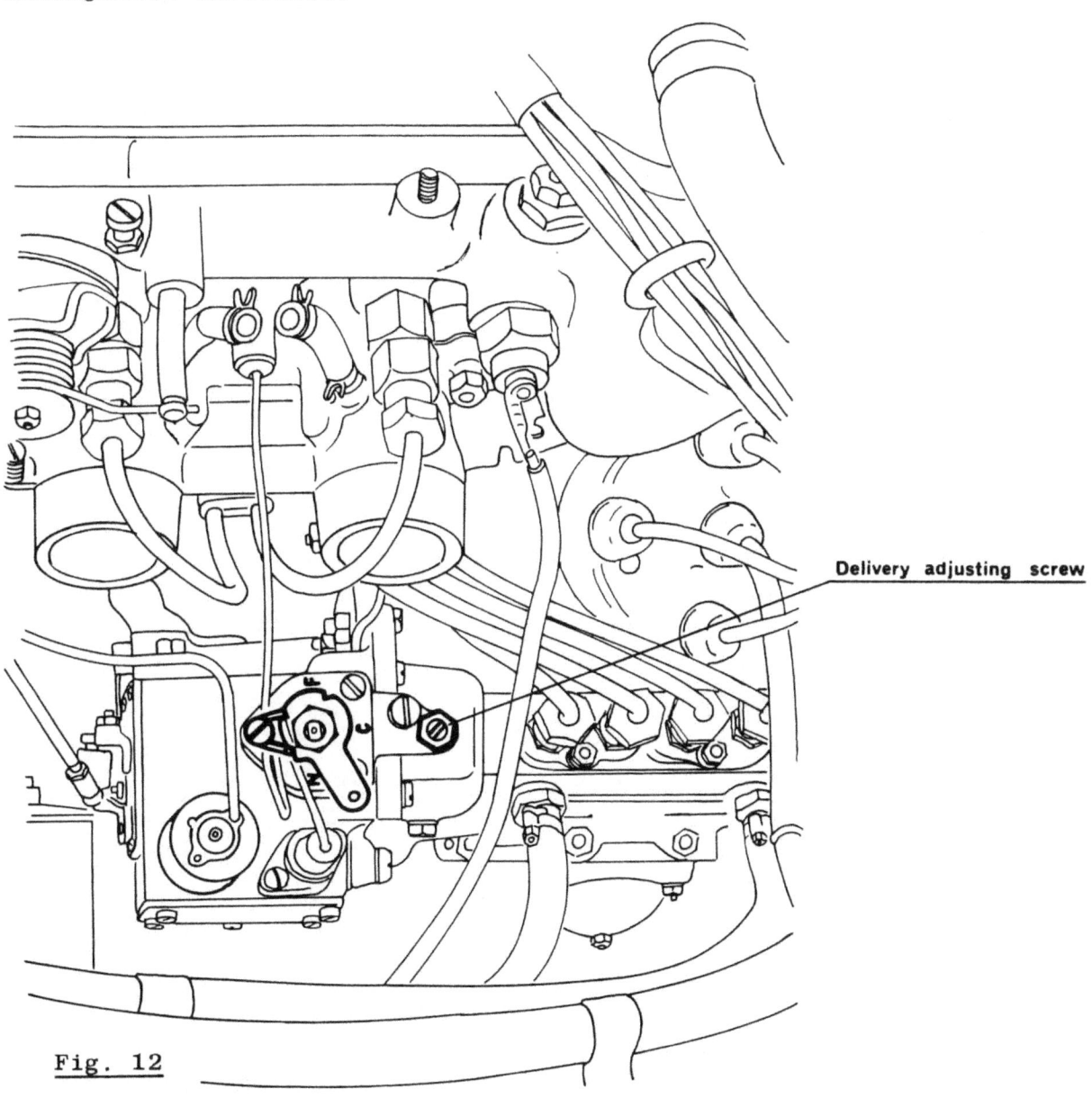

Fig. 12

INDEX OF SPECIFIC ADJUSTMENTS

Installing the ignition distributor . . . . page   25

Check the relationship between throttle angles and
control unit lever angles . . . .   "   25

Installing the thermostatic actuator on control
unit . . . .   "   28

Removal and reinstallation of the injection pump . . .   "   29

Timing the injection pump . . . .   "   30

Adjusting the fuel cut off regulating device . . . . .   "   31

Testing the injectors . . . .   "   31

Replacing the altitude compensator (in-car) . . . . .   "   32

Replacing the oil filter in the injection pump . . . .   "   34

Checking and adjusting the throttle control linkage . . "   35

SPECIFIC ADJUSTMENTS

INSTALLING THE IGNITION DISTRIBUTOR

When reinstalling or renewing the distributor, perform the following procedure:

- rotate the crankshaft to bring no. 1 cylinder piston to the compression stroke that is with both valves closed;

- by slightly rotating the crankshaft bring the fixed advance mark F on pulley into line with the reference pointer;

- fit the supporting clamp onto the distributor body and tighten the clamp just snug;

- remove distributor cap and rotate the drive shaft by hand to bring the rotor arm in line with the contact for no. 1 cylinder;

- as a trial installation place the distributor on engine and move the supporting clamp so that the stud is centered in the clamp slot when the contact-breaker points are about to open for no.1 cylinder

- then, remove the distributor with its supporting clamp, taking care not to disturb the distributor body/clamp setting and lock the clamp in place;

- reinstall the distributor and adjust timing as directed on page 16.

CHECK THE RELATIONSHIP BETWEEN THROTTLE ANGLES AND CONTROL UNIT LEVER ANGLES

Perform this check when the engine is cold; the air cleaner must then be removed from engine (see under "Replace the air cleaner elements"), the procedure for disconnecting the rods (7) and (8)(see fig. 2) must be repeated as well as the removal of thermostatic actuator (taking care not to distort excessively the small pipe).

At this point check the positioning of linkage at idle and full throttle setting with the special tool no. A.4.0121 and fit the dummy actuator, tool no. A.4.0120. Reconnect the rod and check for a clearance of .012 to .024" (the nearer to .019" the better) between the control unit lever and its reference screw (if necessary, adjust the rod length by acting on the threaded clevis).

WARNING

Never disturb the reference screw of control unit input lever.

Fit the fixed protractor (tool no. C.6.0140) onto rear end of control unit, using the cover attaching screws, and the pointer (tool no. C.6.0141) aligned with the zero on the scale (see fig. 13); to take read ings use the suitable built-in light mirror.

Reconnect the rod (7) and check for a proper closure of throttles as directed under "Check the positioning of throttle/control unit linkage".

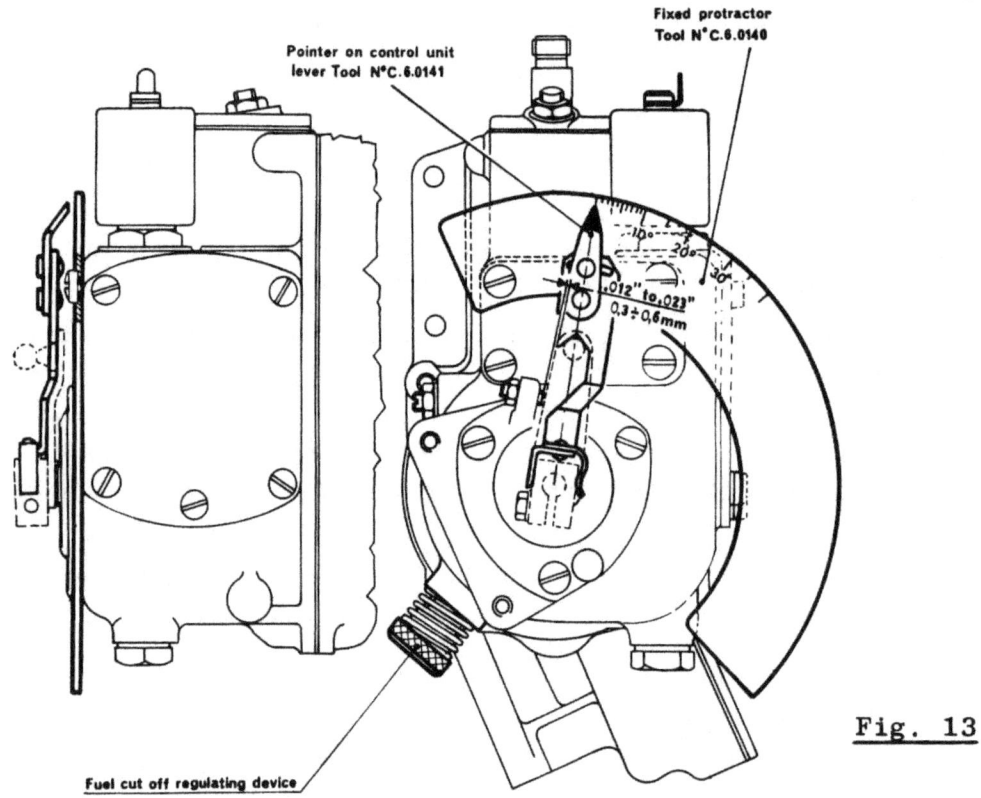

Fig. 13

Place the movable protractor (tool no. C.6.0142) on the spindle of rear throttle valve pair and set to zero in correspondence of the pointer (tool no. C.6.0143) see fig. 14.

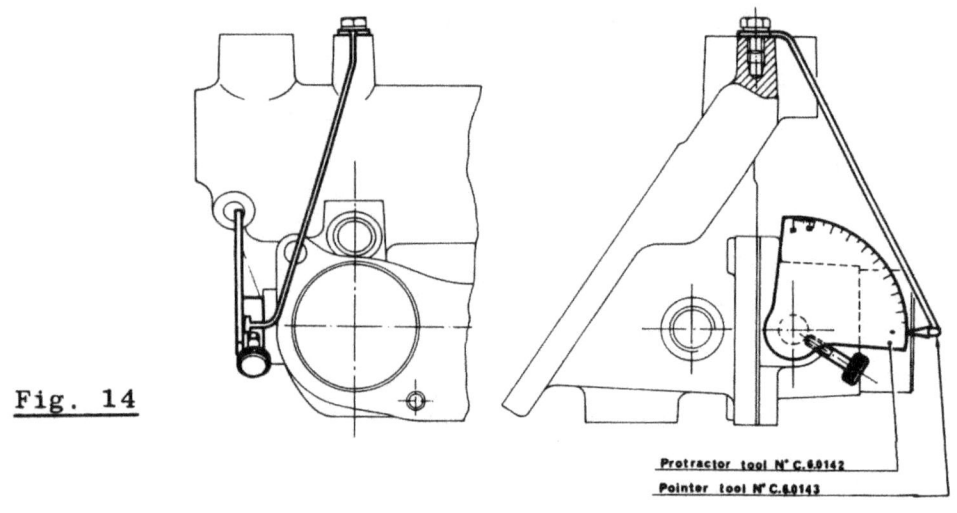

Fig. 14

Install the tool no. A.2.0181 using the cable sheath clips and gradually rotate the relay crank by acting on the adjuster (See fig. 15).

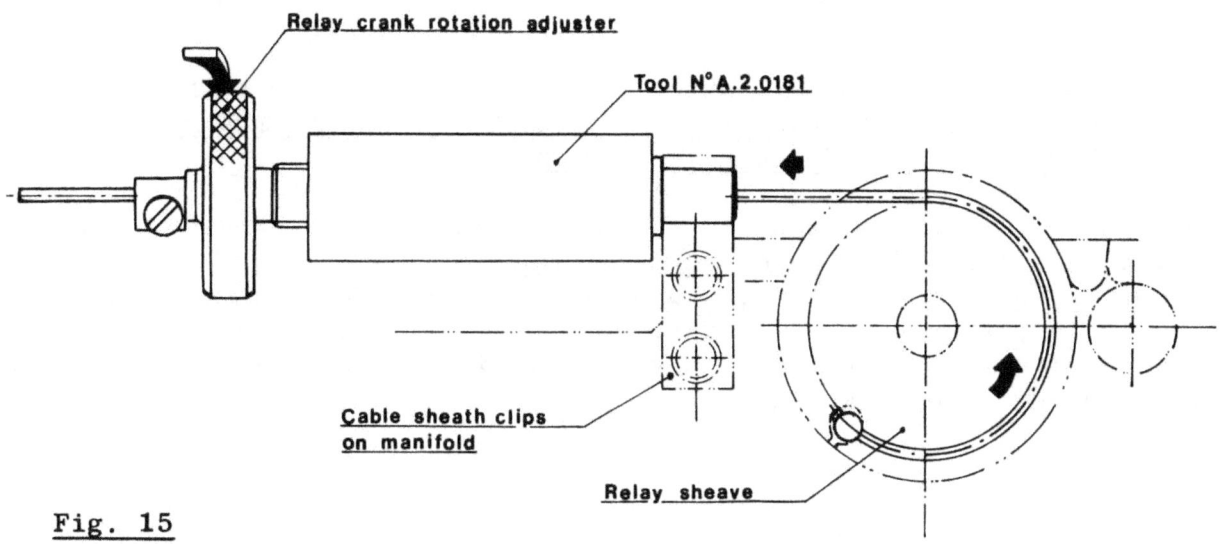

Fig. 15

Open the throttle valves to predetermined angles (2, 4, 6 degrees - see table) and read the corresponding rotations of control unit lever.

THROTTLE ANGLES/CONTROL UNIT LEVER ANGLES RELATIONSHIP TABLE

α	β	Tolerance on β
0°	0°	
2°	8° 13'	± 20'
4°	14° 40'	
6°	20° 09'	
10°	29° 30'	± 1°
15°	39° 20'	
20°	47° 54'	
25°	55° 33'	
30°	62° 30'	
35°	68° 51'	
40°	74° 41'	± 2°
50°	84° 55'	
60°	93° 25'	
70°	100° 12'	
82°	106° 08°	

α = throttle rotation angle

β = control unit lever rotation angle

28

In the event the throttle angles and control unit lever angles are out of the specified relation, it is likely that checking procedure has not been perfectly accomplished; therefore, try once more; if again it will not satisfy, inspect carefully any component of control linkage, or parts directly affecting it, replace any defective part and repeat the procedure.

When the above checks are over, lengthen the rod (8) until there is a clearance of .035 to .051" (0.9 - 1.3 mm) or 1° to 1° 30' between the control unit lever and the reference screw.

On completion of adjustments, reinstall the standard thermostatic actuator and check for a clearance of .012 to .024" (.3 to .6 mm) with a hot engine (coolant temperature above 158°F - 70°C) between the control unit lever and its reference screw; if necessary, adjust the length of rod (8) by acting on the clevis thread (the same footnote as given on page 19 applies).

INSTALLING THE THERMOSTATIC ACTUATOR ON CONTROL UNIT

If the engine shows too fast an idle and black smoke at the exhaust or stalls easily at idle while emitting black smoke or if an excessive fuel consumption is experienced, the cause is probably a malfunction of the thermostatic actuator on the injection pump control unit.

To replace the thermostatic actuator, proceed as follows:

- remove the air cleaner as outlined under "Replace the air cleaner elements";

- drain about one gallon of coolant from cooling system and remove the defective thermostat assembly;

- install the new thermostat assembly by fitting first the bulb on manifold, then the actuator pipe anchoring grommet and finally the actuator on control unit taking care not to distort excessively the small pipe. Replace the "O"ring on thermostat bulb, if necessary;

- check that clearance between control unit lever and the reference screw is .146 to .165" (3.7 to 4.2 mm) when the coolant temperature is about 68°F (20°C). Should this clearance not fall in the above specified limits, screw in or unscrew the adjuster in the control unit (to gain access to adjuster, take the actuator off) to respectively increase or diminish the clearance;

- on completion of thermostat installation, replenish the cooling system.

REMOVAL AND REINSTALLATION OF THE INJECTION PUMP

After having removed the air cleaner (see relevant directions) perform the following steps:

- disconnect the negative battery terminal;
- disconnect the lead from cold starting device selenoid;
- remove the two screws on the thermostat actuator mounting flange and the two screws clamping the actuator pipe anchoring grommet (do not remove the thermostat bulb); then withdraw the actuator from the control unit, taking care not to distort excessively the pipe;
- disconnect the fuel hoses from injection pump;
- detach the push-pull rod from the control unit.

Proceed by timing the injection pump with the engine (instant in which fuel injection starts); to do this, bring the no.1 piston at 70° BTDC of the induction stroke by aligning the mark "I" cut in the crankshaft pulley with the pointer on crankcase front cover (doing so will facilitate the reinstallation on the injection pump to the engine).

Finally, unscrew the three attaching nuts and remove the drive belt cover; then take the drive belt off the injection pump pulley.

Now, perform the removal of the injection pump proper as follows:

- fully slacken the injection pipe nuts on pump outlet fittings (use the wrench tool no. A.5.0164), without removing the pipes;
- unscrew the nuts on the two bolts attaching the pipe cluster plate and the injection pump slanting bracket;
- loosen the two screws attaching the control unit to its bracket at the engine mount;
- unscrew, from the underside of car, the four nuts (use tool A.5.0167 for the front ones) attaching the injection pump support to the engine front cover.

Withdraw the injection pump and its support as a unit by tilting it suitably.

To reinstall the injection pump, reverse the removal procedure.

In case of injection pump renewal, the new injectors, supplied with the new pump, must be installed on the engine in place of the old ones. The new injectors bring a location number and must be installed accordingly.

CAUTION: owing to the special construction of the injection pump, the pump plungers must on no account be operated directly with a lever or any other tool.

WARNING: on reinstallation, align the reference marks on the injection pump and the drive pulley (with the engine previously timed for injection in no.1 cylinder), then fit the drive belt onto the pulley avoiding the use of tools that might damage the belt.

TIMING THE INJECTION PUMP

To check the injection pump timing proceed as follows:

rotate the crankshaft until the mark "I" is aligned with the pointer on crankcase front cover corresponding to 70° BTDC of the induction stroke; to do this easier, turn the crankshaft over counterclockwise until the no. 1 cylinder intake valve (as seen through the spark plug hole) closes; then, go on in revolving the shaft until the above mentioned mark and pointer line up.

Now, check that the mark on the injection pump pulley is aligned with the reference on the injection pump itself (to gain access to the reference on the injection pump remove the protective cover).

N.B. - The reference marks can be out of alignment within a tolerance of about ± .2" (5 mm) corresponding to half pitch of pulley splines.

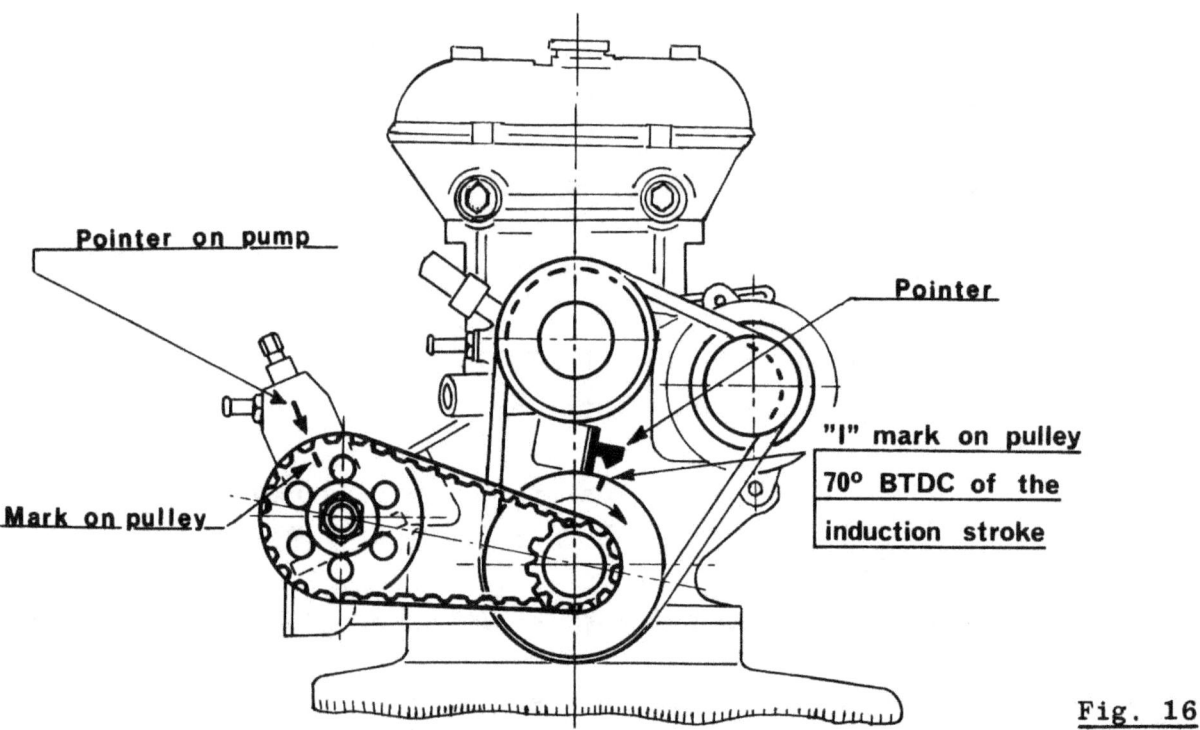

Fig. 16

If the pump is out of timing:

- remove the drive belt;
- line up the reference marks of the injection pump and refit the drive belt by rotating the pulley in either direction to engage the nearest spline.

On completion of the alignment, refit the protective cover.

ADJUSTING THE FUEL CUT OFF REGULATING DEVICE

The injection pump control unit is provided with a device, located at the bottom of unit (see fig. 13), that regulates the rate at which fuel cut off ceases on decelerations with a fully released accelerator pedal, thus preventing exhaust emissions and detonations from taking place due to incomplete combustion.

If, when releasing the accelerator pedal fully with the engine either under load or in neutral, exhaust detonations occur, the cause may be an improper adjustment of the fuel cut off device.

In this event, progressively screw in the knurled knob until the trouble is remedied, taking care that the engine does not stop when, hot and in neutral, is decelerated from about 4000 RPM.

If, on the contrary, the engine stops when the accelerator pedal is released fully in neutral, then progressively unscrew the knurled knob until the engine keeps running when it is decelerated, again hot and in neutral, from about 4000 RPM taking care, however, not to give rise to detonations.

NOTE: to adjust this device gain access from the underside of car.

TESTING THE INJECTORS

Since the operating conditions of the injectors are not so heavy (being located in the air intake ports and therefore not subject to the high pressures and temperatures of the combustion chamber) and since the life of the injectors is expected to be the same as that of the car, they should undergo a test only when the cause for malfunctions is unquestionably attributed to the injectors themselves.

To test the injectors use a handpump like that for testing Diesel injectors but supplied with gasoline and provided with a pressure gage whose top dial reading is 700-1000 psi (50-70 Kg/cm^2).

The procedure for checking the spray shape, injection pressure and leaks is as follows:

- connect the test pump pipe to the injector inlet fitting which has a 12 x 1.5 mm metric thread;
- pump quickly to prime pump and injector;
- pump slowly until injector nozzle opens; this must take place at 360-400 psi (25-28 Kg/cm^2) for new injectors and at no less than 260 psi (18 Kg/cm^2) for used injectors;
- again pumping slowly, bring the pressure to 15-30 psi (1-2 Kg/cm^2) below the rating pressure taken as directed above and make sure that there is no drip from the nozzle within five seconds;
- pump quickly and check that the spray is narrow, deeply plunging and has good vaporization even at minimum delivery. At a distance of 4" (100 mm) from the nozzle orifice the spray cone diameter should be about .8" (20 mm). If the injector does not meet these requirements, replace it with a new one;
- The injectors must be tightened in place with a torque of 20.2-23.1 lb-ft (2.8 - 3.2 Kgm).

N.B. - To remove the injectors use the wrench tool no. A.5.0165.

REPLACING THE ALTITUDE COMPENSATOR (in-car)

If the engine runs at idle but stops as soon as it is accelerated the cause of that is lean mixture due to a failure in the altitude compensator which must therefore be replaced.

The replacement procedure is the following:
- remove the air cleaner;
- bring the temperature setting lever to N position.

Then remove in this sequence:
- the relay crank-to-control unit rod;
- the rear inspection cover from the control unit;
- the altitude compensator with its mounting flange, taking care not to disturb the position of the setting lever (N position).

CAUTION: do not move the control unit input lever (even better tape it in place) nor disturb the inside devices of control unit or serious damage and out-of-adjustment may result.

Measure the dimension A between the bottom face of compensator mounting flange and the top of bellows: such a dimension should fall between .16 and .21" (4 - 5.5 mm).

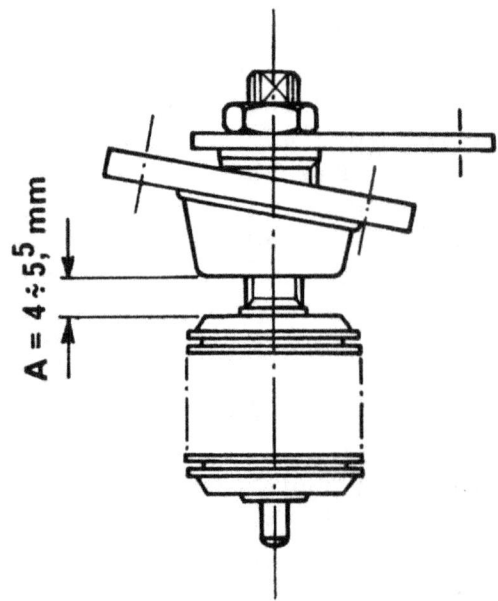

Loosen the locknut and unscrew the capsule taking care not to rotate the setting lever with respect to the mounting flange.
Screw in the new capsule until the dimension previously taken is obtained; then slightly tighten the locknut.
NOTE: if, because of any reason, the dimension A does not fall within the specified limits, screw in the new capsule to a dimension of 5 mm irrespective of the dimension previously read.
Install capsule, and mounting flange assembly on the control unit making sure the setting lever spring is properly positioned and the setting lever itself is in "N" position.

Refit the rear inspection cover and the rod.

Start the engine and warm it up until the coolant has reached a temperature of no less than 158° F (70°C) then race the engine a few times up to 4000 rpm and fully release the throttle pedal each time.

Stop the engine, again remove the rear inspection cover and (with the aid of a suitable mirror and a lamp to light the inside of control unit) see whether the wire at the end of link engages the notch corresponding to the actual atmospheric pressure as listed below (notches to be counted starting from the top of the notched lever):

- atmospheric pressure falling between 29.9 - 30.7 in Hg: the wire should engage the 3rd notch.
- pressure falling between 29.1 - 29.9 in Hg: the wire should engage the 4th notch.
- pressure between 28.3 - 29.1 in Hg: the wire should engage the 5th notch.
- pressure between 27.6 - 28.3 in Hg: the wire should engage the 6th notch.

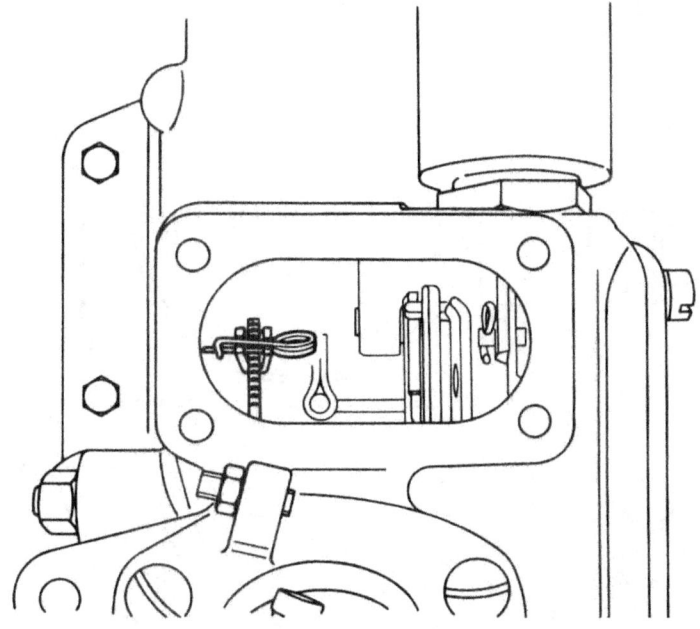

If the above conditions are not fulfilled, adjust the position of the capsule so that, when the engine is started again (before that refit the rear inspection cover on control unit) and the warming up procedure (racing the engine followed by a complete release of accelerator) is repeated, the wire positions itself correctly: screw in the capsule to cause the wire to engage notches of higher numbers and unscrew the capsule to engage notches of lower numbers. Keep in mind that a rotation of about 150 degrees corresponds to one notch.

Tighten securely the locknut on the capsule, place the temperature setting lever in the position corresponding to the ambient conditions and reinstall the air cleaner.

REPLACING THE OIL FILTER IN THE INJECTION PUMP

On performing the engine major overhaul, on removing the injection pump (or after 50000 miles whichever occurs first) or on replacing the engine oil in case of contamination by water or similar, the additional oil filter located in the injection pump support must be renewed.

To do so, proceed as follows:

clean very carefully the filter housing cover and the surrounding areas to prevent any foreign matter from entering the filter housing.

remove the cover and withdraw the element; wash thoroughly the filter housing with gasoline, then insert the new element in such a way that the spring faces the cover; renew the cover gasket, if necessary.

To facilitate the air bleed and the quick filling up of filter housing with oil, slightly tighten the two upper cover retaining nuts; crank the engine a few seconds (even by means of the starter) until the oil just oozes out; then lock the nuts fully.

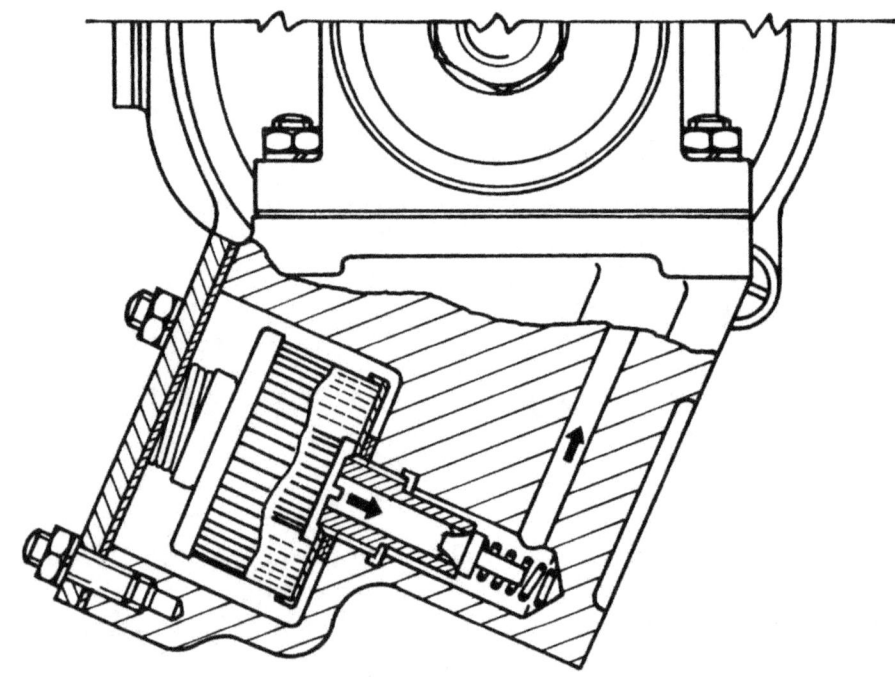

CHECKING AND ADJUSTING THE THROTTLE CONTROL LINKAGE

Engine cold.

Disconnect the relay crank-to-control unit rod 8 (see fig. 2) at the crank-side joint.

When the relay crank is at rest against the idle limit stop, there should be a .04 - .06" (1-1.5 mm) free travel at the pedal lever (see page 5, point "a") in the engine compartment with respect to the reference screw on the cable anchoring bracket; if not so, adjust the reference screw until the specified free travel is obtained.

Depress the accelerator pedal to the floor and check that the clearance between relay crank lug and full throttle limit stop is .08" (2 mm): if not so, adjust the pedal stop on floor until the specified clearance is obtained.

Reconnect the rod 8.

Engine hot (coolant temperature higher than 158°F - 70°C).

With the accelerator pedal fully released, check that the free travel at the pedal lever (see page 5, point "a") is .04 - .06"(1- 1.5 mm).

NOTE: if the adjustments of the reference screw are not enough to obtain the correct free travel of pedal lever, loosen the cable setscrew and tighten it again on the cable at a more suitable position.

TROUBLE SHOOTING

The following chart lists several malfunctions, possible cause for each of them and remedies.

If deficiencies or malfunctions are experienced in the fuel system, it is absolutely essential to make sure they are not caused nor affected by the incorrect operation of the ignition system: in fact it is impossible to distinguish "a priori" whether a failure of fuel or ignition system is the cause for the deficiencies; therefore, first inspect the ignition system for the following and remedy, if necessary

- spark plugs for proper operation and type;
- contact-breaker points conditions and gap.
- ignition coil for continuity or leakage;
- ignition distributor for correct timing using a timing light; adjust timing or replace the ignition distributor, if necessary.

Should any of the troubles listed below be experienced, it is recommended to clean thoroughly the affected areas of both engine and engine compartment with a suitable solvent; this to the purpose of preventing any foreign matter from entering, on removal or reinstallation, the mechanical components and specifically the fuel feed circuit.

Soon after cleaning, inspect the mechanical units for loose attaching or joining parts, the pipes for loose fittings and the brackets for sound conditions.

TROUBLE	POSSIBLE CAUSE	REMEDY
Low fuel pressure warning light does not flash on when ignition key is turned	Fuse no. 6 blown Warning light bulb burnt out Pressure switch faulty (jammed open)	Replace fuse Replace bulb Check switch and replace, necessary

TROUBLE	POSSIBLE CAUSE	REMEDY
Low fuel pressure warning light stays on (fuel pump operates properly)	Pressure switch faulty (jammed closed)	Replace switch
	Low fuel pump outlet pressure due to:	
	- tank to pump lines clogged or air seeping thru them	- Inspect fuel lines
	- tank fuel filter clogged	- Remove and clean filter
	- main fuek filter clogged	- Clean filter and replace element (see page 12)
	- main filter pressure relief valve defective or stuck open	- Check relief valve and replace, if necessary
	Fuel pump delivery too low	Have fuel pump checked or replaced.
Low fuel pressure warning light stays on (fuel pump fails to operate)	Fuse blown (in the additional fuse box)	Replace fuse
	Electric wires to pump disconnected	Check and reconnect
	Fuel pump faulty	Have the pump checked or replaced
Engine will not start from cold	Selenoid-actuated cold start device fails to operate	- check electric connections - Have the device checked or replaced
Engine misfires; rough idle	One injector defective	Trace the cylinder by grounding each spark plug and replace the injector, if necessary
	Injection pipe fittings leaking	Tighten fittings
	Injection pipes cracked	Check and replace, if necessary
Rough idle (hunting)	Lean mixture	Remedy possible air seepage downstream throttles. Refer to page 21
Too fast an idle and smoky exhaust	Faulty thermostatic actuator	Replace thermostatic actuator
Engine keeps running at idle but stops on accelerating	Altitude compensator faulty	Replace altitude compensator (see page 32)

TROUBLE	POSSIBLE CAUSE	REMEDY
Idle too fast	Accelerator linkage fails to return fully	Check: - flexible cable - linkage joints and pivot pins for free movement - pedal return spring for sound conditions - pedal and linkage limit stop for proper adjustment Clean linkage joints and pack with grease
Unsatisfactory driveability and road performance; hesitations	Control linkage out of adjustment	Check throttle/control unit linkage (see page 18)
	Fuel pump outlet pressure too low (warning light comes on while running at high rpm.)	Refer to remedies as under "Low fuel pressure warning light stays on"
	Air induction clogged	Check and replace air cleaner elements, if necessary
	Injector defective	Refer to remedies as under "Engine misfires; rough idle"
	Injection pump or control unit/ defective	Have them checked and replaced, if necessary, by an authorized workshop
Excessive fuel consumption	Fuel feed circuit leaks	Check pipes, fittings, seals and replace defective parts
	Thermostatic actuator defective; also refer to causes as under "Too fast an idle"	Have the thermostatic actuator checked and replaced, if necessary, by an authorized workshop
	Defective carburation	Have the injection pump adjusted by an authorized workshop
Engine stalls in positions other than idle	Defective altitude compensator or excessive vibrations of injection pump and control unit	Have the altitude compensator checked (see page 32); also check injection pump and control unit brackets for sound conditions and firm attachment
Engine stalls flat	Injection pump driving belt defective	Replace belt

TROUBLE	POSSIBLE CAUSE	REMEDY
Detonations in the exhaust pipe on deceleration	Both throttles and control unit lever fail to return fully on deceleration	Check: - flexible cable - linkage joints and pivot pins for free movement - pedal and linkage return springs for sound conditions - pedal and linkage limit stops for proper adjustment - clean linkage joints and pack them with grease suitable for low temperatures
	Control unit lever out of adjustment does not return fully on deceleration	Check throttle/control unit linkage (see page 18)
	Fuel cut off regulator device out of adjustment	Screw in knurled knob on control unit bottom (see fig. 13) until no more detonations occur; take care that engine does not stop when, hot and unloaded, is decelerated from about 4,000 rpm
Engine stops frequently on deceleration	Fuel cut off regulator device out of adjustment	Unscrew knurled knob (see fig. 13) so as to remedy the trouble without giving rise to detonations on deceleration
Noisy electric fuel pump	Line between pump and main filter distorted or forced in the rubber mountings or against the recovery pipe	Reset the line making certain it is centered in the rubber mountings without forcing against the recovery pipe
	Tank filter and hoses improperly fitted	Check that the filter is properly fitted and that hoses have a correct run

A.R. PUMP POLICY

Injection pumps are not to be opened for any reason. An exchange pump service is available for complete pump units. Pumps that have been tampered with will forfeit any core valve.

Always before removing a pump consult your Alfa Romeo representative or zone office.

NOTES

Direzione Assistenza

INSTRUCTION AND MAINTENANCE MANUAL

FOR ALFA ROMEO 1750

FUEL INJECTION MODELS

U.S.A. VERSION

1971 MODEL YEAR

This manual contains the specifications and the instructions covering the fuel injection system installed on Alfa Romeo 1750 automobiles 1971 Model year.

Special care should be given to the regular servicing and maintenance directions, particularly as far as the efficiency of the system is concerned.

It is important that any maintenance and repair work be entrusted only to an authorized Alfa Romeo Dealer as such Dealers are equipped with the proper tools and staffed by specially trained mechanics.

ALFA ROMEO
Direzione Assistenza

CONTENTS

Important note . . . . page 1

A - DESCRIPTION OF FUEL INJECTION SYSTEM

1. General . . . . " 2
2. Fuel feed system. Operating diagram . . . . " 2
3. General arrangement of fuel system . . . . " 3
4. Air induction system . . . . " 4
5. Injection pump . . . . " 4
6. Cold start device . . . . " 4
7. Air induction system and throttle-control unit linkage . . . . " 5
8. Initial running device . . . . " 6
9. Crankcase ventilating system . . . . " 6
10. Crankcase ventilating circuit . . . . " 7
11. Fuel vapor recovery system and tank ventilation . . " 8

B - RECOMMENDATIONS ON THE USE

1. Starting the engine . . . . " 9
2. Utilization directions . . . . " 9
3. Temperature setting . . . . " 10
4. Deceleration . . . . " 10

C - REGULAR SERVICING

1. Schedule . . . . " 11
2. Replace the air cleaner elements . . . . " 12
3. Replace the main fuel filter element . . . . " 12
4. Check spark plugs (Lodge HL) and replace, if necessary . . . . " 13
5. Check the alternator and fan driving belt . . . . . " 14
6. Check valve timing chain tension . . . . " 14
7. Check the distributor (Marelli S 103 B) and the ignition timing . . . . " 15
8. Valve clearance checking and adjustment . . . . . . " 17
9. Replace the tank fuel filter . . . . " 17
10. Clean the throttle valve throats . . . . " 17
11. Check the positioning of throttle-control unit linkage . . . . " 18
12. Check the positioning and alignment of throttles . " 20
13. Idle adjustment . . . . " 21
14. Checking and adjusting the throttle control linkage " 22
15. Road test . . . . " 23

D - SPECIAL ADJUSTMENTS

1 Installing the ignition distributor	page 25
2 Check the relationship between throttle angles and control unit lever angles	" 25
3 Throttle angles-control unit lever angles relationship table	" 27
4 Installing the thermostatic actuator on control unit	" 28
5 Removal and reinstallation of the injection pump	" 29
6 Timing the injection pump	" 30
7 Testing the injectors	" 31
8 Replacing the altitude compensator (in car)	" 32
9 Replacing the oil filter in the injection pump	" 34
10 Checking and adjusting the throttle control linkage	" 35
11 Replacing the fuel cut off solenoid	" 35

E - TROUBLE SHOOTING

1 Alfa Romeo Spica pump policy	" 37
2 Trouble chart	" 38

I M P O R T A N T   N O T E

The fuel injection system for the 1750 model has been designed not only to attain high performance and low fuel consumption but also to keep the exhaust emissions below the levels permitted by U.S.A. regulations.

The low exhaust emission levels have therefore been obtained by improving the distribution and the combustion. No devices to burn the unburned gases downstream of the exhaust valves are required.

Of course, even with the fuel injection system fitted to the Alfa 1750, the exhaust emissions of cars sold to Customers will not continue to meet U.S. specification unless the owner himself provides to have the prescribed servicing outlined on page 11 regularly carried out by authorized workshops and provided that, when remedying troubles or performing any maintenance work on the engine or fuel feed system, the workshops strictly follow the factory prescribed procedure.

DESCRIPTION OF FUEL INJECTION SYSTEM

A 1 GENERAL

Fuel is supplied to the engine by injection into the intake port of each cylinder by means of four pumping elements (one per cylinder) whose delivery is controlled by a "control unit". A cam in the control unit provides a "base" delivery according to the opening of throttles and to RPM range; the "base" delivery is varied by compensating devices giving proper corrections for atmospheric pressure, engine temperature, cold starting, initial running and fuel cut off on deceleration.

A 2 FUEL FEED SYSTEM

Operating diagram (see fig. 1)

Inserting the key in the ignition switch (1) and rotating clockwise to the first click will operate the electric pump (2). The gasoline flows from the tank (3) thru tank filter (4) and main filter (5) and feeds the injection pump (6).

The excess fuel, acting also as a coolant for the injection pump (6), before returning to the tank, passes thru a calibrated orifice (7) which regulates the fuel pressure within the injection pump. A pressure switch (8) inserted in the delivery pipe will switch on the warning light (10) on dashboard if a pressure drop occurs in fuel lines; the pressure should never be lower than 7.1 psi - 0.5 Kg/cm^2.

A pressure relief valve (9) on filter (5) limits the fuel pump outlet pressure bypassing fuel to the recovery pipe at 16 - 18 psi (1.1 ÷ 1.3 Kg/cm^2).

A 3   GENERAL ARRANGEMENT OF FUEL SYSTEM

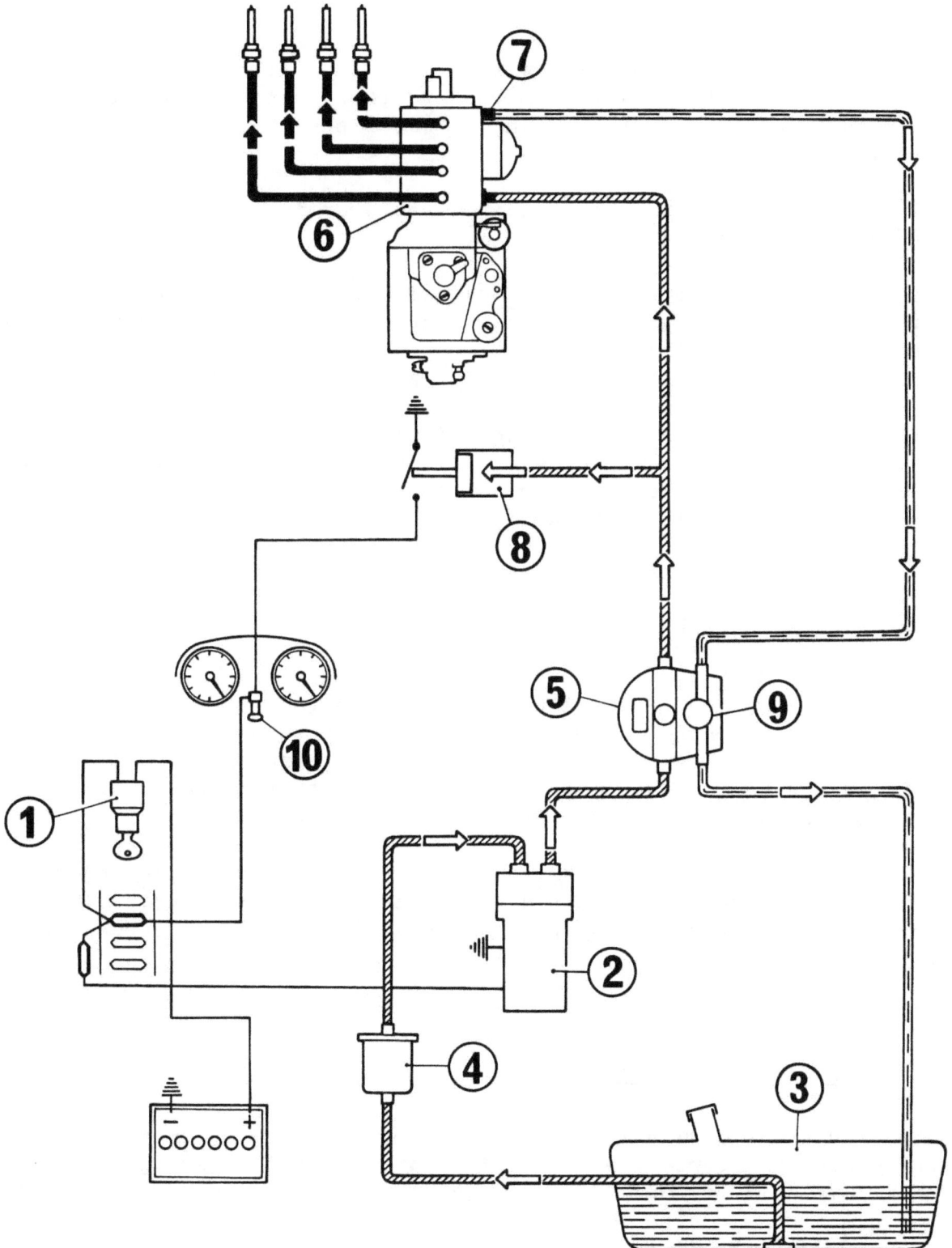

Fig. 1

A 4   AIR INDUCTION SYSTEM (see fig. 2)

The air induction system consists of a silencer (1), incorporating an air cleaner (2), directly connected to the throttle valve throats (3).

The air cleaner is connected with a hose to a front ram intake port at the side of the radiator; moreover, the cleaner is provided with an automatic device for draining of water possibly entered thru the air intake port.

The filtered air enters the engine thru four intake ports each with a throttle valve.

The idling air (throttle valves closed) is fed thru a separate circuit consisting of a filtered air supply pipe (10), an adjuster ring fitted to the equalizer (11) and four small hoses connecting the equalizer to the intake ports downstream of the throttle valves.

The accelerator pedal (5) is mechanically linked thru a relay crank to both the throttle valve lever (4) and the control unit lever (6). Therefore, any position of accelerator pedal corresponds to an exact position of throttle valve and control unit levers.

A 5   INJECTION PUMP

The injection pump, SPICA AIBB 4C.S.75, has four variable displacement plungers controlled by the control unit thru a rack. The plungers are actuated by conn. rods driven by a crankshaft revolving at half engine speed. The pump is lubricated with the engine oil drawn from the main gallery just after the main filter.

The lubricating oil, filtered further by a filter in the injection pump mount, seeps past the plungers, lubricates the various moving parts then returns to the pan thru a suitable port in the pump mount itself.

A 6   COLD START DEVICE

The cold start device incorporates a solenoid which, energized when the engine is started, enriches the mixture by increasing the injection pump delivery thru an additional movement of control unit rack.

The cold start device cuts off gradually, according to engine temperature, when the ignition key is released from cranking position.

A 7 AIR INDUCTION SYSTEM AND THROTTLE-CONTROL UNIT LINKAGE

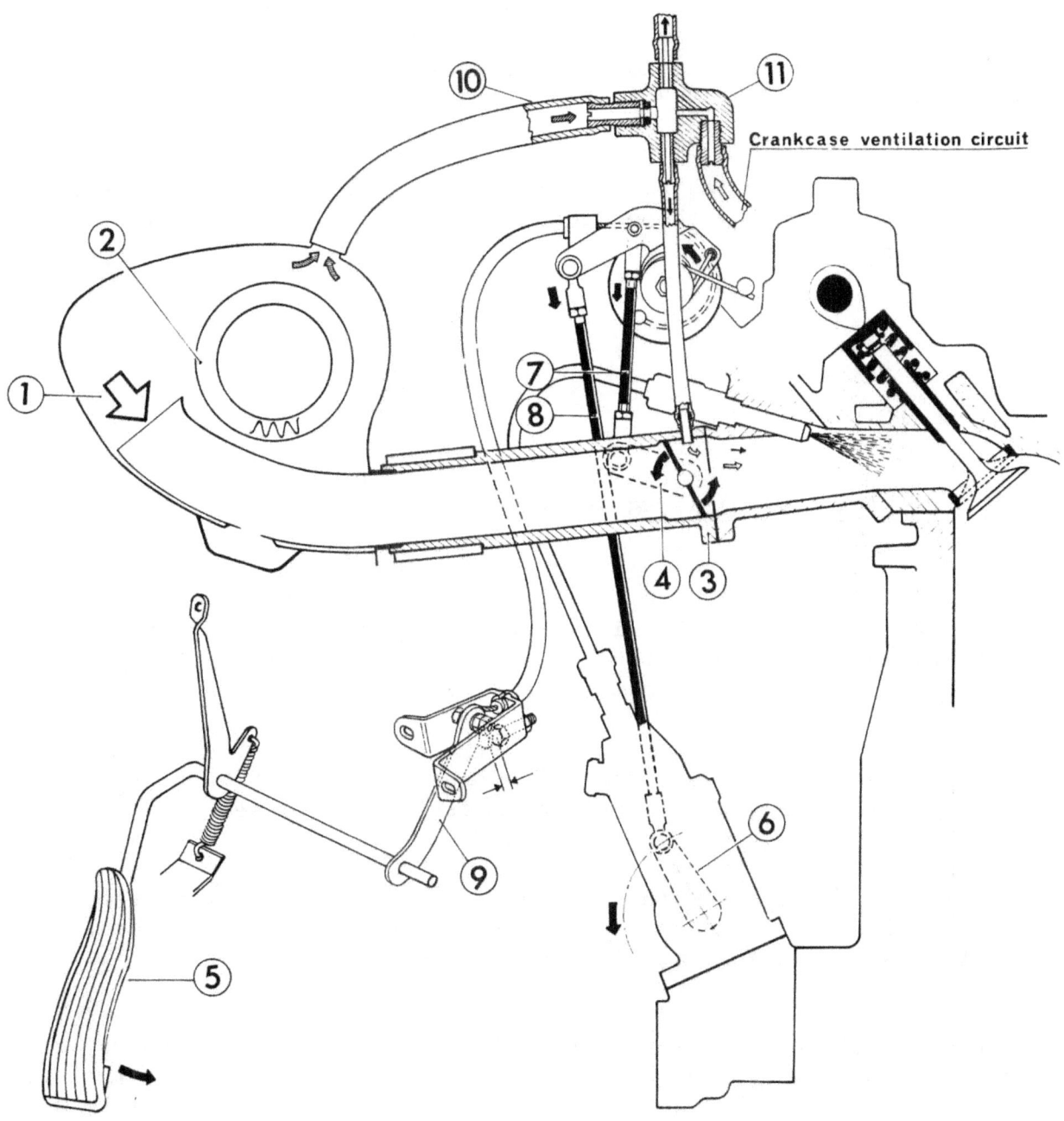

Fig. 2

A 8   INITIAL RUNNING DEVICE

This device provides for a smooth operation of the engine soon after a cold start; it consists of a thermostat which, sensing engine coolant temperatures, acts thru a linkage on the control unit rack so as to increase the injection pump delivery in accord with the decrease in temperature and at the same time, thru rods 7 and 8 outside the control unit, opens the throttles so that the engine can be properly fed.

The device cuts off automatically and progressively as the engine warms up to operating temperature thus restoring the standard idling conditions.

A 9   CRANKCASE VENTILATING SYSTEM

The exhaust gases and the oil vapors developed during engine operation and gas vapors from the fuel tank are sucked thru the camshaft cover in the combustion chambers and burned (see Fig. 3).

The crankcase ventilating system controls gases both at high engine RPMs and at idling speed when the throttles are closed.

When the throttles are fully opened the vapors flow thru the hose (1) to the oil separator (2) and thru hose (3) into the manifold chamber (4) communicating with the intake ports (5)

When the trottles are closed or partially opened, the secondary circuit (9) comes into operation; such a circuit starts from the oil separator and conveys unburned gases and vapors directly into the chamber of the idling air equalizer (6) downstream of the adjuster.

Inside the equalizer, exhaust gases and gas vapors are mixed with fresh air then properly distributed among cylinders thru pipes (10). The oil collected in the oil separator returns to the pan via the hose (8).

A 10   CRANKCASE VENTILATING CIRCUIT

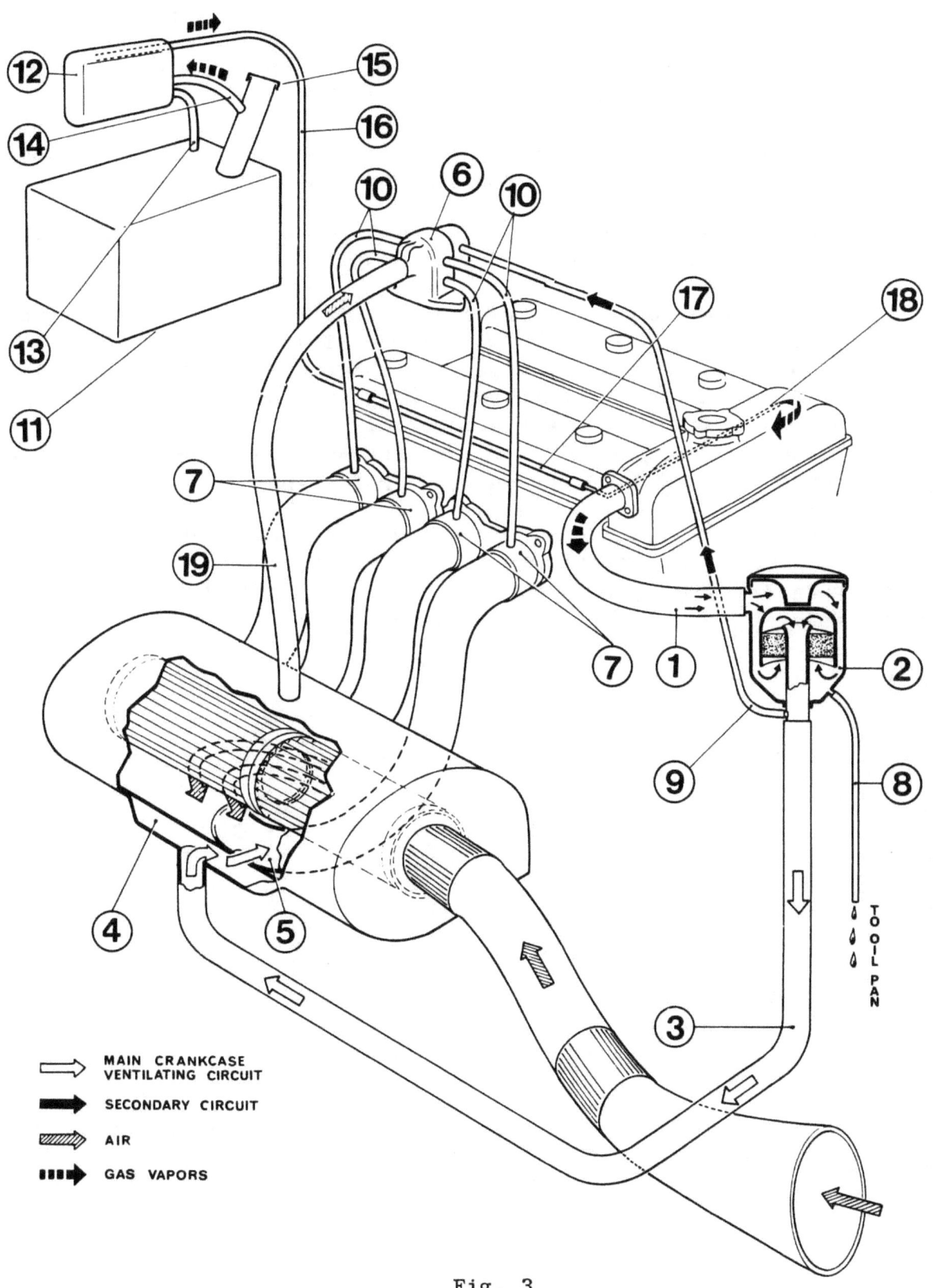

⇨ MAIN CRANKCASE VENTILATING CIRCUIT
⬛⇨ SECONDARY CIRCUIT
▨ AIR
▰▰⇨ GAS VAPORS

Fig. 3

A 11 FUEL VAPOR RECOVERY SYSTEM AND TANK VENTILATION (see fig. 3)

Gas vapors, emanating from fuel tank (11) both during engine operation and hot soak period after engine shutdown, are collected in the vapor storage tank (12) which acts also as a liquid-vapor separator returning the condensate to the fuel tank via the pipe (13) located at the bottom of separator.

The pipe (14) serves to make a proper connection between the fuel tank, when fully replenished, and the gas vapor tank.

To prevent gas vapors from escaping in the open air, an air tight filler cap (15) is provided.

Gas vapors coming to the vapor separator flow out of the separator from the top and, passing thru the pipes (16) and (17), enter the cylinder head, then, via the pipe (18) which extends into the cylinder head, get into the crankcase: during the hot soak period, the crankcase is used as a storage volume while during engine operation the crankcase is purged of vapors by the action of the ventilation system as outlined at the beginning of paragraph.

It the event that, after engine shut down, the pressure in the vapor separator tends to diminish as a consequence of drop in temperature, gas vapors will flow back thru pipes (18) (17) (16) thus keeping the vapor separator at atmospheric pressure.

RECOMMENDATIONS ON THE USE

B 1   STARTING THE ENGINE

- Insert the key in the ignition switch and turn it clockwise to the first click; wait a few seconds to make sure the low fuel pressure warning light goes off.

- Turn the ignition key further clockwise to operate the starter.

- As soon as the engine fires release the key.

WARNING: if the warning light does not flash on or stays on, this is an indication of failure of the indicating device or fuel feed system; therefore have them checked as soon as possible.

Automatic devices act as a standard choke usually does, namely, facilitate the initial running of engine after a cold start until the proper operating temperature is reached.

As an aid in starting from cold, partially depress the accelerator pedal slowly. After a cold start and particularly when the ambient temperature is below freezing point, wait a fairly long time before getting away so as to warm up properly all engine parts and allow the oil to reach all points requiring lubrication.

To performance must never be demanded of the car until coolant temperature is about 158°F (70°C).

When the engine is already hot or with very high ambient temperatures (above 77°F - 25°C) slowly depress the accelerator pedal to facilitate starting.

CAUTION: owing to the special construction of the injection pump, the pump plungers must on no account be operated directly with a lever or any other tool.

B 2   UTILIZATION DIRECTIONS

The fuel injection system allows the engine to be used in the widest RPM range; however, in gears higher then the second, the best performance and emission control as well, can only be attained by exceeding 2200 RPM. It is recommended that all driving be done above 2200 RPM, shifting to a lower gear when below this engine speed.

B 3 TEMPERATURE SETTING

To keep a constant fuel/air ratio even when the ambient temperature varies as the seasons change, the temperature compensator lever on the control unit shall be shifted to:

- "N" (normal) for ambient temperatures exceeding 59°F (15°C).
- "C" (cold) for temperatures between 59°F (15°C) and 32°F (0°C).
- "F" (freezing) for temperatures below 32°F (0°C).

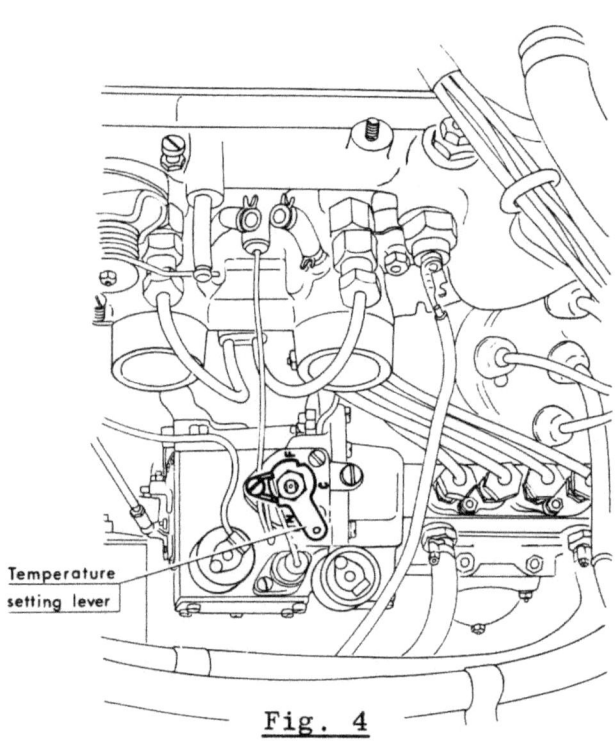

Fig. 4

B 4 DECELERATION

On deceleration, the injection pump delivery is automatically cut off by means of an electromagnetic device fed thru a microswitch which, being actuated by a particular profile suitably shaped in the control unit cam, closes when the accelerator pedal is released; this not only eliminates the unburned gases in a condition which is critical for the emission levels, but also favorably affects the fuel consumption.

As the engine speed reaches about 1300 rpm, the fuel delivery restores to prevent stopping the engine. Of course, the fuel delivery restores even if the engine is re-accelerated before it slows down to 1300 rpm.

REGULAR SERVICING

C 1 SCHEDULE OF REGULAR SERVICING REQUIRED TO KEEP THE EXHAUST EMISSION LEVEL WITHIN LIMITS PRESCRIBED BY U.S. REGULATIONS

In order to maintain the fuel injection system in good operating conditions and the exhaust emissions below the limits specified by Federal regulations, the servicing items listed below must be performed at the prescribed period; each item will be set out in details on the following pages.

Every 6,000 miles

Replace air cleaner elements	page 12
Replace main fuel filter element	" 12

Every 12,000 miles (or once a year whichever comes first)

Check spark plugs and replace, if necessary	" 13
Check the alternator and fan driving belt	" 14
Check valve timing chain tension	" 14
Check the distributor and the ignition timing	" 15
Check valve clearance and adjust, if necessary	" 17
Replace air cleaner elements	" 12
Replace main fuel filter element	" 12
Replace tank fuel filter (throw away type)	" 17
Clean throttle valve throats	" 17
Check positioning of throttle/control unit linkage	" 18
Check positioning and alignment of throttles	" 20
Idle adjustment	" 21
Road test	" 23

C 2   REPLACE THE AIR CLEANER ELEMENTS

To provide room for subsequent operations, the air cleaner shall be removed as a whole; to do so, remove the pipe (17) (see fig. 3); detach the two upper anchoring straps at manifold side; loosen at the engine side the four clamps on the intake hoses; free the crankcase ventilation hose (3) from the oil separator; disconnect the idle hose (19) from the idling air equalizer (6); remove the hose connecting the air cleaner to the ram intake port.

Then the cover of cleaner housing can be removed and the elements replaced after having cleaned the inside of air cleaner housing. Do not reinstall the air cleaner on engine at this point.

C 3   REPLACE THE MAIN FUEL FILTER ELEMENT

This operation, to be performed after the previous one has already been accomplished, should be carried out as follows:

- disconnect the battery negative terminal;

- disconnect the starter positive cable if necessary;

- CAUTION: first of all clean carefully the outside of filter body to make sure no foreign matter could enter the filter on reassembly;

- slacken the bolt securing the filter to its bracket and remove the filter;

- withdraw the filter element;

- get rid of foreign matter that may have collected in the housing and fit a new element; also replace the housing gasket and the bolt washer, if damaged.

WARNING: extreme cleanliness is required in the area of the fuel filter.

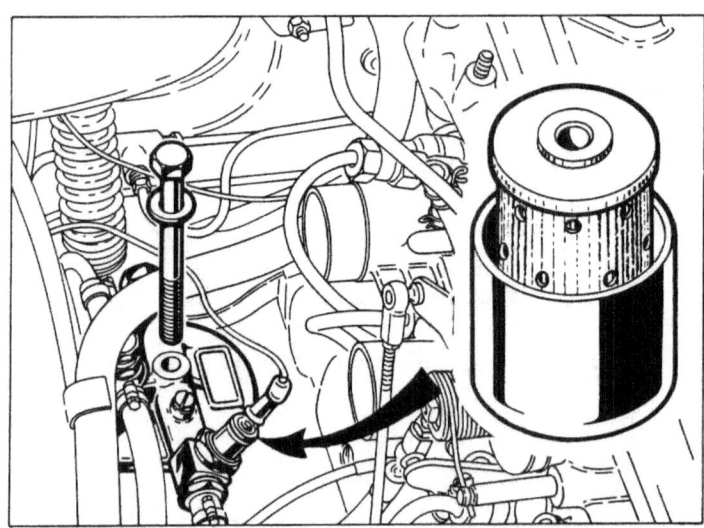

Fig. 5

C 4   CHECK SPARK PLUGS (Lodge HL) AND REPLACE, IF NECESSARY

The spark plugs are of the surface gap type with four points and a central electrode. The only maintenance required is occasional cleaning with a brush of the central electrode and points. <u>No routine adjustment is necessary</u> of the gap between the electrode and points.

If the ceramic insulator is cracked or the electrodes are excessively worn away, the spark plugs must be replaced.

The spark plugs should be tightened when cold to a torque of <u>18 - 25.3 lb-ft</u> (2.5 ÷ 3.5 kgm); lubricate the threads with graphite grease before fitting.

The standard plugs fitted to the engine are LODGE HL. A decal, giving the specifications for these plugs, is attached under the hood; here below, the text of the decal is repeated.

In order to comply with the Federal rule regarding the control of air pollution the engine is fitted with <u>LODGE-HL</u> spark plugs.

These plugs are completely adequate when the automobile is driven at speeds not exceeding the speed limiting regulations. If the automobile is driven at sustained speeds higher than the said speed limits, <u>LODGE-2HL</u> spark plugs must be used.

Under no condition can substitute spark plugs be used, unless they are specifically advised and approved by Alfa Romeo. Use of other plugs can promote serious engine damage, as well as alter emission levels.

C 5   CHECK THE ALTERNATOR AND FAN DRIVING BELT

The belt should be tightened enough to drive the fan and alternator pulley without slipping and without overloading the bearings.

The tension is correct when, on pressing the belt down, the sag is about 1/2" (10-15 mm).

To tighten the belt unscrew the nut on the adjusting arm and move the alternator outwards.

C 6   CHECK VALVE TIMING CHAIN TENSION

Unscrew the camshaft cover retaining nuts and remove the cover; slacken the chain tensioner setscrew and check that the tensioner spring is working properly; crank the engine for a few seconds to allow the tensioner to tighten the chain and then lock the tensioner setscrew firmly.

On refitting the camshaft cover, make sure the gasket is in sound conditions or replace, if necessary. Moderately tighten the cover retaining nuts in diagonal order.

C 7   CHECK THE DISTRIBUTOR (Marelli S 103 B) AND THE IGNITION TIMING

Dwell meter should read between 57 and 63 degrees, with new points closed, corresponding to .017 to .019" (.43 to .48 mm) gap.

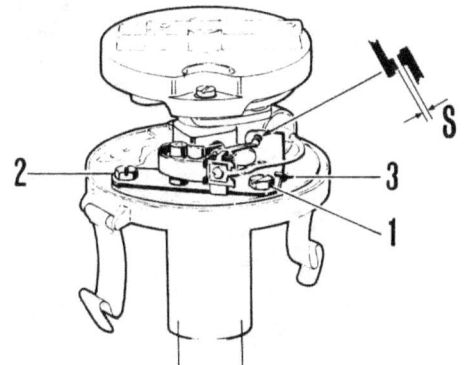

To adjust, loosen the screws 1 and 2, insert a screwdriver in the adjustment slot 3 and pry the stationary-point plate.

S = .017 - .019 in.

Smear the distributor cam with grease. Check the inside of distributor cap for any sign of moisture, carbon deposits or cracks and the central power electrode for free movement in its seat and for effective spring action. Finally, check cap terminals for good conditions.

The ignition timing should be checked when the engine is warmed up to operating temperature (coolant exceeding 158°F; 70°C) and running at idle speed by using a timing light.

The timing should be retarded by one to three degrees ATDC (mark F cut in the pulley in line with the pointer) see fig. 6.

With the engine running with no load at 5,000 RPM, the ignition advance should be 31 to 37 degrees, that is the mark "M" on the pulley should be in line with the pointer or .12" (3 mm) apart either side.

Timing at idle speed must be adjusted with special care as it affects more greatly the emission levels.

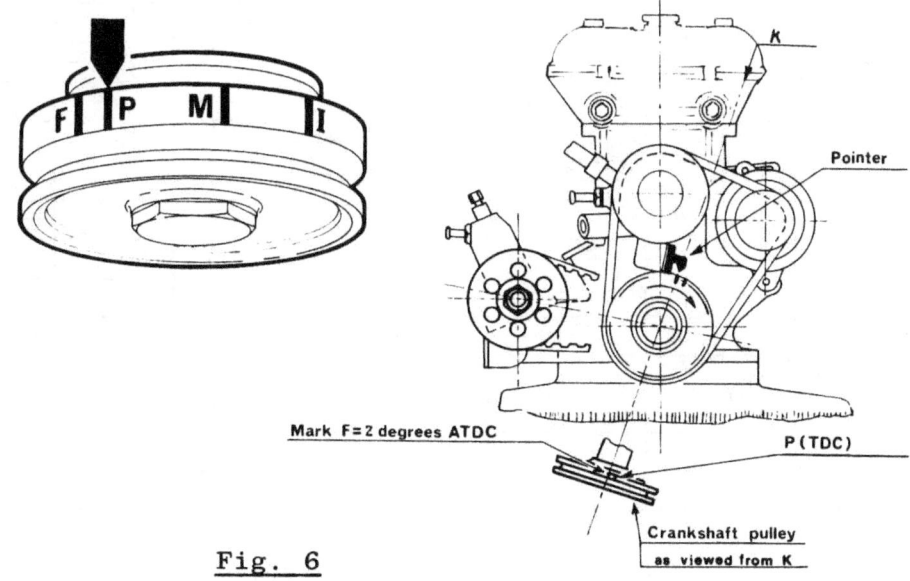

Fig. 6

Timing adjustment (maximum accuracy required)

If the timing requires adjustment, proceed as follows:

1 - unscrew the distributor securing nut 1 on the stud so as to allow the distributor to be rotated together with its supporting clamp;
2 - rotate the distributor body counterclockwise or clockwise according to whether it is necessary to respectively advance "A" or retard "R" the ignition setting;
3 - retighten the nut, taking care not to move the distributor body;
4 - recheck timing.

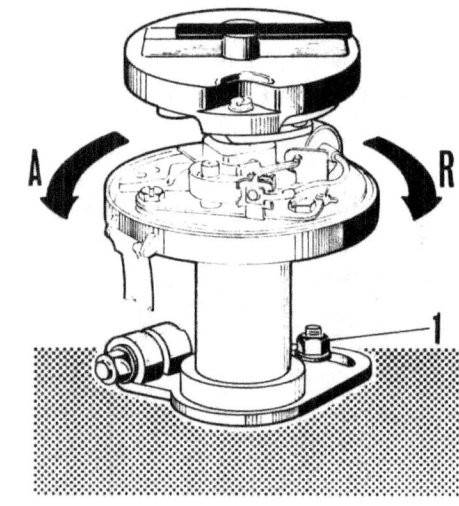

In the event of reinstallation or renewal of the distributor, refer to the directions given on page 25.

Automatic advance graph and specifications of Marelli S 103 B distributor

Contact gap . . . . .017 - .019"
Contact opening angle . . . . 30° $\pm$ 3°
Dwell angle . . . . 60° $\pm$ 3°
Contact pressure . . . . 18 - 21 oz

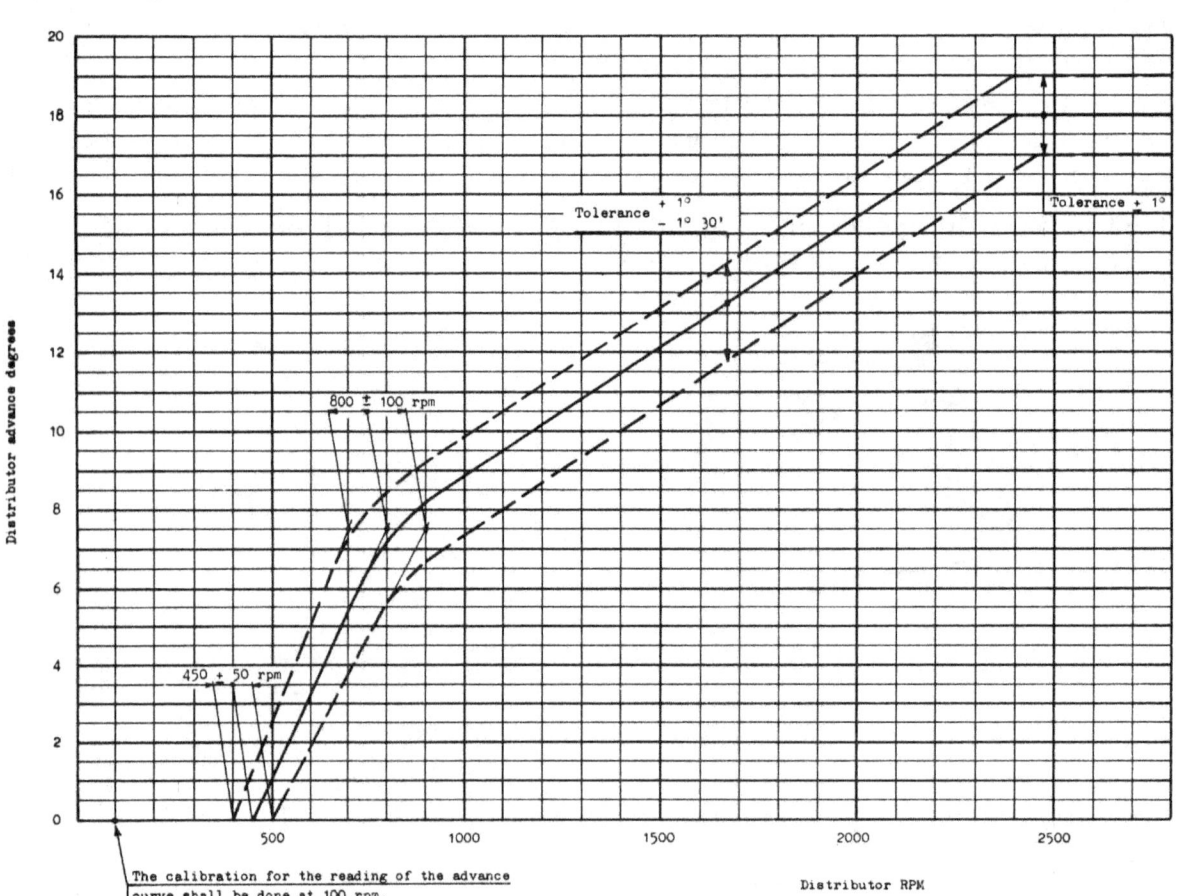

The calibration for the reading of the advance curve shall be done at 100 rpm.

Distributor RPM

C 8 VALVE CLEARANCE CHECKING AND ADJUSTMENT

The V-mounted overhead valves are directly operated by two camshafts acting thru oil bath cups.

When the engine is cold, carefully measure the clearance "G" with a feeler gage. If the clearance is not as specified, remove camshafts and valve cups; measure the thickness "S" of the adjusting pad on each valve stem and replace it with another of proper thickness so that the clearance is the correct one shown in the diagram.

To facilitate this adjustment the pads are made available in a series of thicknesses ranging from .05 to .014" (1.3 to 3.5 mm) in increments of .001" (.025 mm).

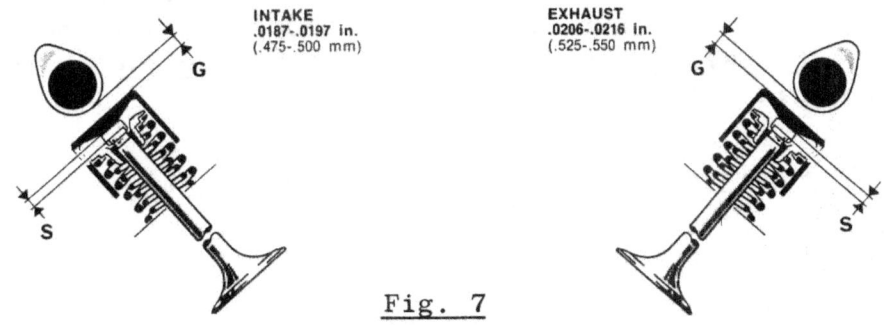

Fig. 7

C 9 REPLACE THE TANK FUEL FILTER

To replace the tank fuel filter (throw-away type) (see 4, fig. 1), located on the rear underbody of car, proceed as follows:

- slacken the bolt on the clamp securing the filter to the underbody;
- loosen the clamps securing the hoses to the filter inlet and outlet adapters; it is advisable to stop the pipe from fuel tank provisionally.

Remove the filter and replace it with a new one by proceeding in reverse order of removal. Make sure the hoses are properly positioned.

C 10 CLEAN THE THROTTLE VALVE THROATS

Clean the valve throats especially at the areas of contact of throttle valve edges and throat by holding the throttles in full open position and using a brush soaked in gasoline; the cleaning can be completed by rubbing repeatedly the affected areas with a lint-free cloth.

Then, clean in a similar way the throttle valve edges taking care not to strain the spindles.

C 11 CHECK THE POSITIONING OF THROTTLE-CONTROL UNIT LINKAGE

Before performing this, take the air cleaner off the engine (see paragraph "replace the air cleaner elements") and check that the accelerator pedal moves thru a little free-travel before actuating the relay crank (see paragraph C 14 page 22).

With hot engine (over 158°F - 70°C) and the standard thermostat fitted, check with a feeler gauge that clearance between the control unit input lever and its reference screw is .012 to .024" (.3 to .6 mm) (the nearer to .019" the better) when the relay crank is resting against the idle limit stop; if this is not the case, let the engine cool down then proceed as follows: first disconnect the push-pull rods (7) and (8) (see fig. 2), the cable from the relay crank sheave and the battery negative terminal; remove the cable clamps and fit the tool no. A.4.0121 (fig. 8) onto the studs. Adjust the idle stop screw until the ball joint just touches the reference plane of the tool and lock in this position.

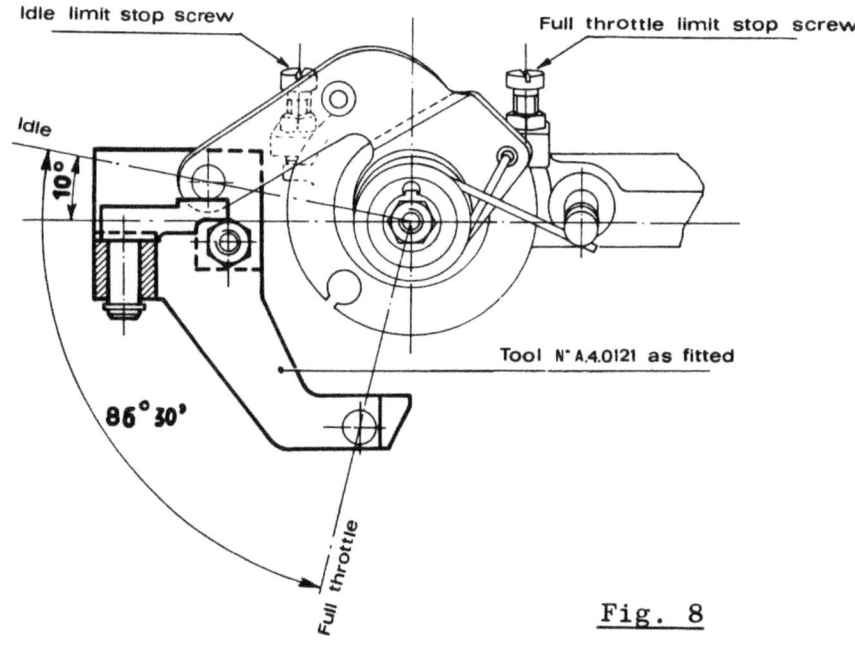

Fig. 8

CAUTION - If the linkage assembly has been removed or if doubts of distortion or straining exist, it is advisable to check also the "full throttle" setting as follows: with the above mentioned tool fitted, rotate the relay crank to bring the ball joint in contact with the "full throttle" reference plane and lock in place the respective limit stop screw.

Now the "actuator" section of the thermostatic control can be removed from the control unit; to do so, remove the two screws retaining the actuator mounting flange and the two screws clamping the actuator pipe anchoring grommet (do not remove the thermostat bulb); then withdraw the actuator taking care not to distort excessively the pipe.

Fit the "dummy actuator" (tool no. A.4.0120 - fig. 9) in place of the standard one just removed. At this point, refit the relay crank/control unit lever rod (8) and, if necessary, adjust the rod length so that the linkage is at rest against the idle limit stop, when, between control unit lever and its reference screw, there is a <u>clearance</u> of .035 - .051" (0.9 ÷ 1.3 mm).

> WARNING
>
> Never tamper with the seal on the reference screw of control unit input lever as this will result in loss of any benefit under warranty

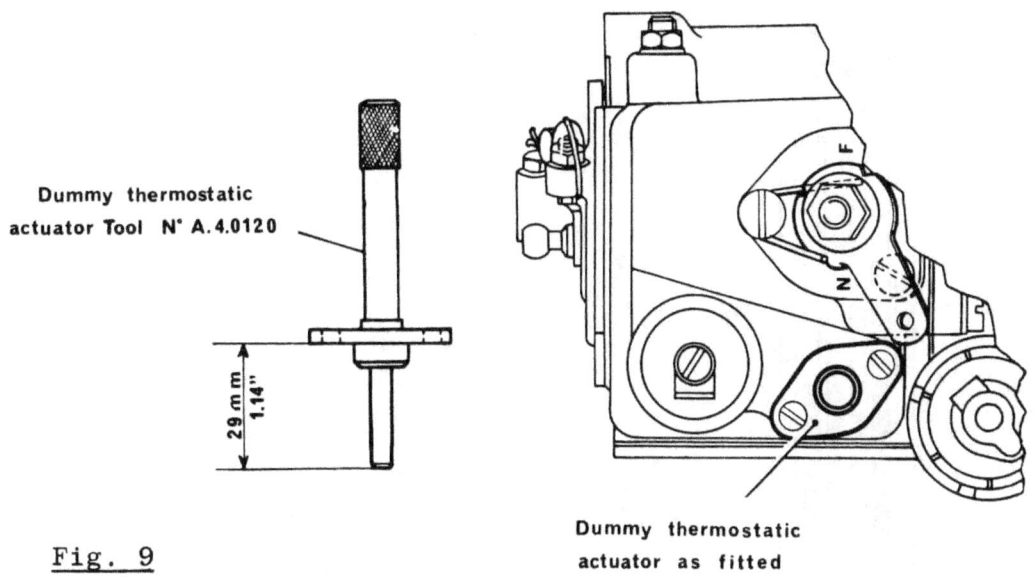

Fig. 9

Dummy thermostatic actuator Tool N° A.4.0120

Dummy thermostatic actuator as fitted

When the above adjustment is over, reconnect the relay crank-to-throttle rod (7) and, if necessary, adjust the rod length so that the throttle valves are just closed when the linkage rest against the idle limit stop ("just closed" means such a position that, when <u>slightly</u> opening the throttle valves and then releasing them, a definite hit of the linkage against the idle limit stop is felt).

Remove the dummy actuator, reinstall the standard one carefully and tighten it in place.

Again check that - <u>with hot engine</u> - the clearance between the control unit input lever and its reference screw is <u>.012 to .024"</u> (the nearer to .019" the better).

If the injection pump has been removed from engine or any doubt exists that the system setting has been disturbed or any component <u>distorted</u> for a collision, etc., an additional adjustment of throttle angles in relation to control unit lever angles, described on page 25, should be performed.

<u>NOTE</u>: to obtain the specified clearance, a twisting within ± 30° from the in-line-position of the plastic sockets of each rod is allowed.

C 12 CHECK THE POSITIONING AND ALIGNMENT OF THROTTLES

To perform this check, the air cleaner body and hoses shall be removed from the engine and the four adapters of tool no. C.2.0012 connected to the idle fittings on the throttle valve throats after having removed the four idle pipes from the fittings; the other end of these adapters shall be connected to the four columns of mercury gage (tool no. C.2.0014) see fig. 10.

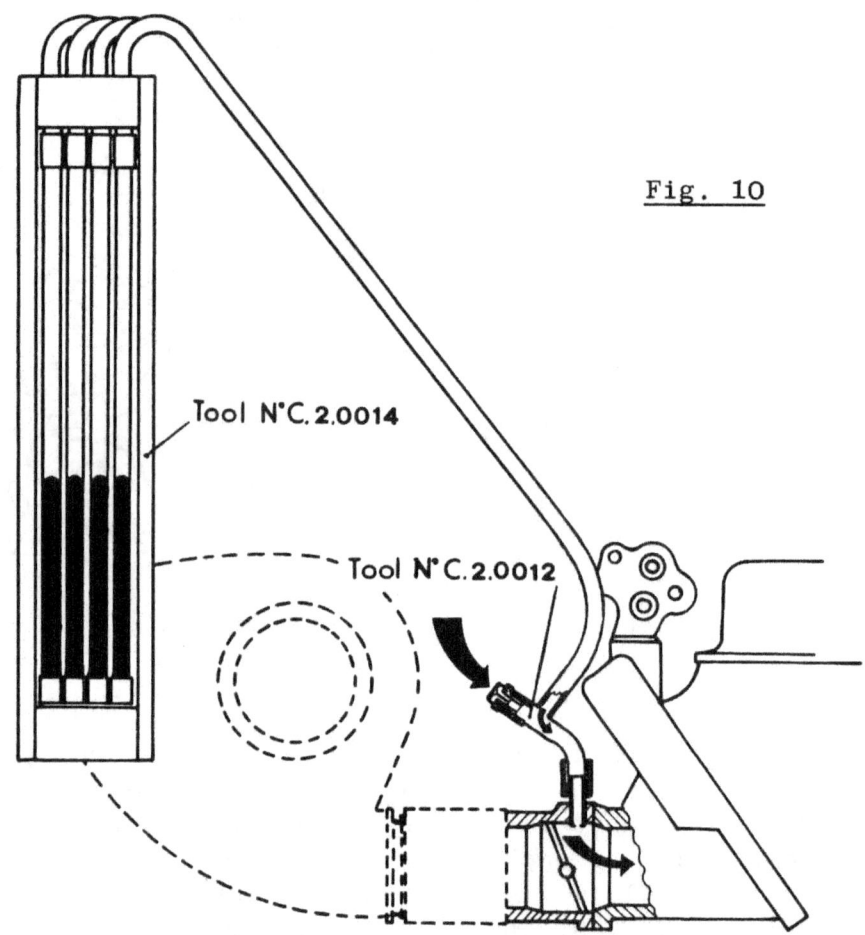

Fig. 10

Start the engine and warm it up until the coolant temperature is at least 158°F (70°C); first check that the clearance between control unit lever and its reference screw is .012 to .024" (the nearer to .019" the better) with hot engine and thermostat actuator fitted.

Now, check that readings on mercury gage columns are much the same (maximum difference: .4" - 10 mm); if this is not the case, proceed as follows:

- if readings show that vacuum in front pair of cylinders is higher than in the rear, unscrew the throttle coupling adjusting screw so as to close the rear pair of throttles;

- if vacuum in front pair of cylinders is lower than that in rear pair, disconnect the relay crank-to-throttle rod and set the throttle coupling adjusting screw in such a way as to close the front pair of throttles (screw in the adjusting screw); then, reconnect the relay crank-to-throttle rod and adjust its length so that the throttle valves are in the "just closed" condition as outlined in the paragraph: "Check the positioning of throttle/control unit linkage".

If, before commencing the above adjustments, the engine would run unevenly (lean mixture), make sure the throttle valves are in the "just closed" position; if not the relay crank-to-throttle rod must be shortened.

CAUTION: avoid sudden revving up of the engine or too great a vacuum could take place and the mercury might be sucked out of gage columns.

C 13 IDLE ADJUSTMENT

After having disconnected the adapters of gage columns from the idle fittings on throttle valve throats, reinstall the air cleaner, clamping in place the hoses and attaching the two upper anchoring straps; reinstall the gas vapor pipe; reconnect the four pipes from the idle equalizer to the idle fittings downstream of the throttles and the crankcase ventilation hose; do not fit the cleaner-to-equalizer pipe at this stage.

With hot engine, check for a smooth idle and an idle speed not lower than 720 rpm:

- if idle speed is faster than specified and hunting takes place, gradually screw in the adjuster ring at the air inlet port of idle equalizer until smooth idle is obtained provided that idle speed does not fall below 720 rpm;

- if idle speed is slower than specified, gradually unscrew the adjuster ring until the prescribed rpms are obtained.

To take engine speed readings, it is advisable to use an electronic tachometer of proven accuracy.

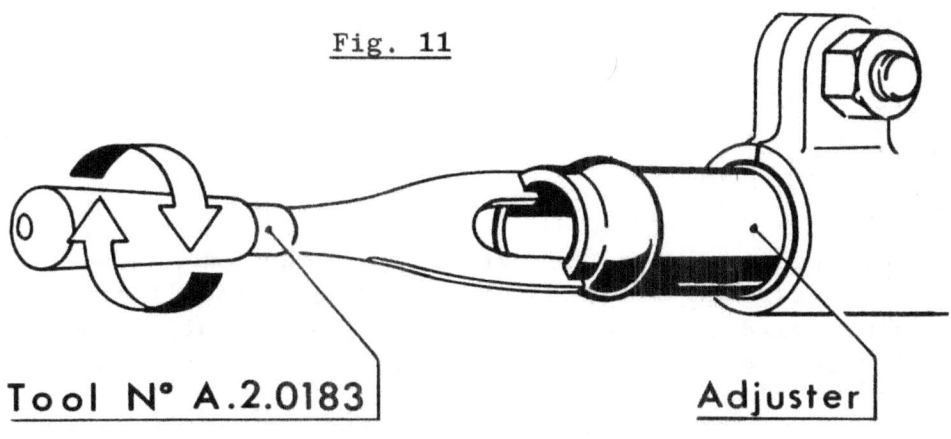

Fig. 11

Tool N° A.2.0183   Adjuster

On completion of the above operations, fit the cleaner-to-equalizer pipe, then perform the check outlined in the paragraph C 14 below.

If during road test no adjustment of carburetion were needed, proceed with the check of the CO rate in the exhaust gases at idle speed; on the contrary, if carburation required adjustment, the idle must again be checked for proper rpm and smoothness before testing the CO emissions.

A CO tester, set in operation and calibrated prior to performing the test, shall be used for checking the CO emissions at idle; readings shall be taken soon after the road test (repeat road test, even on a short run, until idle requires no further adjustments).

The CO rate in exaust gases shall fall within 0.8% and 2.5%, the closer to the lower limit the better.

Only if driveability is completely unsatisfactory at small throttle openings, the CO rate may be set closer to the higher limit.

To set the CO rate, act on the adjuster at the idle equalizer air inlet: screw in the adjuster to increase the CO rate and viceversa.

After the CO rate has been so adjusted, the idle conditions shall again meet the requirements previously specified.

C 14   CHECKING AND ADJUSTING THE THROTTLE CONTROL LINKAGE

With engine still hot, proceed as follows:

- With the accelerator pedal fully released, check that the free travel of the lever (9) (see fig. 2 page 5) is:

    .04 - .06" (1 ÷ 1.5 mm)

    If not so, adjust the pedal stop on floor until the specified clearance is obtained.

- Depress the accelerator pedal to the pedal stop on floor and check that the clearance between relay crank lug and full throttle limit stop screw is .08" (2 mm).

C 15   ROAD TEST

With a hot engine, drive the car hard for a few miles, using high revs and low gears in order to burn off any deposit from the spark plugs; then, drive the car at a constant speed of 30 mph in third gear to see whether the engine operates smoothly, without any hesitation.

If hesitations are experienced, they can be remedied <u>by unscrewing</u> the fuel cut off solenoid to get a <u>richer mixture</u> (see also fig. 20).

Proceed as follows:

- Countermark the cut off solenoid for angular position; to this purpose the solenoid has 8 reference notches on its top (without damaging the solenoid, mark one of the notches with respect to a fixed point on the control unit);

- Disconnect the terminal of solenoid feed wire;

- Slacken the ring nut at the solenoid bottom with the suitable wrench (special tool no. A.5.0177) taking care not to rotate the solenoid body or the reference marks will go out of alignment;

- Unscrew by hand the solenoid by one notch (one eighth of a turn);

- Retighten the ring nut and check that the reference marks previous<u>l</u>y made are properly lined up; reconnect the feed wire.

If the mixture is not enough rich, further <u>enrich it</u> by one eighth of a turn at a time until driveability is satisfactory.

In the event the mixture is excessively rich, proceed as outlined above except that the solenoid <u>must be screwed in</u>, again by one eighth of a turn at a time, <u>to lean out</u> the mixture.

NOTE - The solenoid is not to be adjusted before all previous steps are completed. It will not correct for ignition timing inaccuracy or maladjusted throttles.

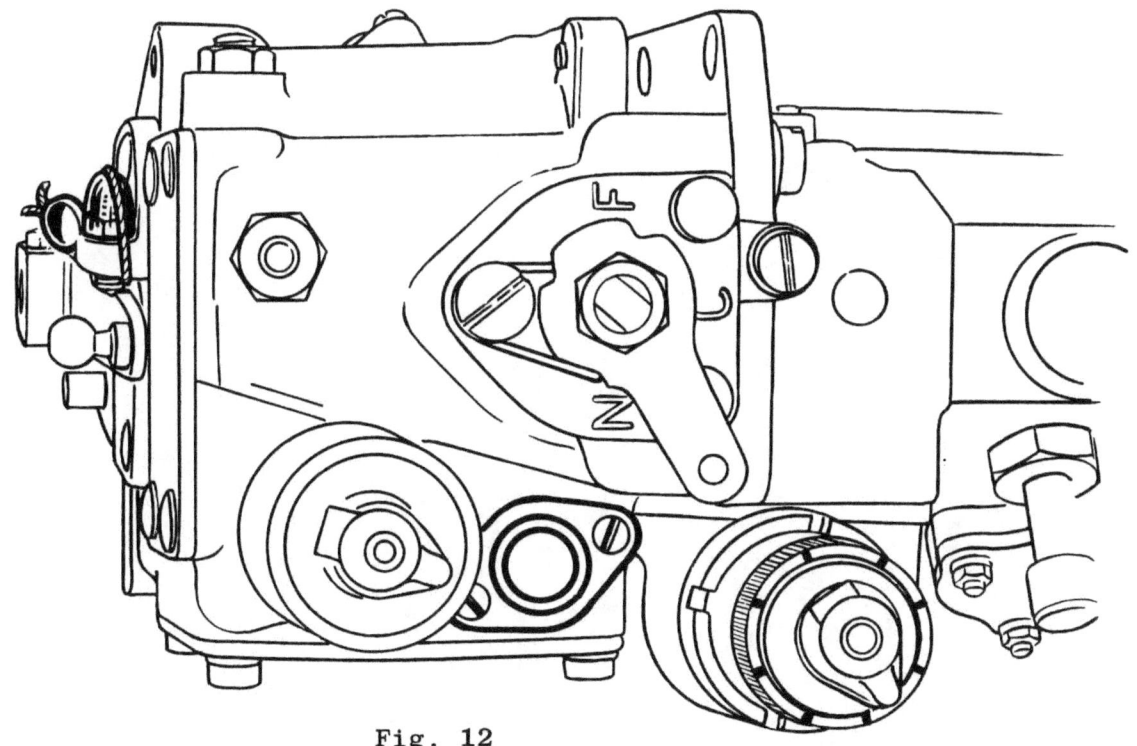

Fig. 12

INDEX OF SPECIAL ADJUSTMENTS

D 1 Installing the ignition distributor . . . . page 25

D 2 Check the relationship between throttle angles and control unit lever angles . . . . " 25

D 3 Throttle angles control unit lever angles relationship table . . . . " 27

D 4 Installing the thermostatic actuator on control unit " 28

D 5 Removal and reinstallation of the injection pump . . " 29

D 6 Timing the injection pump . . . . " 30

D 7 Testing the injectors . . . . " 31

D 8 Replacing the altitude compensator (in-car) . . . . . " 32

D 9 Replacing the oil filter in the injection pump . . . " 34

D 10 Checking and adjusting the throttle control linkage . " 35

D 11 Replacing the fuel cut off solenoid . . . . " 35

SPECIAL ADJUSTMENTS

D 1 INSTALLING THE IGNITION DISTRIBUTOR

When reinstalling or renewing the distributor, perform the following procedure:

- rotate the crankshaft to bring no. 1 cylinder piston to the compression stroke that is with both valves closed;

- by slightly rotating the crankshaft bring the fixed advance mark F on pulley into line with the reference pointer;

- fit the supporting clamp onto the distributor body and tighten the clamp just snug;

- remove distributor cap and rotate the drive shaft by hand to bring the rotor arm in line with the contact for no. 1 cylinder;

- as a trial installation place the distributor on engine and move the supporting clamp so that the stud is centered in the clamp slot <u>when the contact-breaker points are about to open for no. 1 cylinder</u>;

- then, remove the distributor with its supporting clamp, taking care not to disturb the distributor body/clamp setting and lock the clamp in place;

- reinstall the distributor and adjust timing as directed on page 16.

D 2 CHECK THE RELATIONSHIP BETWEEN THROTTLE ANGLES AND CONTROL UNIT LEVER ANGLES

Perform this check when the engine is cold; the air cleaner must then be removed from engine (see under "Replace the air cleaner elements"), the procedure for disconnecting the rods (7) and (8) (see fig. 2) must be repeated as well as the removal of thermostatic actuator (taking care not to distort excessively the small pipe).

At this point check the positioning of linkage at idle and full throttle setting with the special tool no. A.4.0121 and fit <u>the dummy actuator</u>, tool no. A.4.0120. Reconnect the rod and check for a <u>clearance of .012 to .024"</u> (the nearer to .019" the better) between the control unit lever and its reference screw (if necessary, adjust the rod length by acting on the threaded clevis).

WARNING

Never tamper with the seal on the reference screw of control unit input lever as this will result in loss of any benefit under warranty.

Fit the fixed protractor (tool no. C.6.0140) onto rear end of control unit, using the cover attaching screws, and the pointer (tool no. C.6.0141) aligned with the zero on the scale (see fig. 13); to take readings use the suitable built-in light mirror.

Reconnect the rod (7) and check for a proper closure of throttles as directed under "Check the positioning of throttle/control unit linkage"

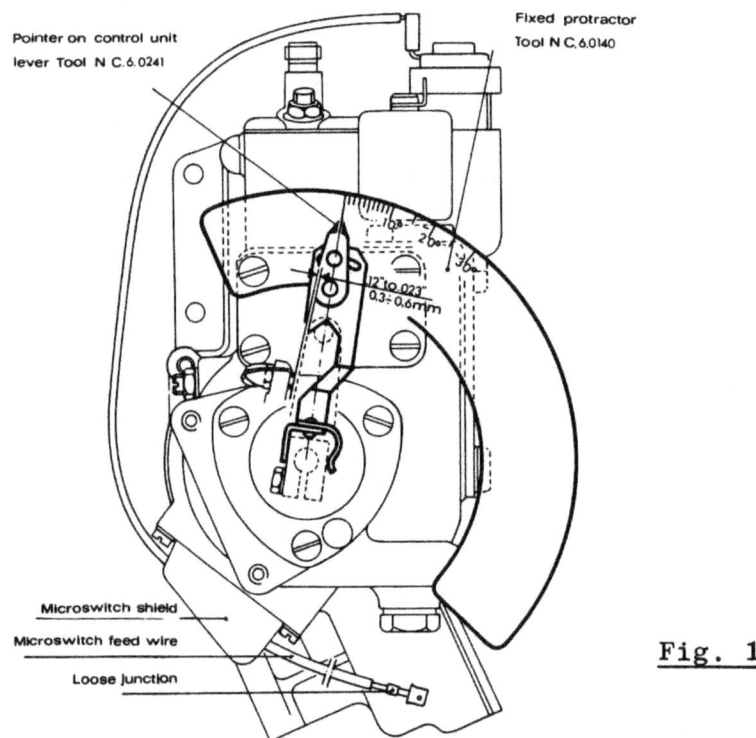

Fig. 13

Place the movable protractor (tool no. C.6.0142) on the spindle of rear throttle valve pair and set to zero in correspondence of the pointer (tool no. C.6.0143) see fig. 14.

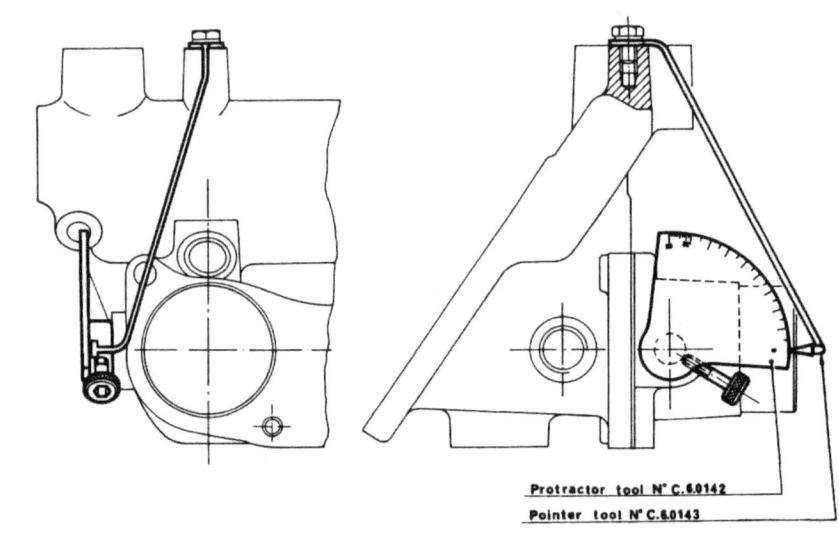

Fig. 14

Install the tool no. A.2.0181 using the cable sheath clips and gradually rotate the relay crank by acting on the adjuster (See fig. 15).

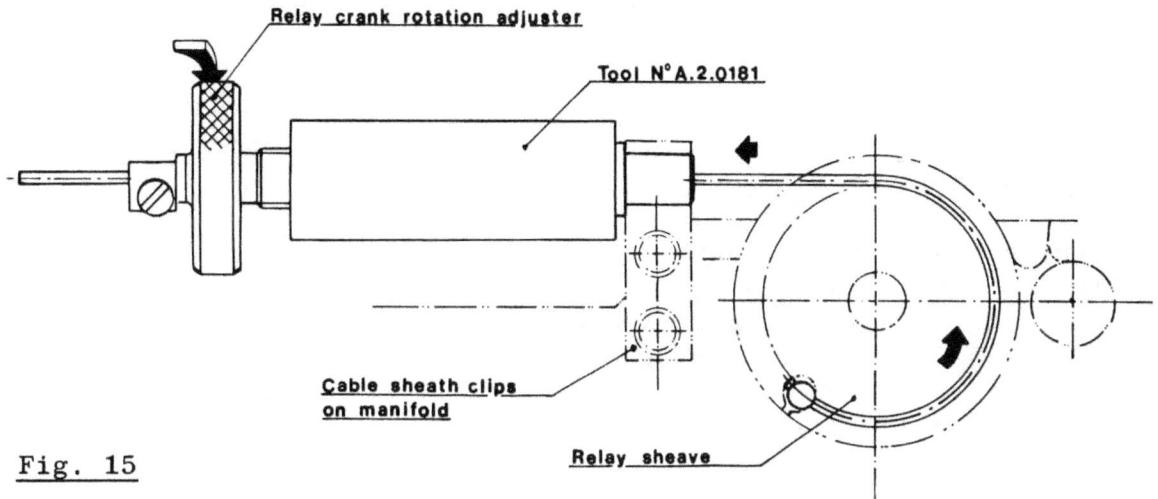

Fig. 15

Open the throttle valves to predetermined angles (2, 4, 6 degrees - see table) and read the corresponding rotations of control unit lever.

THROTTLE ANGLES-CONTROL UNIT LEVER ANGLES RELATIONSHIP TABLE

α	β	Tolerance on β
0°	0°	
2°	8° 13'	$\pm$ 20'
4°	14° 40'	
6°	20° 09'	
10°	29° 30'	$\pm$ 1°
15°	39° 20'	
20°	47° 54'	
25°	55° 33'	
30°	62° 30'	
35°	68° 51'	
40°	74° 41'	$\pm$ 2°
50°	84° 55'	
60°	93° 25'	
70°	100° 12'	
82°	106° 08'	

α = throttle rotation angle

β = control unit lever rotation angle

In the event the throttle angles and control unit lever angles are out of the specified relation, it is likely that checking procedure has not been perfectly accomplished; therefore, try once more; if again it will not satisfy, inspect carefully any component of control linkage, or parts directly affecting it, replace any defective part and repeat the procedure.

When the above checks are over, lengthen the rod (8) until there is a clearance of .035 to .051" (0.9 ÷ 1.3 mm) or 1° to 1°30' between the control unit lever and the reference screw.

On completion of adjustments, reinstall the standard thermostatic actuator and check for a clearance of .012 to .024" (.3 to .6 mm) with a hot engine (coolant temperature above 158°F - 70°C) between the control unit lever and its reference screw; if necessary, adjust the length of rod (8) by acting on the clevis thread (the same footnote as given on page 19 applies).

D 4 INSTALLING THE THERMOSTATIC ACTUATOR ON CONTROL UNIT

If the engine shows too fast an idle and black smoke at the exhaust or stalls easily at idle while emitting black smoke or if an excessive fuel consumption is experienced, the cause is probably a malfunction of the thermostatic actuator on the injection pump control unit.

To replace the thermostatic actuator, proceed as follows:

- remove the air cleaner as outlined under "Replace the air cleaner elements";

- drain about one gallon of coolant from cooling system and remove the defective thermostat assembly;

- install the new thermostat assembly by fitting first the bulb on manifold, then the actuator pipe anchoring grommet and finally the actuator on control unit taking care not to distort excessively the small pipe. Replace the "O" ring on thermostat bulb, if necessary;

- check that clearance between control unit lever and the reference screw is .146 to .165" (3.7 to 4.2 mm) when the coolant temperature is about 68°F (20°C). Should this clearance not fall in the above specified limits, screw in or unscrew the adjuster in the control unit (to gain access to adjuster, take the actuator off) to respectively increase or diminish the clearance;

- on completion of thermostat installation, replenish the cooling system.

D 5   REMOVAL AND REINSTALLATION OF THE INJECTION PUMP

After having removed the air cleaner (see relevant directions) perform the following steps:
- disconnect the negative battery terminal;
- disconnect the lead from cold starting device solenoid and the loose junction on the wire feeding the microswitch (see fig. 13) of fuel cut-off solenoid;
- remove the two screws on the thermostat actuator mounting flange and the two screws clamping the actuator pipe anchoring grommet (do not remove the thermostat bulb); then withdraw the actuator from the control unit, taking care not to distort excessively the pipe;
- disconnect the fuel hoses from injection pump;
- detach the push-pull rod from the control unit.

Proceed by timing the injection pump with the engine (instant in which fuel injection starts); to do this, bring the no. 1 piston at 70° BTDC of the induction stroke by aligning the mark "I" cut in the crankshaft pulley with the pointer on crankcase front cover (doing so will facilitate the reinstallation on the injection pump to the engine).

Finally, unscrew the three attaching nuts and remove the drive belt cover; then take the drive belt off the injection pump pulley.

Now, perform the removal of the injection pump proper as follows:
- fully slacken the injection pipe nuts on pump outlet fittings (use the wrench tool no. A.5.0164), without removing the pipes;
- unscrew the nuts on the two bolts attaching the pipe cluster plate and the injection pump slanting bracket;
- loosen the two screws attaching the control unit to its bracket at the engine mount;
- unscrew, from the underside of car, the four nuts (use tool A.5.0167 for the front ones) attaching the injection pump support to the engine front cover.

Withdraw the injection pump and its support as a unit by tilting it suitably.

To reinstall the injection pump, reverse the removal procedure.

In case of injection pump renewal, the new injectors, supplied with the new pump, must be installed on the engine in place of the old ones. The new injectors bring a location number and must be installed accordingly.

CAUTION: owing to the special construction of the injection pump, the pump plungers must on no account be operated directly with a lever or any other tool.

WARNING: on reinstallation, align the reference marks on the injection pump and the drive pulley (with the engine previously timed for injection in no. 1 cylinder), then fit the drive belt onto the pulley avoiding the use of tools that might damage the belt.

D 6 TIMING THE INJECTION PUMP

To check the injection pump timing proceed as follows:

Rotate the crankshaft until the mark "I" is aligned with the pointer on crankcase front cover corresponding to 70° BTDC of the induction stroke; to do this easier, turn the crankshaft over counterclockwise until the no. 1 cylinder intake valve (as seen through the spark plug hole) closes; then, go on in revolving the shaft until the above mentioned mark and pointer line up.

Now, check that the mark on the injection pump pulley is aligned with the reference on the injection pump itself (to gain access to the reference on the injection pump remove the protective cover).

N.B. - The reference marks can be out of alignment within a tolerance of about ± .2" (5 mm) corresponding to half pitch of pulley splines.

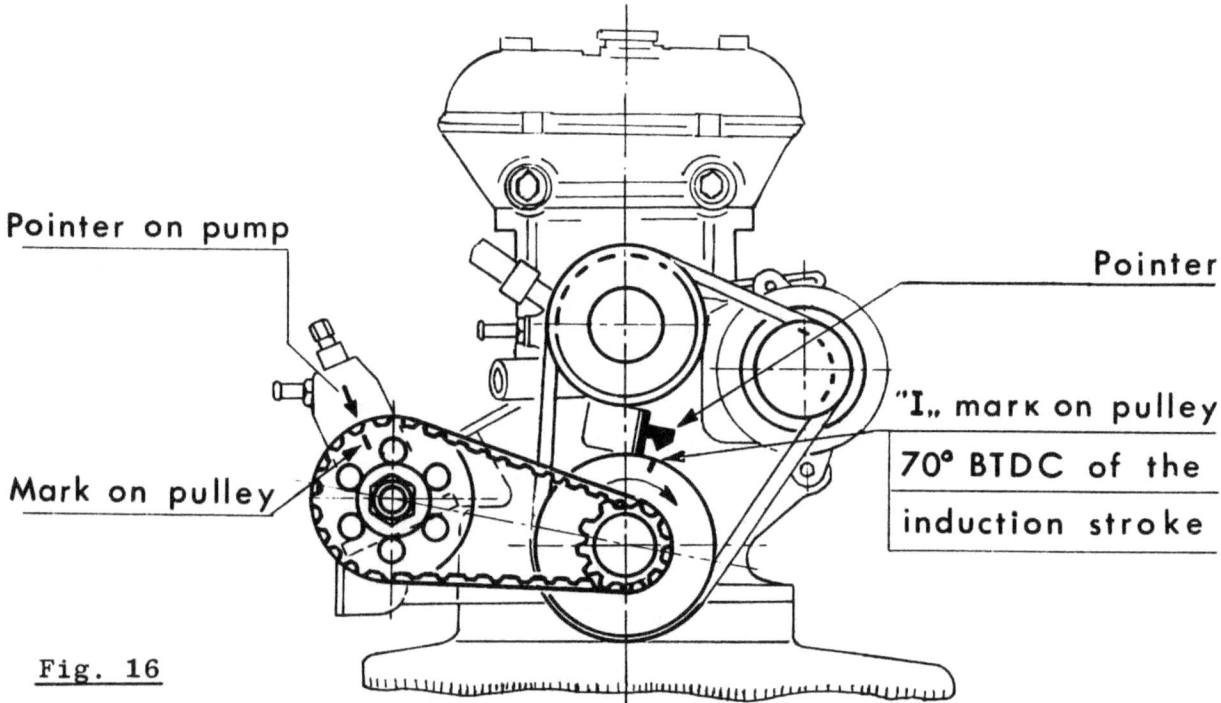

Fig. 16

If the pump is out of timing:

- remove the drive belt;
- line up the reference marks of the injection pump and refit the drive belt by rotating the pulley in either direction to engage the nearest spline.

On completion of the alignment, refit the protective cover.

D 7   TESTING THE INJECTORS

Since the operating conditions of the injectors are not so heavy (being located in the air intake ports and therefore not subject to the high pressures and temperatures of the combustion chamber) and since the life of the injectors is expected to be the same as that of the car, they should undergo a test only when the cause for malfunctions is unquestionably attributed to the injectors themselves.

To test the injectors use a handpump like that for testing Diesel injectors but supplied with gasoline and provided with a pressure gage whose top dial reading is 700 - 1000 psi (50 ÷ 70 Kg/cm^2).

The procedure for checking the spray shape, injection pressure and leaks is as follows:

- connect the test pump pipe to the injector inlet fitting which has a 12 x 1.5 mm metric thread;

- pump quickly to prime pump and injector;

- pump slowly until injector nozzle opens; this must take place at 360 - 400 psi (25 ÷ 28 Kg/cm^2) for new injectors and at no less than 260 psi (18 Kg/cm^2) for used injectors;

- again pumping slowly, bring the pressure to 15-30 psi (1÷2 Kg/cm^2) below the rating pressure taken as directed above and make sure that there is no drip from the nozzle within five seconds;

- pump quickly and check that the spray is narrow, deeply plunging and has good vaporization even at minimum delivery. At a distance of 4" (100 mm) from the nozzle orifice the spray cone diameter should be about .8" (20 mm). If the injector does not meet these requirements, replace it with a new one;

- The injectors must be tightened in place with a torque of 20.2-23.1 lb-ft (2.8 ÷ 3.2 Kgm).

N.B. - To remove the injectors use the wrench tool no. A.5.0165.

D 8   REPLACING THE ALTITUDE COMPENSATOR (in-car)

If the engine runs at idle but stops as soon as it is accelerated the cause of that is lean mixture due to a failure in the altitude compensator which must therefore be replaced.

Proceed as detailed below after having removed in this sequence:

- The air cleaner;
- The relay crank-to-control unit rod;
- The rear inspection cover from the control unit;
- The altitude compensator with its mounting flange.

CAUTION: do not move the control unit input lever (even better tape it in place) nor disturb the inside devices of control unit or serious damage and out-of-adjustment may result.

Measure the dimension "A" between the mounting flange face on which the spring rests and the top of bellows: such a dimension should fall between .35 and .41" (9 ÷ 10.5 mm) when the temperature setting lever is in "N" position.

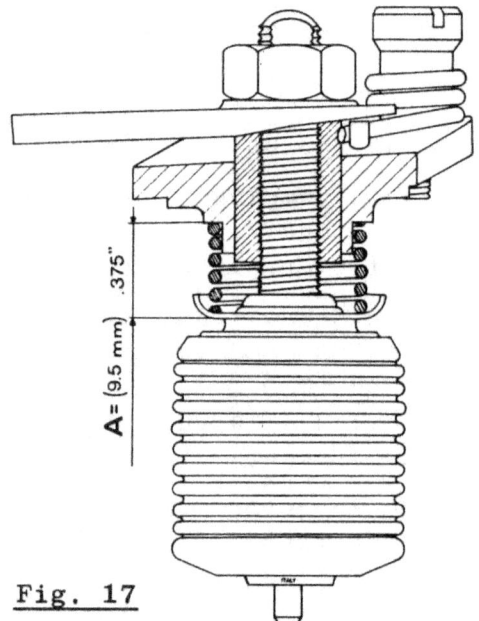

Fig. 17

Loosen the locknut and unscrew the capsule taking care not to rotate the setting lever with respect to the mounting flange.

Screw in the new capsule until the dimension previously taken is obtained; then slightly tighten the locknut.

NOTE: if, because of any reason, the dimension "A" does not fall within the specified limits, screw in the new capsule to a dimension of .37" (9.5 mm) irrespective of the dimension previously read.

Install capsule, and mounting flange assembly on the control unit making sure the setting lever spring is properly positioned and the setting lever itself is in "N" position.

Refit the rear inspection cover and the rod.

Start the engine and warm it up until the coolant has reached a temperature of no less than 158°F (70°C) then race the engine a few times up to 4000 rpm and fully release the throttle pedal each time.

Stop the engine, again remove the rear inspection cover and (with the aid of a suitable mirror and a lamp to light the inside of control unit) see whether the wire at the end of link engages the notch corresponding to the actual atmospheric pressure as listed below (notches to be counted starting from the top of the notches lever):

- atmospheric pressure falling between 29.9 - 30.7 in Hg: the wire should engage the 7th notch;

- pressure falling between 29.1 - 29.9 in Hg: the wire should engage the 8th notch;

- pressure between 28.3 - 29.1 in Hg: the wire should engage the 9th notch;

- pressure between 27.6 - 28.3 in Hg: the wire should engage the 10th notch.

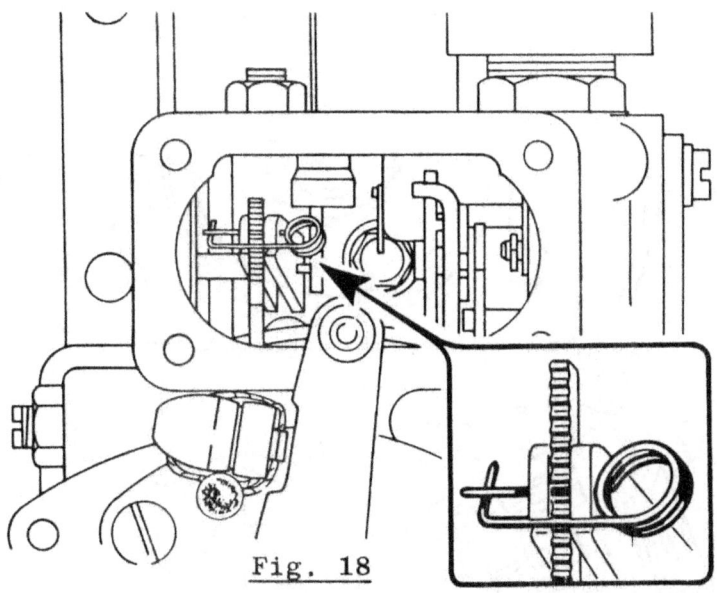

Fig. 18

If the above conditions are not fulfilled, adjust the position of the capsule so that, when the engine is started again (before that refit the rear inspection cover on control unit) and the warming up procedure (racing the engine followed by a complete release of accelerator) is repeated, the wire positions itself correctly: screw in the capsule to cause the wire to engage notches of higher numbers and unscrew the capsule to engage notches of lower numbers. Keep in mind that a rotation of about 150 degrees corresponds to one notch.

Tighten securely the locknut on the capsule, place the temperature setting lever in the position corresponding to the ambient conditions and reinstall the air cleaner.

D 9   REPLACING THE OIL FILTER IN THE INJECTION PUMP

On performing the engine major overhaul, on removing the injection pump (or after 50000 miles whichever occurs first) or on replacing the engine oil in case of contamination by water or similar, the additional oil filter located in the injection pump support must be renewed.

To do so, proceed as follows:

clean very carefully the filter housing cover and the surrounding areas to prevent any foreign matter from entering the filter housing.

remove the cover and withdraw the element; wash thoroughly the filter housing with gasoline, then insert the new element in such a way that the spring faces the cover; renew the cover gasket, if necessary.

To facilitate the air bleed and the quick filling up of filter housing with oil, slightly tighten the two upper cover retaining nuts, crank the engine a few seconds (even by means of the starter) until the oil just oozes out; then lock the nuts fully.

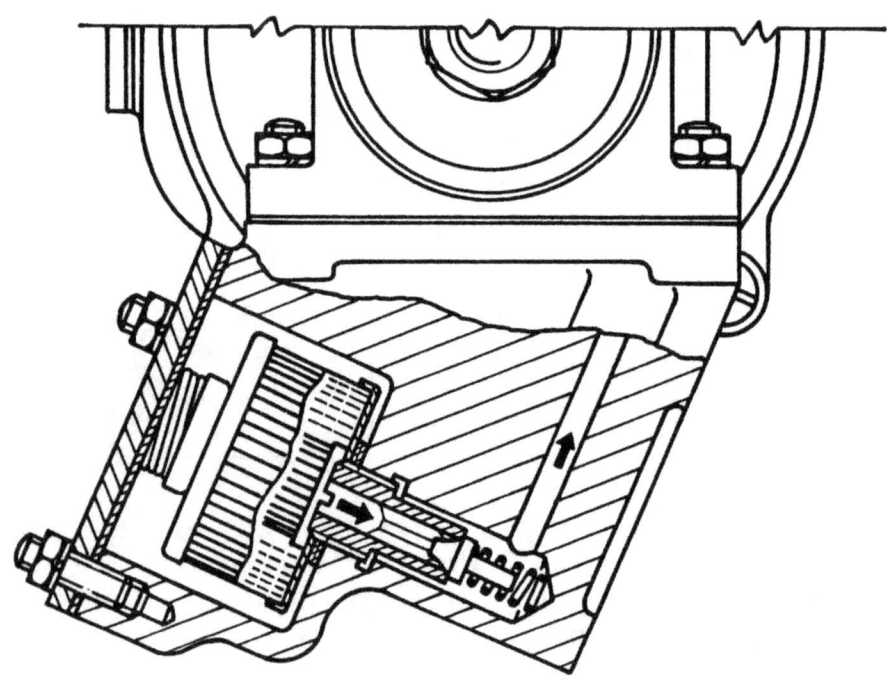

Fig. 19

D 10   CHECKING AND ADJUSTING THE THROTTLE CONTROL LINKAGE

Engine cold

Disconnect the relay crank-to-control unit rod 8 (see fig. 2) at the crank-side joint.

When the relay crank is at rest against the idle limit stop, there should be a .04 - .06" (1 - 1.5 mm) free travel at the pedal lever (see page 5) in the engine compartment with respect to the reference screw on the cable anchoring bracket; if not so, adjust the reference screw until the specified free travel is obtained.

Depress the accelerator pedal to the pedal stop on floor and check that the clearance between relay crank lug and full throttle limit stop screw is .08" (2 mm): if not so, adjust the pedal stop on floor until the specified clearance is obtained.

Reconnect the rod 8.

Engine hot (coolant temperature higher than 158°F - 70°C).

With the accelerator pedal fully released, check that the free travel at the pedal lever (see page 5) is .04 - .06" (1 ÷ 1.5 mm).

NOTE: if the adjustments of the reference screw are not enough to obtain the correct free travel of pedal lever, loosen the cable setscrew and tighten it again on the cable at a more suitable position.

D 11   REPLACING THE FUEL CUT OFF SOLENOID (See fig. 20)

On deceleration, if detonations take place or the engine stops occasionally or wholly, the cause may be an improper operation or a failure of the fuel cut off solenoid.

To renew the solenoid, proceed as follows:
- Remove the air cleaner.
- Disconnect the terminal of solenoid feed wire.
- Keep a record of the projection "A" of solenoid body from the ring nut top.
- Slacken the ring nut with the special tool no. A.5.0177 taking care not to cock the solenoid.
- Unscrew the solenoid by hand and take it away.
- Test the solenoid by energizing it with a 12 Volt D.C. supply. When energized, the solenoid plunger must protrude by .185 − .20" (4.7 ÷ 5 mm); when the solenoid is de-energized, the plunger must back up fully with no sluggishness.

Repeat the test several times, each time rotating the plunger to make certain it moves freely in any position.

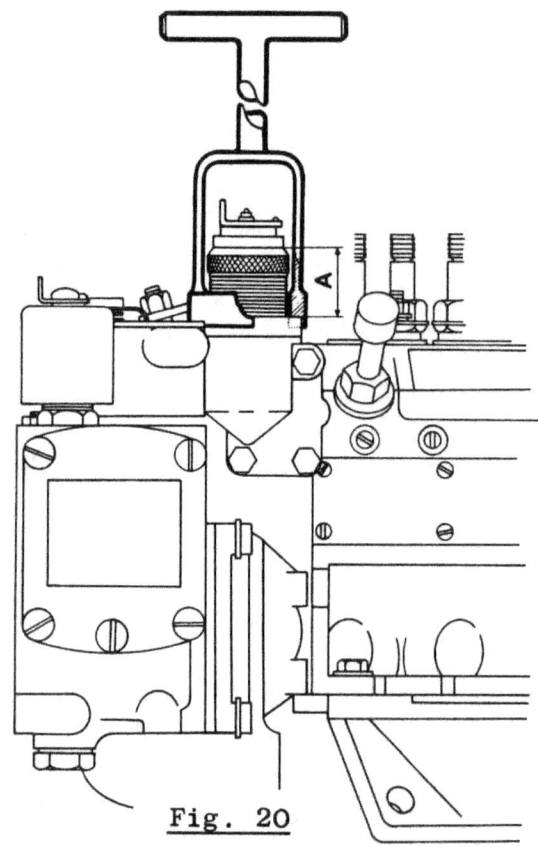

Fig. 20

* If the solenoid is operating properly, screw it in again to the projection previously recorded (tighten the ring nut before checking for correct dimension "A")

** If the solenoid is not operating properly, change it with a new one and screw it in until projection "A" (ring nut tightened) is <u>1 inch</u> (25.4 mm)

- **Reconnect the feed wire**
- **Refit the air cleaner**

Road test the car to check that driveability is satisfactory:

* If the solenoid has not been renewed and the driveability is not completely satisfactory, this may be due to a slight misalignment of the solenoid on reinstallation; in this case, merely <u>unscrew</u> the solenoid by one eighth of a turn (one reference notch as suitably provided)

** If the solenoid has been renewed and the driveability is not satisfactory, <u>unscrew</u> the solenoid by one notch at a time until the appropriate carburation is obtained

*** If the solenoid has been renewed and if the driveability is satisfactory, <u>screw in</u> the solenoid by one notch at a time until slight hesitations take place: at this point <u>unscrew</u> the solenoid by one notch so as to put it back into the next former setting giving good driveability

<u>CAUTION</u>: When tightening or slackening the ring nut, take care not to rotate the solenoid or it will go out of correct setting.

TROUBLE SHOOTING

The following chart lists several malfunctions, possible cause for each of them and remedies.

If deficiencies or malfunctions are experienced in the fuel system, it is absolutely essential to make sure they are not caused nor affected by the incorrect operation of the ignition system: <u>in fact it is impossible to distinguish "a priori" whether a failure of fuel or ignition system is the cause for the deficiencies</u>; therefore, first inspect the ignition system for the following and remedy, if necessary

- spark plugs for proper operation and type;
- contact-breaker points conditions and gap;
- ignition coil for continuity or leakage;
- ignition distributor for correct timing using a timing light; adjust timing or replace the ignition distributor, if necessary.

Should any of the troubles listed below be experienced, it is recommended to clean thoroughly the affected areas of both engine and engine compartment with a suitable solvent; this to the purpose of preventing any foreign matter from entering, on removal or reinstallation, the mechanical components and specifically the fuel feed circuit.

Soon after cleaning, inspect the mechanical units for loose attaching or joining parts, the pipes for loose fittings and the brackets for sound conditions.

E 1   ALFA ROMEO SPICA PUMP POLICY

Injection pumps are not to be opened for any reason. An exchange pump service is available for complete pump units. Pumps that have been tampered with will forfeit any core valve.

Always before removing a pump consult your Alfa Romeo representative or zone office.

E 2 TROUBLE CHART

TROUBLE	POSSIBLE CAUSE	REMEDY
Low fuel pressure warning light does not flash on when ignition key is turned	Fuse no. 6 blown Warning light bulb burnt out Pressure switch faulty (jammed open)	Replace fuse Replace bulb Check switch and replace, if necessary
Low fuel pressure warning light stays on (fuel pump operates properly)	Pressure switch faulty (jammed closed) Low fuel pump outlet pressure due to: - tank to pump lines clogged or air seeping thru them - tank fuel filter clogged - main fuel filter clogged - main filter pressure relief valve defective or stuck open Fuel pump delivery too low	Replace switch - Inspect fuel lines - Replace filter - Clean filter and replace element (see page 12) - Check relief valve and replace, if necessary Have fuel pump checked or replaced
Low fuel pressure warning light stays on (fuel pump fails to operate)	Fuse blown (in the additional fuse box) Electric wires to pump disconnected Fuel pump faulty	Replace fuse Check and reconnect Have the pump checked or replaced
Engine will not start from cold	Solenoid-actuated cold start device fails to operate	- check electric connections - have the device checked or replaced
Engine misfires; rough idle	One injector defective Injection pipe fittings leaking Injection pipes cracked	Trace the cylinder by grounding each spark plug and replace the injector, if necessary Tighten fittings Check and replace, if necessary
Rough idle (hunting)	Lean mixture	Remedy possible air seepage downstream of throttles. Refer to page 21

TROUBLE	POSSIBLE CAUSE	REMEDY
Rough idle	Idle equalizer out of adjustment	Adjust idle
Too fast an idle and smoky exhaust	Faulty thermostatic actuator	Replace thermostatic actuator
Engine keeps running at idle but stops on accelerating	Altitude compensator faulty	Replace altitude compensator (see page 32)
Idle too fast	Accelerator linkage fails to return fully	Check: - flexible cable - linkage joints and pivot pins for free movement - pedal return spring for sound conditions - pedal and linkage limit stop for proper adjustment Clean linkage joints and pack with grease
Unsatisfactory driveability; hesitations	Control linkage out of adjustment	Check throttle/control unit linkage (see page 18)
	Fuel pump outlet pressure too low (warning light comes on while running at high speed)	Check and replace, if necessary, tank fuel filter and/or main filter element
	Injector defective	Refer to remedies as under "Engine misfires; rough idle"
	Injection pump or control unit/defective	Have them checked and replaced, if necessary, by an authorized workshop
	Temperature setting lever improperly positioned	Position the lever correctly
Unsatisfactory road performance	Temperature setting lever improperly positioned	Position the lever correctly
	Control linkage out of adjustment	Check throttle/control unit linkage (see page 18)
	Fuel pump outlet pressure too low (warning light comes on while running at high speed)	Check and replace, if necessary, tank fuel filter and/or main filter element
	Air induction clogged	Check and replace air cleaner elements, if necessary
	Injector defective	Refer to remedies as under "Engine misfires; rough idle"
	Injection pump or control unit/defective (defective carburation)	Have them checked and replaced, if necessary, by an authorized workshop

TROUBLE	POSSIBLE CAUSE	REMEDY
Excessive fuel consumption	Fuel feed circuit leaks	Check pipes, fittings, seals and replace defective parts
	Thermostatic actuator defective; also refer to causes as under "Too fast an idle"	Have the thermostatic actuator checked and replaced, if necessary, by an authorized workshop
	Defective carburation	Have the injection pump adjusted by an authorized workshop
Engine stalls in positions other than idle	Defective altitude compensator or excessive vibrations of injection pump and control unit	Have the altitude compensator checked (see page 32); also check injection pump and control unit brackets for sound conditions and firm attachment
Engine stalls flat	Injection pump driving belt broken	Replace belt (check for proper injection pump timing. See page 30)
Engine does not slow down to idle on deceleration (fast idle)	Both throttles and control unit lever fail to return fully on deceleration	Check: - flexible cable - linkage joints and pivot pins for free movement - pedal and linkage return springs for sound conditions - pedal and linkage limit stops for proper adjustment - clean linkage joints and pack them with grease suitable for low temperatures
Detonations in the exhaust pipe on deceleration	Fuse no. 6 blown	Replace fuse
	Feed wire disconnected at fuel cut off solenoid	Re-connect wire
	Loose junction of fuel cut off device feed wire disconnected	Re-connect junction
	Defective fuel cut off solenoid	Have the fuel cut off solenoid checked and replaced, if necessary
	Defective fuel cut off device micro switch	Have the fuel cut off device checked by an authorized workshop

TROUBLE	POSSIBLE CAUSE	REMEDY
Engine stops: - wholly or occasionally on deceleration in neutral - occasionally or wholly when re-accelerating after a deceleration Engine fires again suddenly and with delay when re-accelerating after a deceleration	Fuel cut off solenoid stuck in cut off position or sluggish in backing up	Have the fuel cut off solenoid checked and replaced, if necessary
Noisy electric fuel pump	Line between pump and main filter distorted or forced in the rubber mountings or against the recovery pipe Tank filter and hoses improperly fitted	Reset the line making certain it is centered in the rubber mountings without forcing against the recovery pipe Check that the filter is properly fitted and that hoses have a correct run

NOTES

Direzione Assistenza

INSTRUCTION AND MAINTENANCE MANUAL

FOR ALFA ROMEO 2000

FUEL INJECTION MODELS

U.S.A. VERSION

1972 MODEL YEAR

CONTENTS

IMPORTANT NOTE . . . . Page 1

A - FUEL INJECTION SYSTEM

    A1 General . . . . " 2
    A2 Fuel feed system . . . . " 2
    A3 Air induction system . . . . " 2
    A4 Injection pump . . . . " 3
    A5 Cold start device . . . . " 3
    A6 Initial running device . . . . " 4
    A7 Crankcase ventilating system . . . . " 4
    A8 Fuel vapor recovery system and tank ventilation . . . . " 5

B - RECOMMENDATIONS ON THE USE

    B1 Starting the engine . . . . " 6
    B2 Temperature setting . . . . " 7
    B3 Deceleration . . . . " 7

C - REGULAR SERVICING

    C1 Schedule of regular servicing required to keep the exhaust emission
        level within limits prescribed by U.S. regulations . . . . " 8
        - Index of servicing operations . . . . " 8
    C2 Replacing the air filter elements . . . . " 9
    C3 Replacing the main fuel filter element . . . . " 9
    C4 Checking the spark plugs and replacing . . . . " 10
    C5 Checking the alternator and fan driving belt . . . . " 11
    C6 Checking the valve timing chain tension . . . . " 11
    C7a Checking the distributor and the ignition timing . . . . " 11
        - Condenser capacity test . . . . " 12
        - Timing adjustment . . . . " 13
    C7b Replacing the distributor . . . . " 13
        - Automatic advance graph and specifications of Marelli S 113 B dis-
          tributor . . . . " 14
    C8 Checking the valve clearance . . . . " 15
    C9 Replacing the tank fuel filter . . . . " 15
    C10 Cleaning the throttle valve throats . . . . " 16
    C11 Replacing the injection pump oil filter . . . . " 16
    C12 Checking the positioning of throttle-control unit linkage . . . . . " 17
    C13 Checking the positioning and alignment of throttles . . . . " 19
    C14 Idle adjustment-mixture adjustment . . . . " 20
        - First step: preliminary idle adjustment . . . . " 21
        - Second step: road test and operating mixture adjustment . . . . . " 22
                   adjusting the fuel mixture . . . . " 22
        - Third step: speed and CO adjustment . . . . " 23

D - INJECTION PUMP REPAIRS

    D1 Removal and reinstallation of the injection pump . . . . " 24
    D2 Timing the injection pump . . . . " 25
    D3 Replacement of thermostatic actuator . . . . " 26
    D4 Replacing the fuel cut of solenoid . . . . " 27
    D5 Replacement of cold start solenoid and plunger removal . . . . . . " 29
    D6 Testing the injectors . . . . " 30
    D7 Replacing the altitude compensator . . . . " 31
    D8 Check the relationship between throttle angles and control unit lever
        angles . . . . " 33
    D9 Replacing the rotating seal and the motor of the electric pump . . " 36

E - TROUBLE SHOOTING

    E1 Alfa Romeo Spica pump policy . . . . " 38
    E2 Trouble chart . . . . " 39

IMPORTANT NOTE

The fuel injection system for the 2000 model has been designed not only to attain high performance and low fuel consumption but also to keep the exhaust emissions below the levels allowed by U.S.A. regulations.

The low exhaust emission levels have been obtained by improving the distribution and combustion. No devices to burn the unburned gases downstream of the exhaust valves are required.

Simple and efficient systems for controlling crankcase and evaporative emissions are fitted.

Of course, even with the mentioned systems fitted to the Alfa 2000 the emissions will not continue to meet Federal and State regulations unless the owner himself provides to have the prescribed servicing, carried out by authorized Alfa Romeo Dealers and provided that, when remedying troubles or performing any maintenance work on the engine or fuel feed system, the factory prescribed procedures are strictly followed.

Alfa Romeo warrants to the original and each subsequent owner of a 1972 Alfa Romeo passenger vehicle, that the vehicle:

1 - has been designed and built to conform at the time of sale with those emission requirements issued under the Clean Air Act, section 202 (a) applicable at the time of manufacture;

2 - is free from defects in material and workmanship which would cause it not to conform with those regulations for a period of 50,000 miles or 5 years, whichever occurs first.

By express terms of Federal Law, the emission control system warranty applies only to those vehicles which have been used and maintained according to Alfa Romeo's instructions published in the owner's manual and service coupon booklet. Maintenance records are the responsibility of the vehicle owner, as are the costs of these services.

Federal Law prohibits manufactures and dealers from knowingly removing or rendering an emission control system inoperative or ineffective after sale and delivery to an ultimate purchaser.

WARNING - Dealers are adviced that owners must furnish evidence of compliance with the Alfa Romeo instructions relating to exhaust emission maintenance.

The evidence of compliance is provided by the coupons and stubs contained in the Service Coupon Booklet [45 CFR 1201.160 (b)].

NOTES

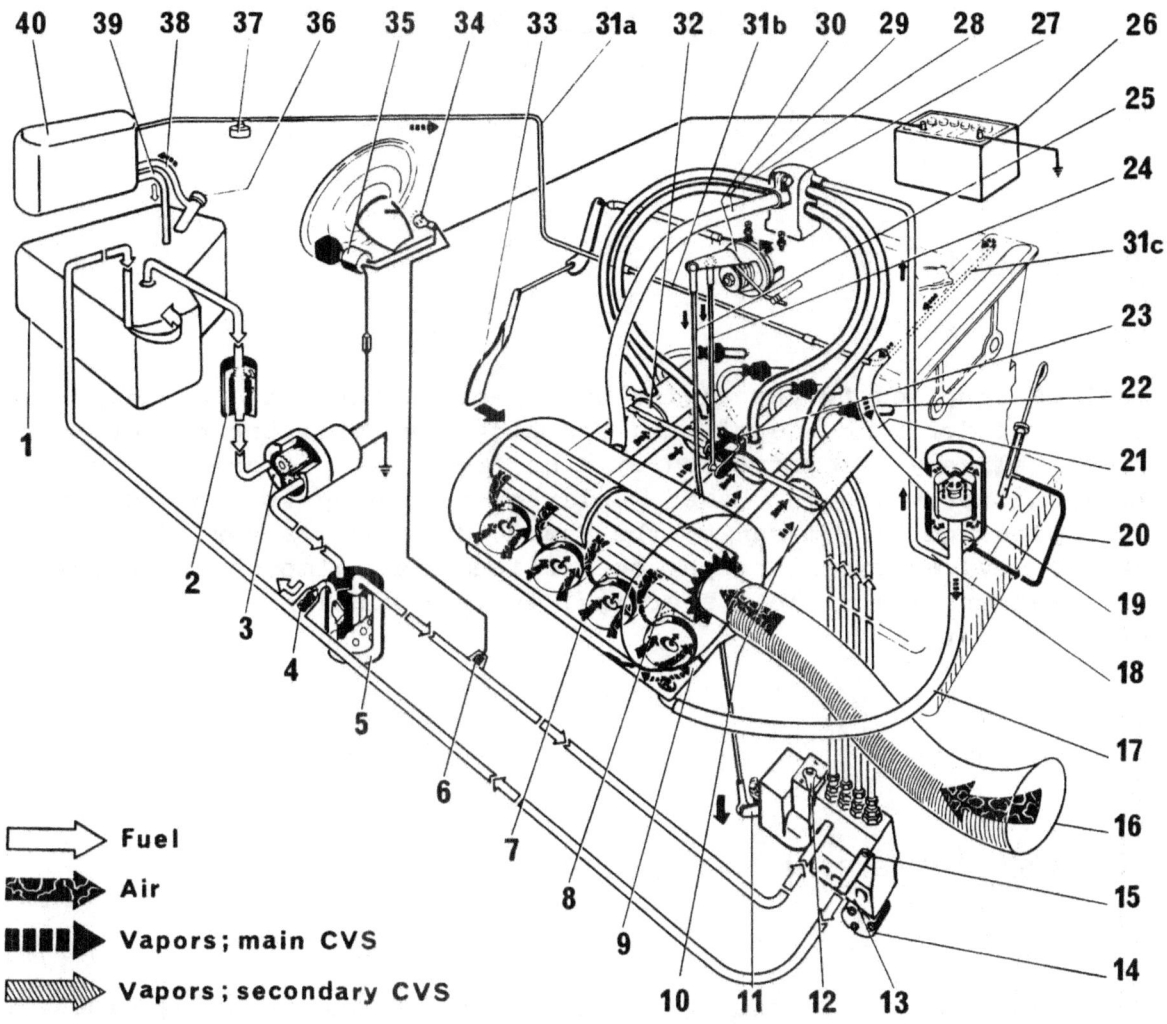

Fig. 1 - GENERAL ARRANGEMENT OF FUEL INJECTION SYSTEM

1 Fuel tank
2 Tank filter
3 Electric pump
4 Pressure relief valve
5 Main filter
6 Pressure switch
7 Filter housing
8 Filter element
9 Manifold gallery
10 Intake duct
11 Control unit lever
12 Average seasonal temperature compensator, hand operated
13 Injection pump
14 Injection pump oil filter
15 Calibrated orifice
16 Air hose
17 Main crankcase ventilating system hose
18 Secondary crankcase ventilating system hose
19 Oil separator
20 Oil separator draining hose

21 Suction hose for crankcase ventilating systems
22 Injector
23 Throttle lever
24 Relay crank - to - throttle rod
25 Relay crank - to - control unit rod
26 Battery
27 Idle air adjuster and equalizer
28 Idle air hoses
29 Idle air supply pipe
30 Relay crank
31a ⎫
31b ⎬ Fuel tank vent pipe
31c ⎭
32 Throttles
33 Accelerator pedal
34 Low fuel pressure warning light
35 Ignition switch
36 Sealed filler cap
37 Air inlet valve
38 Fuel tank - expansion connection
39 Liquid return hose
40 Expansion tank (vapor-liquid separator)

A FUEL INJECTION SYSTEM

A1 GENERAL

Fuel is supplied to the engine by injection into the intake port of each cylinder by means of four pumping elements (one per cylinder) whose delivery is controlled by a control unit. A cam in the control unit provides a "base" delivery according to the opening of throttles and to rpm range; the "base" delivery is varied by compensating devices giving proper corrections for atmospheric pressure, engine temperature, cold starting, initial running and fuel cut off on deceleration.

A2 FUEL FEED SYSTEM (see fig. 1)

Inserting the key in the ignition switch (35) and rotating clockwise to the first click will operate the electric pump (3). The gasoline flows from the fuel tank (1) thru tank filter (2) and main filter (5) and feeds the injection pump (13).

The excess fuel, acting also as a coolant for the injection pump (13), before returning to the tank, passes thru a calibrated orifice (15) which regulates the fuel pressure within the injection pump. A pressure switch (6) inserted in the delivery pipe will switch on the warning light (34) on instrument panel if a pressure drop occurs in fuel lines; the pressure should never be lower than 7.1 psi -(0.5 kg/cm^2).

A pressure relief valve (4) on filter (5) limits the fuel pump outlet pressure bypassing fuel to the recovery pipe at 16 - 18 psi (1.1 ÷ 1.3 kg/cm^2).

A3 AIR INDUCTION SYSTEM (see fig. 1)

The air induction system consists of the housing (7) incorporating two filtering elements (8), directly connected to the intake ducts (10) which deliver air to the throttles (32); an air hose (16) connects the housing (7) to a ram intake port at the front of the car (an automatic device provides for the draining of water possibly entered thru the air intake port).

The idling air (throttle valves closed) is fed thru a separate circuit consisting of a filtered air supply pipe (29), an adjuster ring fitted to the equalizer (27) and four small hoses (28) connecting the equalizer to the intake ducts downstream of the throttles.

The accelerator pedal (33) is mechanically linked thru a relay crank (30) to both the throttle lever (23) and the control unit lever (11). Therefore, any position of accelerator pedal corresponds to an exact position of throttle and control unit levers.

A 4 INJECTION PUMP (see fig. 1)

The injection pump (13), (SPICA AIBB. 4C.S.75), has four variable displacement plungers controlled by the control unit thru a rack. The plungers are actuated by conn.rods driven by a crankshaft revolving at half engine speed. The pump is lubricated with the engine oil drawn from the main gallery just after the main filter.

The lubricating oil, filtered further by a filter (14) in the injection pump mount, seeps past the plungers, lubricates the various moving parts then returns to the pan thru a suitable port in the pump mount itself.

A 5 COLD START DEVICE

The cold start device incorporates a solenoid which, energized when the engine is started, enriches the mixture by increasing the injection pump delivery thru an additional movement of control unit rack.

The cold start device cuts off gradually, according to engine temperature, when the ignition key is released from cranking position.

A 6   INITIAL RUNNING DEVICE (see fig. 1)

This device provides for a smooth operation of the engine soon after a cold start; it consists of a thermostat which, sensing engine coolant temperatures, acts thru a linkage on the control unit rack so as to increase the injection pump delivery in accord with the decrease in temperature and at the same time, thru rods (24) and (25) outside the control unit, opens the throttles so that the engine can be properly fed.

The device cuts off automatically and progressively as the engine warms up to operating temperature thus restoring the standard idling conditions.

A 7   CRANKCASE VENTILATING SYSTEM (see fig. 1)

The exhaust gases and the oil vapors developed during engine operation and gas vapors from the fuel tank are sucked thru the camshaft cover in the combustion chambers and burned.

The crankcase ventilating system controls gases both at high engine rpms and at idling speed when the throttles are closed.

The gases and vapors flow from camshaft cover to the oil separator (19) thru the hose (21), then enter either the main or secondary crankcase ventilating system according to the opening of throttles (32):

when throttles are fully opened, the vapors are delivered from the oil separator (19), thru the main system hose (17), to the manifold gallery (9), communicating directly with the four intake ducts (10) and, from here, to the throttle throats; when the throttles are instead closed or partially opened, the oil vapors are delivered from the oil separator (19), via the secondary system hose (18), to the equalizer (27), where they are suitably mixed with fresh air and thence, thru four hoses (28) they are delivered to the intake ducts downstream of the throttles.

The oil collected in the oil separator (19) returns to the pan via the hose (20).

A 8 FUEL VAPOR RECOVERY SYSTEM AND TANK VENTILATION (see fig. 1)

Gas vapors, emanating from fuel tank (1) both during engine operation and hot soak period after engine shutdown, are collected in the expansion tank (40) which acts also as a vapor liquid separator returning the condensate to the fuel tank via the pipe (39) located at the bottom of expansion tank.

The pipe (38) serves to make a proper connection between the fuel tank (1), when fully replenished, and the expansion tank (40).

To prevent gas vapors from escaping in the open air, a sealed filler cap (36) is provided.

Gas vapors coming to the expansion tank (40) flow out of the separator from the top and, passing thru the pipes (31a) and (31b), enter the cylinder head, then, via the pipe (31c) which extends into the cylinder head, get into the crankcase: during the hot soak period, the crankcase is used as a storage volume while during engine operation the crankcase is purged of vapors by the action of the ventilation system as outlined on page 4 at the beginning of paragraph.

In the event that, after engine shut down, the pressure in the vapor separator tends to diminish as a consequence of drop in temperature, gas vapors will flow back thru pipes (31a - b - c) thus keeping the fuel tank (1) and expansion tank (40) at atmospheric pressure.

A valve (37) on the pipe (31a) allows to keep a constant supply of fuel to the engine even if an obstruction should occur in the pipe (31a - b - c) itself.

B RECOMMENDATIONS ON THE USE

B 1   STARTING THE ENGINE

1) <u>Under normal conditions</u>:

   Insert the key in the ignition switch and turn it clockwise to the first click; wait a few seconds to make sure the low fuel pressure warning light goes off.

   <u>WARNING</u>: if the warning light does not flash on or stays on, this is an indication of failure of the indicating device or fuel feed system; therefore have them checked as soon as possible.

   Turn the ignition key further clockwise to operate the starter.

   As soon as the engine fires release the key.

   <u>NOTE</u>: automatic devices act as a standard choke usually does, namely, facilitate the initial running of engine after a cold start until the proper operating temperature is reached.

2) <u>As an aid in starting from cold</u>, proceed as per 1) above taking care to depress slightly the accelerator pedal as soon as cranking motor starts operating (at the second "click"). After a cold start and particularly when the ambient temperature is below freezing point, wait a fairly long time before getting away so as to warm up properly all engine parts and allow the oil to reach all points requiring lubrication.

   Top performance must never be demanded of the car until coolant temperature is about 158°F (70°C).

3) <u>When the engine is already hot</u> or with very high ambient temperatures (above 77°F - 25°C) proceed as per 1) above taking care to depress slightly the accelerator pedal as soon as cranking motor starts operating (at the second "click").

   <u>CAUTION</u>: owing to the special construction of the injection pump the pump plungers must on no account be operated directly with a lever or any other tool.

B2 TEMPERATURE SETTING (see fig. 2)

To keep a constant fuel/air ratio even when the ambient temperature varies as the seasons change, the temperature compensator lever on the control unit shall be shifted to:

- "N" (normal) for ambient temperatures exceeding 59°F (15°C).
- "C" (cold) for temperatures between 59°F (15°C) and 32°F (0°C).
- "F" (freezing) for temperatures below 32°F (0°C).

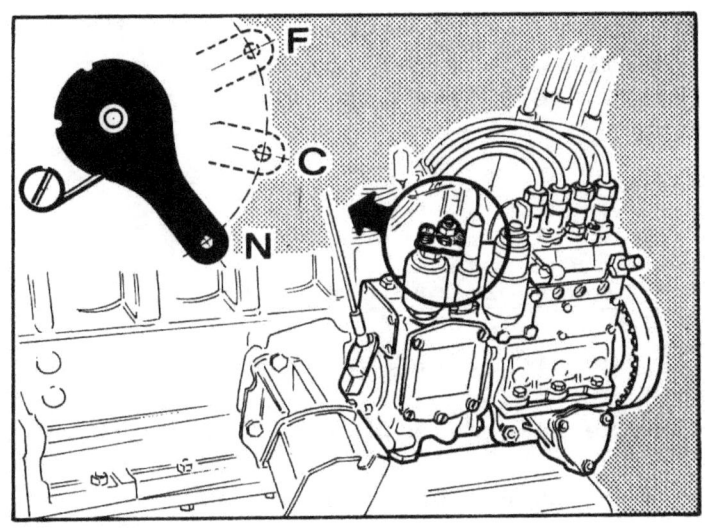

Fig. 2 - TEMPERATURE SETTING LEVER

B3 DECELERATION

On deceleration, the injection pump delivery is automatically cut off by means of an electromagnetic device fed thru a microswitch which, being actuated by a particular profile suitably shaped in the control unit cam, closes when the accelerator pedal is released; this not only eliminates the unburned gases in a condition which is critical for the emission levels, but also favorably affects the fuel consumption.

As the engine speed reaches about 1,300 rpm, the fuel delivery restores to prevent stopping the engine. Of course, the fuel delivery restores even if the engine is re-accelerated before it slows down to 1,300 rpm.

C REGULAR SERVICING

C 1 SCHEDULE OF REGULAR SERVICING REQUIRED TO KEEP THE EXHAUST EMISSION LEVEL WITHIN LIMITS PRESCRIBED BY U.S. REGULATIONS

In order to maintain the fuel injection system in good operating conditions and the exhaust emissions below the limits specified by Federal regulations, the servicing operations listed in the Owner's Manual and in the Service Coupon Book must be performed at the prescribed period.

On the following pages, each operation specifically related to the injection system will be set out in details particularly those requiring the special tools and facilities the authorized workshops are equipped with.

Index of servicing operations

C 2	Replacing the air filter elements	Page	9
C 3	Replacing the main fuel filter element	"	9
C 4	Checking the spark plugs and replacing	"	10
C 5	Checking the alternator and fan driving belt ...	"	11
C 6	Checking the valve timing chain tension	"	11
C 7a	Checking the distributor and the ignition timing .	"	11
C 7b	Replacing the distributor	"	13
C 8	Checking the valve clearance	"	15
C 9	Replacing the tank fuel filter (throw away type) .	"	15
C 10	Cleaning the throttle valve throats	"	16
C 11	Replacing the injection pump oil filter	"	16
C 12	Checking the positioning of throttle/control unit linkage	"	17
C 13	Checking the positioning and alignment of throttles	"	19
C 14	Idle adjustment - Mixture adjustment	"	20

C2 REPLACING THE AIR FILTER ELEMENTS (see Fig. 1)

To provide room for subsequent operations, the air filter elements shall be removed as a whole; to do so, remove the pipe (31b); detach the two upper anchoring straps at manifold side; loosen at the engine side the four clamps on the intake hoses; free the crankcase ventilation hose (17) from the oil separator; disconnect the idle hose (29) from the idling air equalizer (27); remove the hose (16) connecting the air filter housing to the ram intake port.

Then the cover of filter housing can be removed and the elements replaced after having cleaned the inside of air filter housing.

Do not reinstall the air filter on engine at this point.

C3 REPLACING THE MAIN FUEL FILTER ELEMENT (see Fig. 3)

This operation, to be performed after the previous one has already been accomplished, should be carried out as follows:

disconnect the battery negative terminal, disconnect the starter positive cable if necessary.

CAUTION: first of all clean carefully the outside of filter body to make sure no foreign matter could enter the filter on reassembly.

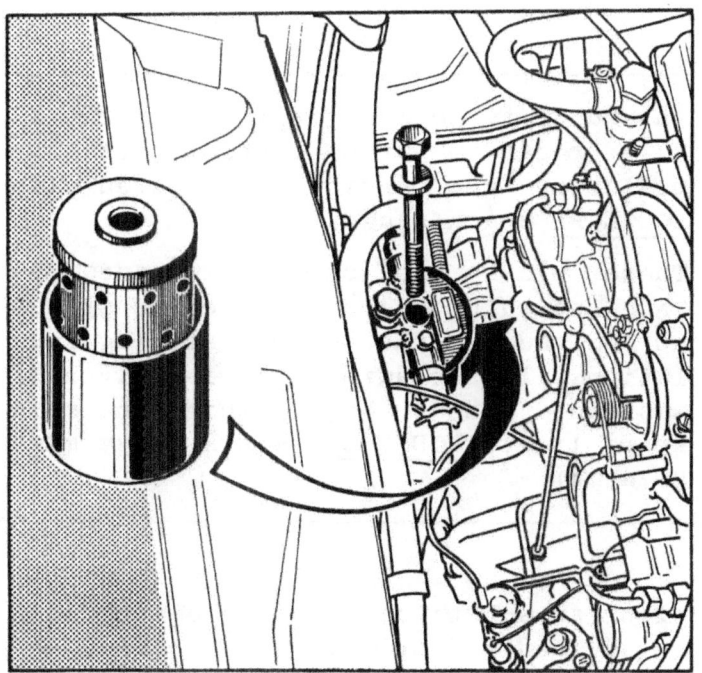

Fig. 3 - MAIN FUEL FILTER ELEMENT

slacken the bolt securing the filter to its bracket and remove the filter,

withdraw the filter element,

get rid of foreign matter that may have collected in the housing and fit a new element; also replace the housing gasket if damaged and the sealing ring on bolt.

WARNING: extreme cleanliness is required in the area of the main fuel filter.

C 4   CHECKING THE SPARK PLUGS (Lodge HL) AND REPLACING

The spark plugs are of the surface gap type with four points and a central electrode. The only maintenance required is occasional cleaning with a brush of the central electrode and points. No routine adjustment is necessary of the gap between the electrode and points.

If the ceramic insulator is cracked or the electrodes are excessively worn away, the spark plugs must be replaced.

The spark plugs should be tightened when cold to a torque of 18 - 25.3 lb-ft (2.5 ÷ 3.5 kgm); lubricate the threads with graphite grease before fitting.

The standard plugs fitted to the engine are LODGE HL. A decal, giving the specifications for these plugs, is attached under the hood; here below, the text of the decal is repeated.

> In order to comply with the Federal rule regarding the control of air pollution the engine is fitted with LODGE-HL spark plugs.
>
> These plugs are completely adequate when the automobile is driven at speeds not exceeding the speed limiting regulations. If the automobile is driven at sustained speeds higher than the said speed limits, LODGE-2HL spark plugs must be used.

Under no condition can substitute spark plugs be used, unless they are specifically advised and approved by Alfa Romeo. Use of other plugs can promote serious engine damage, as well as alter emission levels.

C 5 CHECKING THE ALTERNATOR AND FAN DRIVING BELT

The belt should be tightened enough to drive the fan and alternator pulley without slipping and without overloading the bearings.

The tension is correct when, on pressing the belt down, the sag is about 1/2" (10-15 mm).

To tighten the belt unscrew the nut on the adjusting arm and move the alternator outwards.

C 6 CHECKING THE VALVE TIMING CHAIN TENSION

Run engine at idling speed; while performing the following adjustment any revving up of the engine must be absolutely avoided; slacken off the setscrew securing the chain tensioner; wait a few minutes to allow the tensioner to tighten the chain, then lock the chain tensioner setscrew firmly.

On refitting the camshaft cover, make sure the gasket is in sound conditions or replace, if necessary. Moderately tighten the cover retaining nuts in diagonal order.

C 7a CHECKING THE DISTRIBUTOR (Marelli S 103 B) AND THE IGNITION TIMING

Dwell meter should read between 57 and 63 degrees, with new points closed, corresponding to .017 to .019" (.43 to .48 mm) gap.

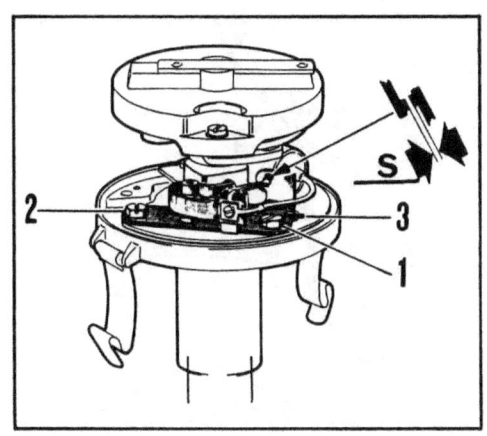

To adjust, loosen the screws (1) and (2), insert a screwdriver in the adjustment slot (3) and pry the stationary-point plate

S = .017 - .019 in.

Fig. 4 - DISTRIBUTOR POINTS GAP CHECK

Smear the distributor cam with grease. Check the inside of distributor cap for any sign of moisture, carbon deposits or cracks and the central power electrode for free movement in its seat and for effective spring action. Finally, check cap terminals for good conditions.

The ignition timing should be checked when the engine is warmed up to operating temperature (coolant exceeding 158°F; 70°C) by using a timing light.

Condenser capacity test

Should an excessive wear of breaker points be experienced, check that the condenser capacity is not lower than 0.20 µF i.e. over 20% less than its rated capacity (0.25 µF) marked on the condenser body.

At idle speed the timing should be 5 to 7 degrees ATDC, that is the mark "F" on the pulley should be in line with the pointer or .04" (1 mm) apart either side.

With the engine running with no load at 5,000 rpm, the ignition advance should be 27 to 33 degrees, that is the mark "M" on the pulley should be in line with the pointer or .12" (3 mm) apart either side.

Timing at idle speed must be adjusted with special care as it affects the emission levels greatly.

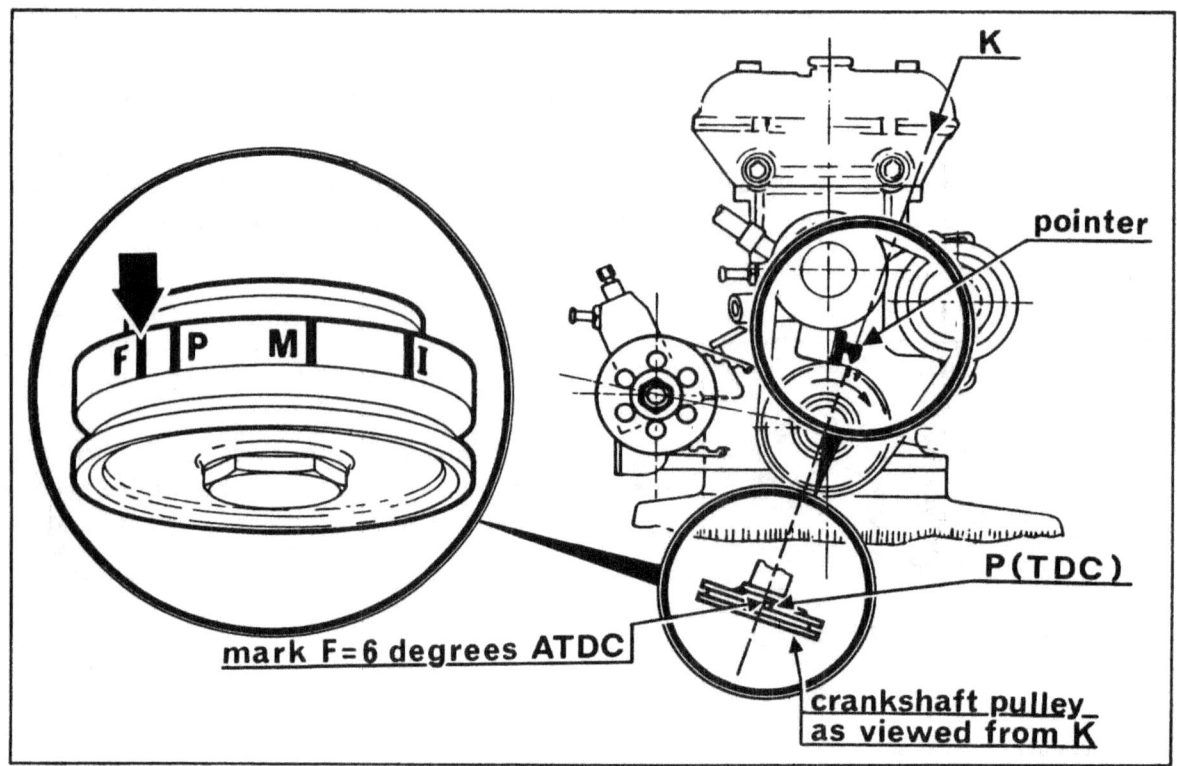

Fig. 5 - IGNITION TIMING

Timing adjustment (maximum accuracy required)

If the timing requires adjustment, proceed as follows:

unscrew the distributor securing nut (1) on the stud so as to allow the distributor to be rotated together with its supporting clamp, then rotate the distributor body counterclockwise or clockwise according to whether it is necessary to respectively advance "A" or retard "R" the ignition setting;

retighten the nut (1), taking care not to move the distributor body;

recheck timing.

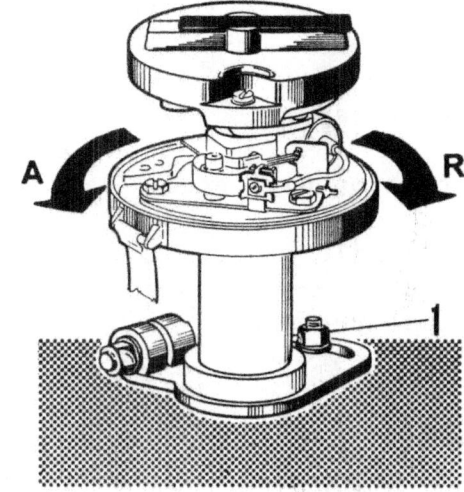

Fig. 6 - IGNITION TIMING ADJUSTMENT

In the event of reinstallation or renewal of the distributor, refer to the directions given on paragraph C7b.

C 7b REPLACING THE DISTRIBUTOR

When reinstalling or renewing the distributor, perform the following procedure:

rotate the crankshaft to bring no. 1 cylinder piston to the compression stroke that is with both valves closed;

by slightly rotating the crankshaft bring the fixed advance mark "F" on pulley into line with the reference pointer;

fit the supporting clamp into the distributor body and tighten the clamp just snug;

remove distributor cap and rotate the drive shaft by hand to bring the rotor arm in line with the contact for no. 1 cylinder;

as a trial installation place the distributor on engine and move the supporting clamp so that the stud is centered in the clamp slot when the contact-breaker points are about to open for no.1 cylinder;

then, remove the distributor with its supporting clamp, taking care not to disturb the distributor body/clamp setting and lock the clamp in place;

reinstall the distributor and adjust timing as directed on paragraph C7a.

Automatic advance graph and specifications of Marelli S 103 B distributor

Contact gap . . . . .017 - .019"

Contact opening angle . . . . 30° ± 3°

Dwell angle . . . . 60° ± 3°

Contact pressure . . . . 18 - 21 oz

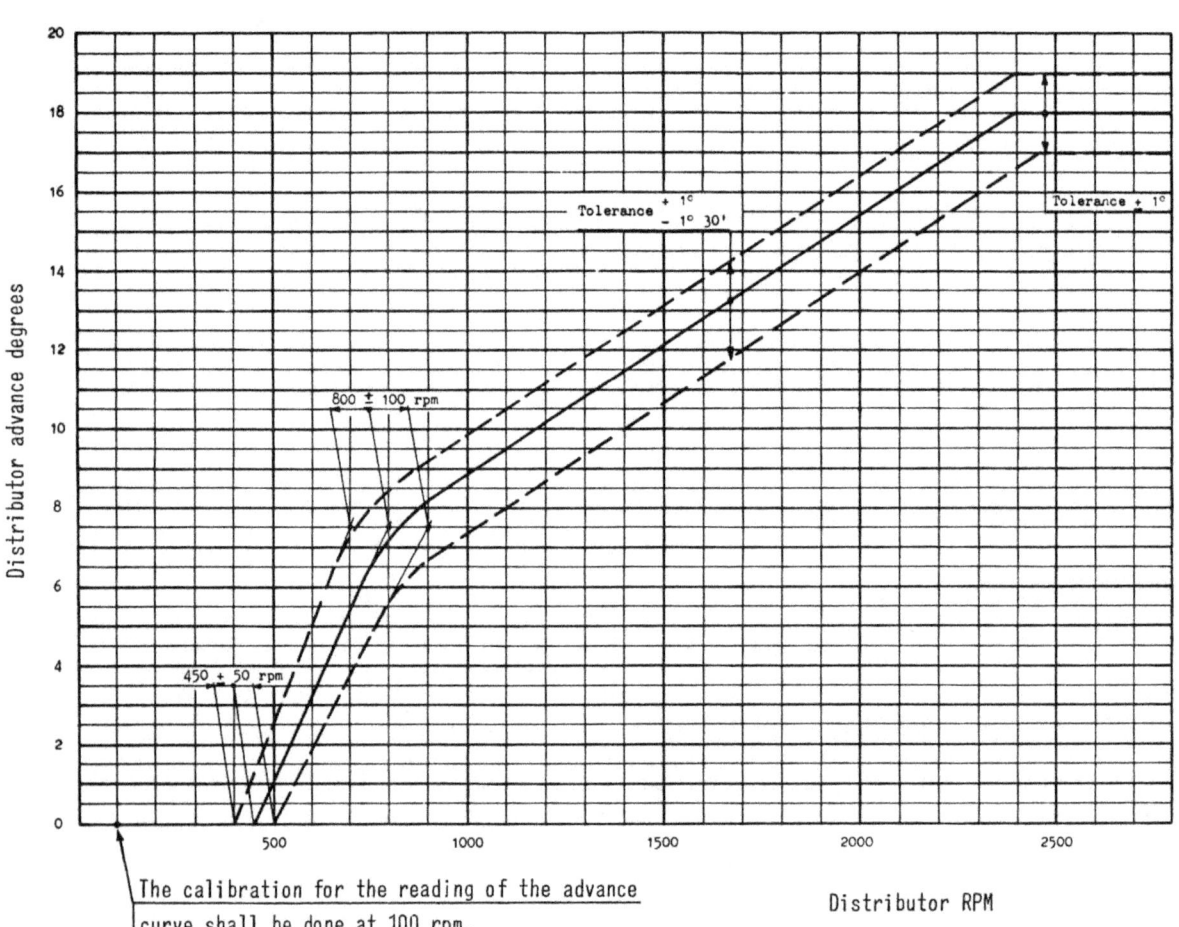

Fig. 7 - DISTRIBUTOR CENTRIFUGAL ADVANCE CURVE

C 8 CHECKING THE VALVE CLEARANCE (see fig. 8)

The V-mounted overhead valves are directly operated by two camshafts acting thru oil bath cups.

When the engine is cold, carefully measure the clearance "G" with a feeler gage. If the clearance is not as specified, remove camshafts and valve cups; measure the thickness "S" of the adjusting pad on each valve stem and replace it with another of proper thickness so that the clearance is the correct one shown in the figure 8.

To facilitate this adjustment the pads are made available in a series of thicknesses ranging from .05 to .014" (1.3 to 3.5 mm) in increments of .001" (.025 mm).

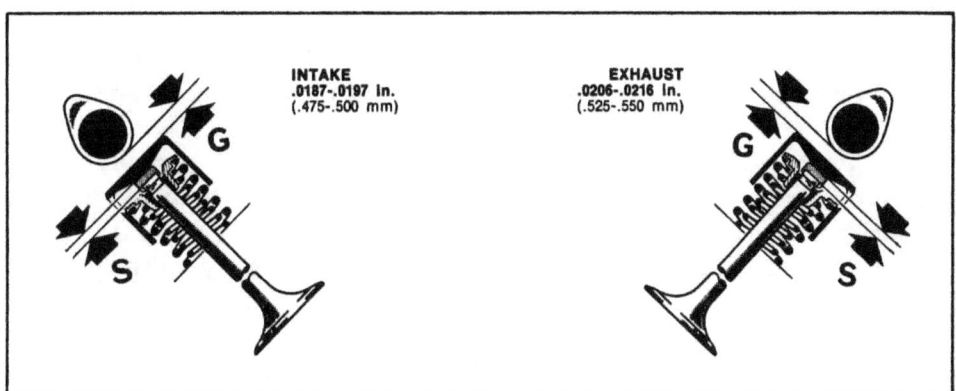

Fig. 8 - VALVE CLEARANCE

C 9 REPLACING THE TANK FUEL FILTER

To replace the tank fuel filter (throw-away type) (see 2, fig. 1), located on the rear underbody of car, proceed as follows:

- slacken the bolt on the clamp securing the filter to the underbody;
- loosen the clamps securing the hoses to the filter inlet and outlet adapters; it is advisable to stop the pipe from fuel tank provisionally.

Remove the filter and replace it with a new one by proceeding in reverse order of removal. Make sure the hoses are properly positioned.

C 10 CLEANING THE THROTTLE VALVE THROATS

Clean the valve throats especially at the areas of contact of throttle valve edges and throat by holding the throttles in full open position and using a brush soaked in gasoline; the cleaning can be completed by rubbing repeatedly the affected areas with a lint-free cloth.

Then, clean in a similar way the throttle valve edges taking care not to strain the spindles.

C 11 REPLACING THE INJECTION PUMP OIL FILTER (see fig. 9)

Clean very carefully the filter housing cover and the surrounding areas to prevent any foreign matter from entering the filter housing.

Remove the cover and withdraw the element; wash thoroughly the filter housing with gasoline, then insert the new element in such a way that the spring faces the cover; renew the cover gasket, if necessary.

To facilitate the air bleed and the quick filling up of filter housing with oil, slightly tighten the two upper cover retaining nuts, crank the engine a few seconds (even by means of the starter) until the oil just oozes out; then lock the nuts fully.

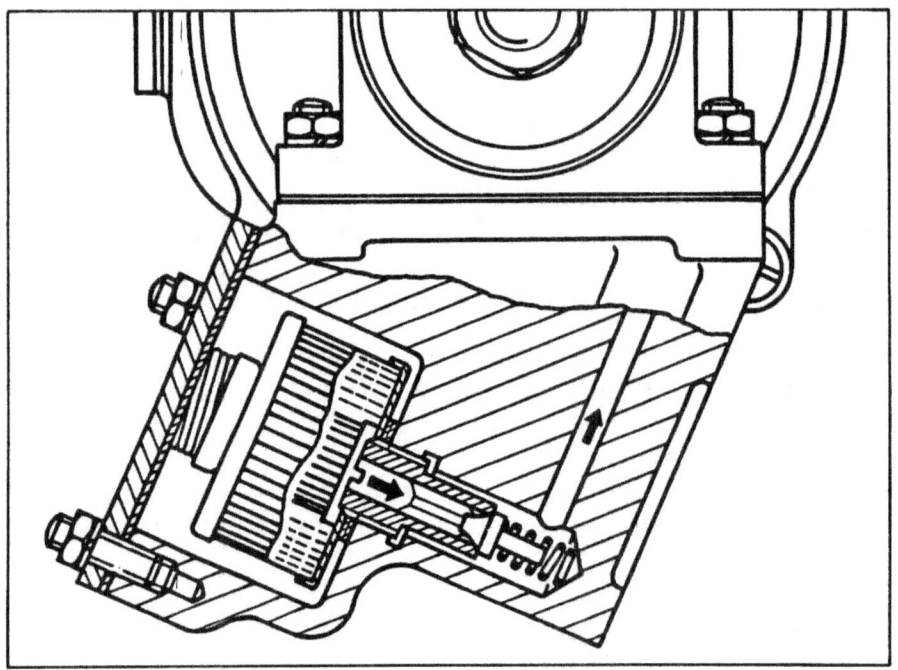

Fig. 9 - INJECTION PUMP OIL FILTER ARRANGEMENT

C 12 CHECKING THE POSITIONING OF THROTTLE-CONTROL UNIT LINKAGE

Proceed as follows:

Disconnect the push-pull rods (5) and (6) (see fig. 10), the cable from the relay crank sheave and the battery negative terminal.

Fit tool A.4.0121 to cable clamp studs (see fig. 11), then adjust idle stop screw until ball joint just touches reference plane of

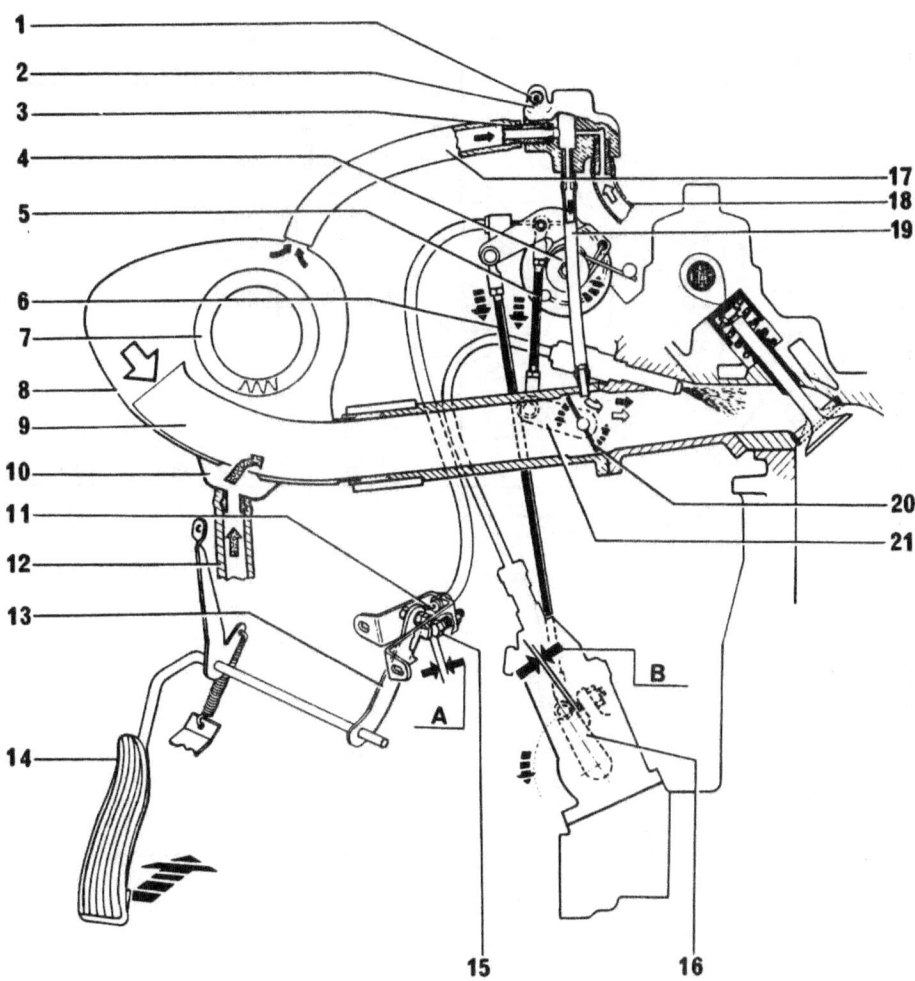

Fig. 10 - THROTTLE-CONTROL UNIT LINKAGE ADJUSTMENT

1 Lockscrew
2 Idle air adjuster and equalizer
3 Adjuster
4 Relay crank
5 Relay crank-to-throttle rod
6 Relay crank-to-control unit rod
7 Filter element
8 Filter housing
9 Intake duct
10 Manifold gallery
11 Throttle cable
12 Main crankcase ventilating system hose
13 Accelerator arm
14 Accelerator pedal
15 Limit screw
16 Control unit lever
17 Idle air supply pipe
18 Secondary crankcase ventilating system hose
19 Idle air hose
20 Throttles
21 Throttle lever

tool and lock in position. Also adjust the full throttle stop screw in the same manner. Now, remove tool and refit throttle cable. Apply grease to cable and pulley.

Check that clearance (see "A" fig. 10) between accelerator arm (13) and limit screw is .040 - .060" as pressure is applied to the pedal while the relay crank is prevented from rotating. Adjust screw if necessary.

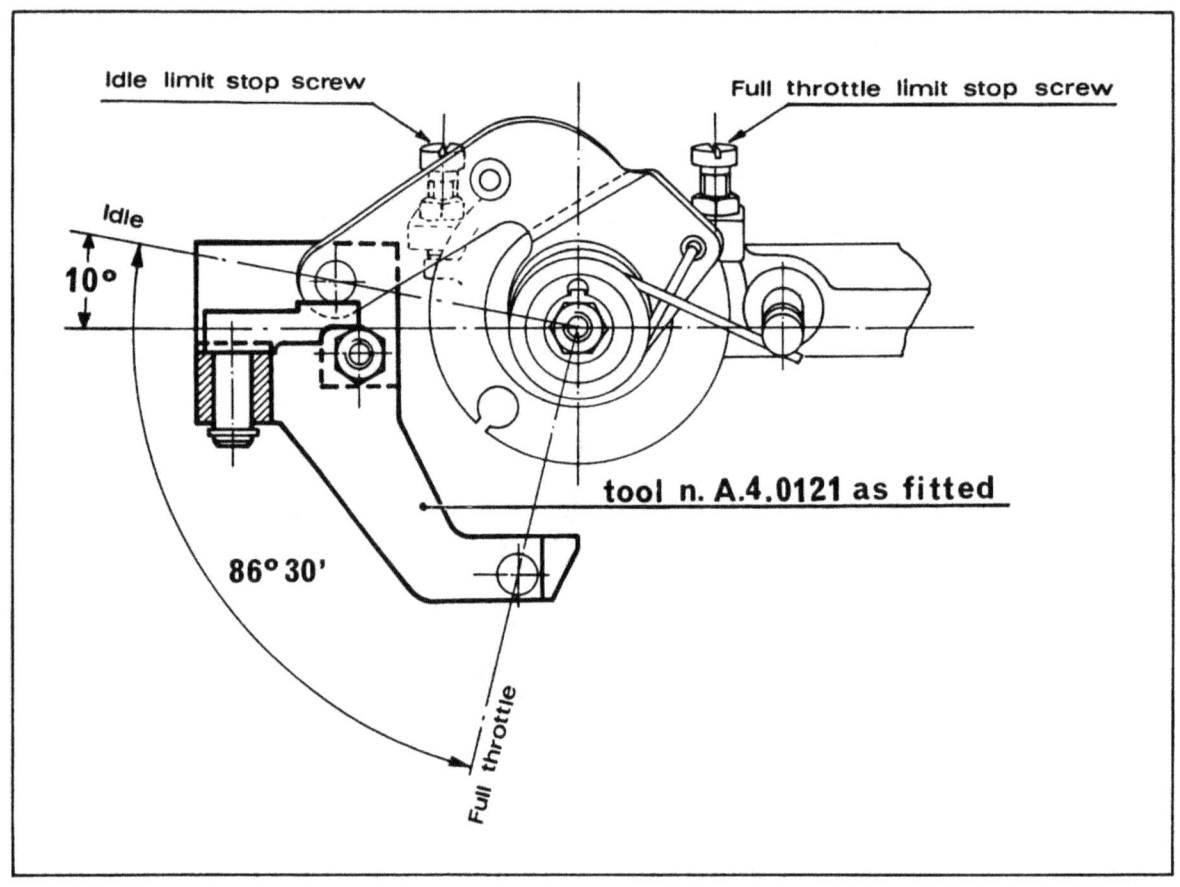

Fig. 11 - POSITIONING OF RELAY CRANK

Depress the accelerator pedal to the floor and check that the clearance between the relay crank lug and full throttle limit stop screw is .080". Adjust the pedal stop screw on floor as required.

Reconnect relay crank-to-throttle rod (5) (see fig. 10) and adjust its length so that throttle are just closed when the relay crank is resting on the idle limit stop screw. "Just closed" can be verified by opening and closing the throttles by hand with the relay crank very slowly. The throttle plates will be felt touching their bores as they close.

When the relay crank is opened slightly and allowed to close under its return spring pressure there will be a click as the crank hits the limit stop screw.

Reconnect the relay crank-to-control unit rod (6), the battery cable start the engine and warm it up to 170°F. (77°C).

Check that clearance (free travel, see "B" fig. 10) between control unit arm and its reference screw is .012 - .024" (0.3 - 0.6 mm) (the closer to .019"/0.5 mm the better).

WARNING: Never tamper with the sealed reference screw on control unit.

Adjust the length of the rod as required. Twisting the rod ends up to 30° off a common plane is permitted to obtain desired clearance.

C 13 CHECKING THE POSITIONING AND ALIGNMENT OF THROTTLES

To perform this check, the air cleaner body and hoses shall be removed from the engine and the four adapters of tool no. C.2.0012 connected to the idle fittings on the throttle valve throats after having removed the four idle pipes from the fittings; the other end of these adapters shall be connected to the four columns of mercury gage (tool no. C.2.0014) (see fig. 12).

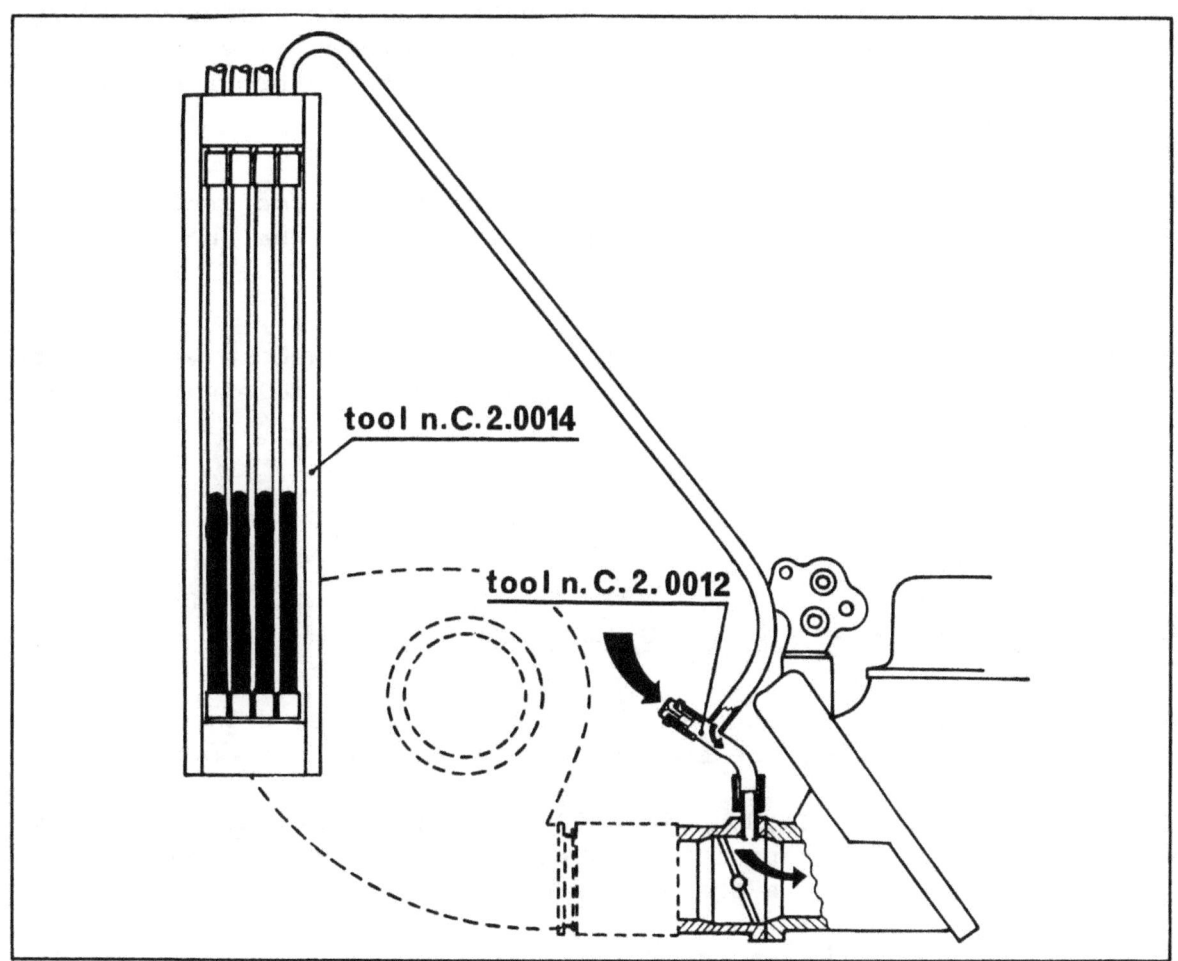

Fig. 12 - THROTTLES ALIGNMENT CHECKING

Start the engine and warm it up until the coolant temperature is at least 158°F (70°C); first check that the clearance between control unit lever and its reference screw is .012 to .024" (the closer to .019" the better) with hot engine and thermostat actuator fitted.

Now, check that readings on mercury gage columns are much the same (maximum difference: .4" - 10 mm); if this is not the case, proceed as follows:

- if readings show that vacuum in front pair of cylinders is higher than in the rear, unscrew the throttle coupling adjusting screw so as to close the rear pair of throttles;

- if vacuum in front pair of cylinders is lower than that in rear pair, disconnect the relay crank-to-throttle rod and set the throttle coupling adjusting screw in such a way as to close the front pair of throttles (screw in the adjusting screw); then, reconnect the relay crank-to-throttle rod and adjust its length so that the throttle valves are in the "just closed" condition as outlined in the paragraph: "Check the positioning of throttle/control unit linkage".

If, before commencing the above adjustments, the engine would run unevenly (lean mixture), make sure the throttle valves are in the "just closed" position; if not the relay crank-to-throttle rod must be shortened.

CAUTION: avoid sudden revving up of the engine or too great a vacuum could take place and the mercury might be sucked out of gage columns.

Disconnect adapters and install air cleaner, crankcase ventilation tube, four idle air tubes, fuel vapor tube and air cleaner-to-equalizer tube.

C 14   IDLE ADJUSTMENT - MIXTURE ADJUSTMENT

To insure control of exhaust emissions and proper driveability it is necessary to adjust the idle and operating mixture correctly.

To obtain proper Carbon Monoxide (CO) percentage at idle the operating mixture must be properly set. Operating mixture can only be set with a road test or on a chassis dyno.

For this reason the steps to follow in adjusting idle and mixture are three.

First   - the idle speed is roughly set.
Second   - the operating mixture is adjusted.
Third   - the idle speed and CO are set accurately.

Note: On cars where it is known that the operating mixture is correct the second step can be eliminated.

FIRST STEP (see fig. 13)

Preliminary idle adjustment

The adjustment procedure is as follows:

warm the engine up to 170°F (77°C). Remove the air cleaner-to-equalizer block hose and loosen adjuster lock screw (1).

Connect accurate electronic tachometer. Act on the adjuster (2) until the engine is idling at as fast a speed as possible, yet with no roughness or hunting (in any case not slower than 600 rpm).

Note: Screw in adjuster to reduce speed; screw out adjuster to increase speed; use tool A.2.0183.

Tighten lock screw (1) and replace hose.

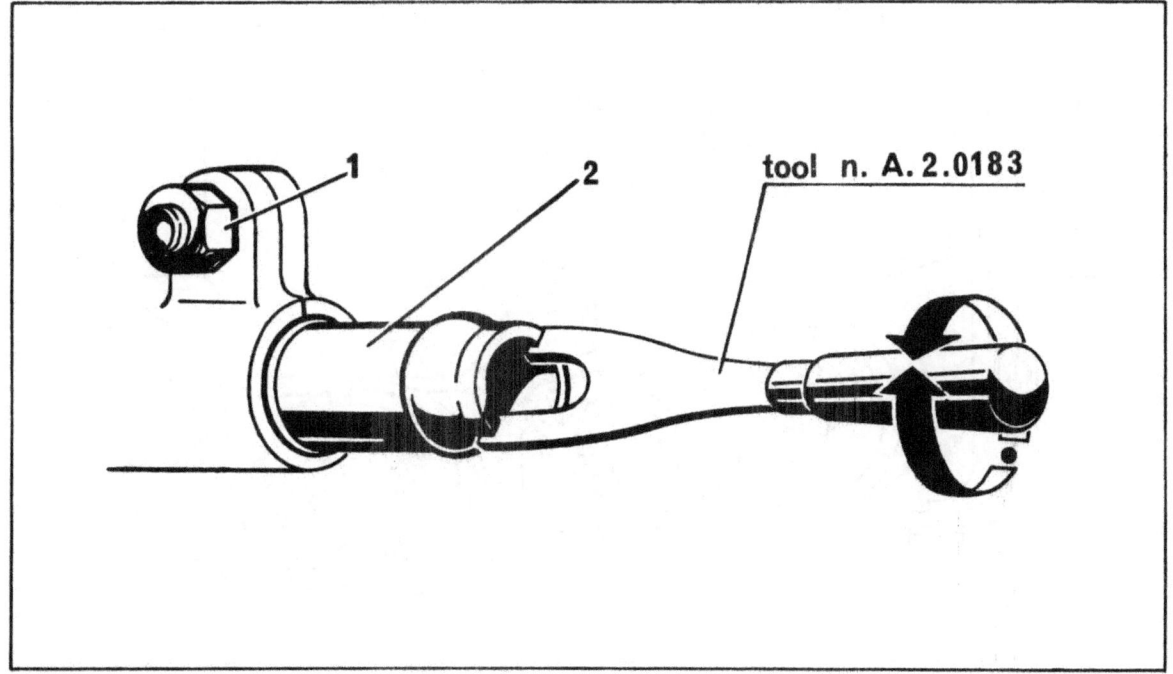

Fig. 13 - IDLE AIR ADJUSTMENT

SECOND STEP

Road test and operating mixture adjustment

With engine at operating temperature drive the car hard for a few miles using high revs and low gears to burn off any deposits from the spark plugs.

Drive the car at a constant speeds of 20-25-30 MPH in third gear and accelerate very slowly to 40-45 MPH. If any hesitation is felt the mixture is too lean and the fuel cut off solenoid must be unscrewed to obtain a richer mixture.

If, instead, during the road test the acceleration is sluggish and the car shows other signs of an over rich mixture such as dirty spark plugs or poor mileage, then the cutoff solenoid must be screwed in until a lean condition is experienced. Then proceed to screw out the solenoid only until the lean hesitation disappears.

Adjusting the fuel mixture (see fig. 14)

Looking down at the top of the fuel cut-off solenoid there are 8 notches around the top edge.

Fig. 14 - MIXTURE ADJUSTMENT

Mark one of the notches with respect to a fixed point on the control unit housing for a reference.

Disconnect the solenoid feed wire.

Loosen the ring nut at bottom of solenoid (tool A.5.0177) taking care not to rotate the solenoid.

Move the solenoid only one notch (1/8 of a turn), in or out, depending on whether mixture is rich or lean.

Retighten ring nut and connect feed wire. Check reference marks to insure that solenoid has been moved one notch.

Install air cleaner, idle air tubes, crankcase breather tubes, air inlet and road test.

THIRD STEP

Speed and CO adjustment

This operation must be done with an accurate electronic tachometer and a CO Meter (Bosch EFAW 173 or equivalent) with engine at normal operating temperature.

Following manufacturer's instructions calibrate and install the CO meter. Attach the tachometer.

Idle speed must not be lower than 600 rpm.

CO percentage must be 0.8 - 2.2% (the closer to 1% the better).

Reading should be taken immediately after the road test.

If adjustment are necessary remove the air cleaner-to-equalizer block hose, loosen the adjuster lock screw (1) (see fig. 13) and adjust the equalizer adjuster accordingly until proper speed and CO are obtained.

Tighten lock screw and replace hose.

N.B.: at idle, HC emissions must not exceed 400 ppm. Should higher levels of HC emissions be experienced after having performed the idle adjustment as above directed, the cause may be found in an improperly operating ignition system component (spark plugs, breaker points, etc.) or in the formation of deposits in the combustion chambers (particularly those fouling the spark plugs).

To burn off such deposits, warm up the engine and drive the car hard for a few miles using high revs and low gears.

D INJECTION PUMP REPAIRS

Only the following repairs are permitted. For any other work the injection pump must be repaired by Alfa Romeo, Inc.

D1 REMOVAL AND REINSTALLATION OF THE INJECTION PUMP

After having removed the air cleaner (see relevant directions) perform the following steps:

- disconnect the negative battery terminal;

- disconnect the lead from cold starting device solenoid and the loose junction on the wire feeding the microswitch of fuel cut-off solenoid;

- remove the two screws on the thermostat actuator mounting flange and the two screws clamping the actuator pipe anchoring grommet (do not remove the thermostat bulb); then withdraw the actuator from the control unit, taking care not to distort excessively the pipe;

- disconnect the fuel hoses from injection pump;

- detach the push-pull rod from the control unit.

Proceed by timing the injection pump with the engine (instant in which fuel injection starts); to do this, bring the no. 1 piston at 70°BTDC of the induction stroke by aligning the mark "I" cut in the crankshaft pulley with the pointer on crankcase front cover (doing so will facilitate the reinstallation on the injection pump to the engine).

Finally, unscrew the three attaching nuts and remove the drive belt cover; then take the drive belt off the injection pump pulley.

Now, perform the removal of the injection pump proper as follows:

- fully slacken the injection pipe nuts on pump outlet fittings (use the wrench tool no. A.5.0164), without removing the pipes;

- unscrew the nuts on the two bolts attaching the pipe cluster plate and the injection pump slanting bracket;

- loosen the two screws attaching the control unit to its bracket at the engine mount;

- unscrew, from the underside of car, the four nuts (use tool A.5. 0167 for the front ones) attaching the injection pump support to the engine front cover.

Withdraw the injection pump and its support as a unit by tilting it suitably.

To reinstall the injection pump, reverse the removal procedure.

In case of injection pump renewal, the new injectors, supplied with the new pump, must be installed on the engine in place of the old ones. The new injectors bring a location number and must be installed accordingly.

Make sure the pump base-to-engine block gasket and O-ring are in place.

CAUTION: Owing to the special construction of the injection pump, the pump plungers must on no account be operated directly with a lever or any other tool.

WARNING: On reinstallation, align the reference marks on the injection pump and the drive pulley (with the engine previously timed for injection in no. 1 cylinder), then fit the drive belt onto the pulley avoiding the use of tools that might damage the belt.

D 2 TIMING THE INJECTION PUMP (see fig. 15)

To check the injection pump timing proceed as follows:

Rotate the crankshaft until the mark "I" is aligned with the pointer on crankcase front cover corresponding to 70° BTDC of the induction stroke: to do this easier, turn the crankshaft over counterclockwise until the no. 1 cylinder intake valve (as seen through the spark plug hole) closes; then, go on in revolving the shaft until the above mentioned mark and pointer line up.

Now, check that the mark on the injection pump pulley is aligned with the reference on the injection pump itself (to gain access to the reference on the injection pump remove the protective cover).

N.B. - The reference marks can be out of alignment within a tolerance of about $\pm$ .2" (5 mm) corresponding to half pitch of pulley splines.

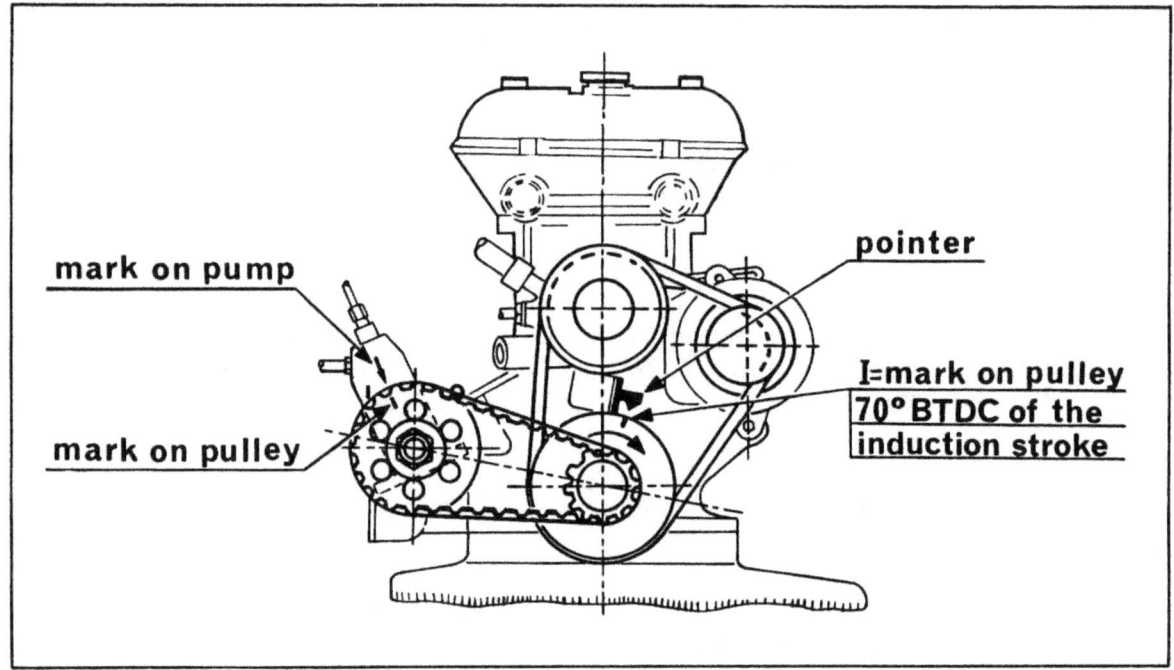

Fig. 15 - INJECTION PUMP TIMING

If the pump is out of timing:

- take the drive belt away from the injection pump pulley;
- line up the reference marks of the injection pump and refit the drive belt by rotating the pulley in either direction to engage the nearest spline.

On completion of the alignment, refit the protective cover.

D 3 REPLACEMENT OF THERMOSTATIC ACTUATOR (see fig. 10)

Remove air filter elements as described in C2.

Drain one gallon of coolant from cooling system and remove thermostatic actuator assembly.

The actuator can be checked by measuring the protrusion of the piston. The measurement is made from the end of the piston to the face of the mounting flange.

With the bulb at a temperature of 20°C, the piston protrusion should be 23 ± 1 mm.

WARNING: Before taking the above measurement, keep the bulb at the specified temperature (20°C) for about five minutes.

Before installing the new actuator, the screw in the control unit upon which the actuator acts should be checked for position.

Disconnect the long rod (6) (see fig.10) from the control unit lever.

Install a 27 mm dummy thermostat (Tool no. A.4.0158).

With the 27 mm dummy in place the clearance "B" between the control unit lever and reference screw should be .5 mm (.020"). Unscrew the screw under the actuator to decrease the clearance or screw it in to increase the clearance.

Install the new thermostatic actuator, connect long rod and refill cooling system.

Start and warm up engine and adjust clearance between control unit arm and reference screw to .012 - .024" (the closer to .019" the better).

Replace air filter elements.

D 4 REPLACING THE FUEL CUT OFF SOLENOID (See fig. 16)

To renew the solenoid, proceed as follows:

Remove the air cleaner.

Disconnect the terminal of solenoid feed wire.

Keep a record of the projection "A" of solenoid body from the ring nut top.

Slacken the ring nut with the special tool no. A.5.0177 taking care not to cock the solenoid.

Unscrew the solenoid by hand and take it away.

Test the solenoid by energizing it with a 12 Volt D.C. supply.

When energized, the solenoid plunger must protrude by .193 - .205" (4.9 ÷ 5.2 mm); when the solenoid is de-energized, the plunger must back up fully with no sluggishness.

Repeat the test several times, each time rotating the plunger to make certain it moves freely in any position.

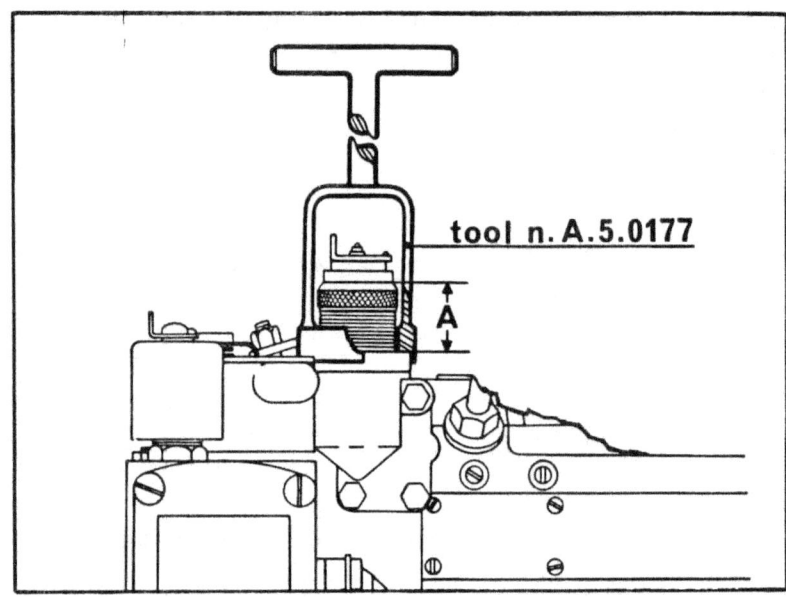

Fig. 16 - FUEL CUT-OFF SOLENOID REMOVAL AND SETTING

1 - If the solenoid is operating properly, screw it in again to the projection previously recorded (tighten the ring nut before checking for correct dimension "A").

2 - If the solenoid is not operating properly, change it with a new one and screw it in until projection "A" (ring nut tightened) is 1 inch (25.4 mm).

- Reconnect the feed wire
- Refit the air cleaner

Road test the car to check that driveability is satisfactory:

1 - If the solenoid has not been renewed and the driveability is not completely satisfactory, this may be due to a slight misalignment of the solenoid on reinstallation; in this case, merely <u>unscrew</u> the solenoid by one eighth of a turn (one reference notch as suitably provided).

2 - If the solenoid has been renewed and the driveability is not satisfactory, <u>unscrew</u> the solenoid by one notch at a time until the appropriate carburation is obtained.

3 - If the solenoid has been renewed and if the driveability is satisfactory, <u>screw in</u> the solenoid by one notch at a time until slight hesitations take place: at this point <u>unscrew</u> the solenoid by one notch so as to put it back into the next former setting giving good driveability.

CAUTION: When tightening or slackening the ring nut, take care not to rotate the solenoid or it will go out of correct setting.

Reset idle speed and CO as described in C 14/3.

D 5 REPLACEMENT OF COLD START SOLENOID AND PLUNGER REMOVAL (see fig. 17)

Removal

Remove the injection pump as described in D1. Remove the side and rear inspection plates from the control unit. Then remove the cotter key (3) and the clevis pin (4) attaching the solenoid to the plunger shaft (5). Measure the distance "H" from bottom of solenoid to control unit.

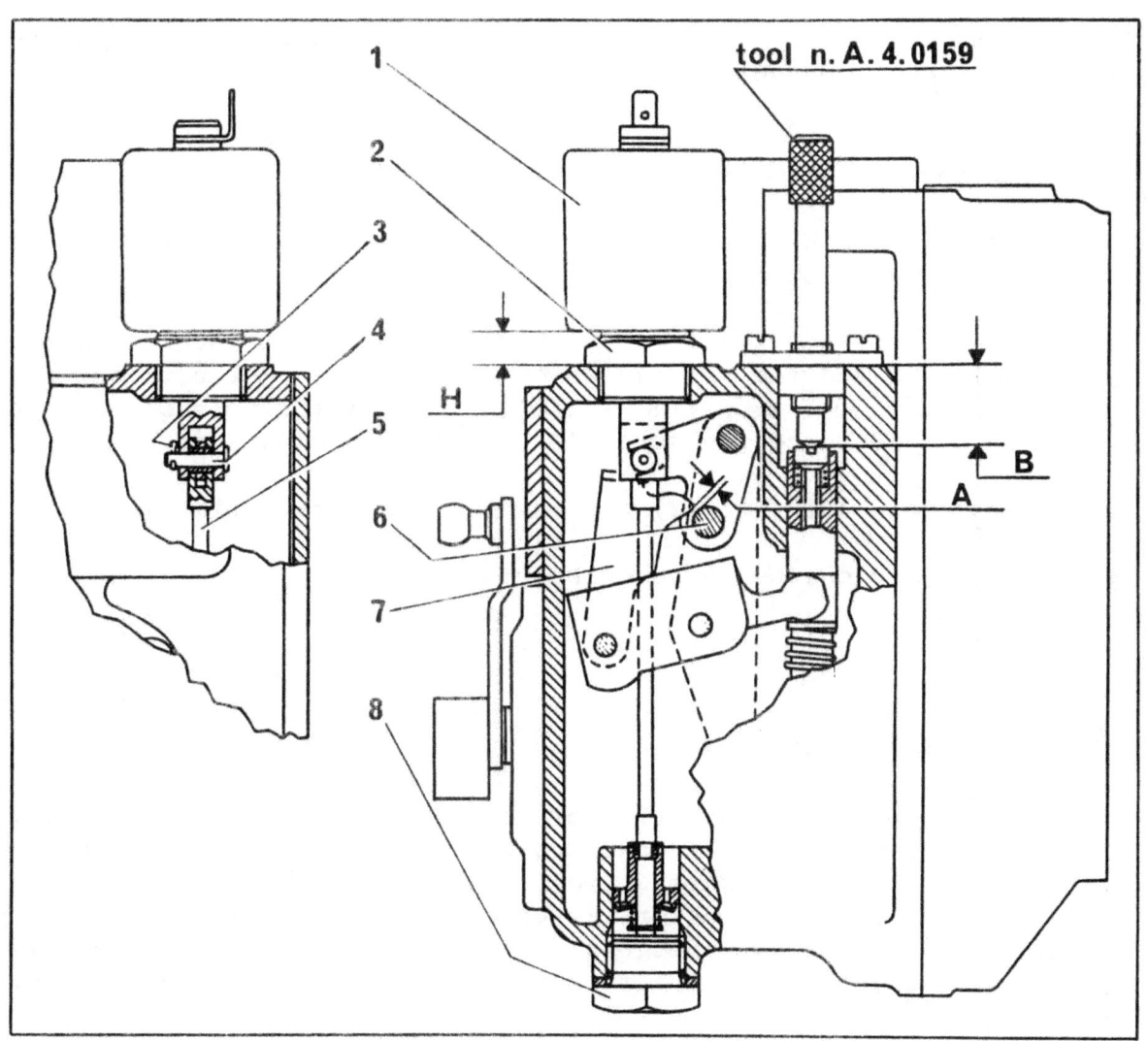

Fig. 17 - COLD START DEVICE AND ITS PLUNGER

Loosen the solenoid lock nut (2) and unscrew the solenoid (1). Then check that the plunger shaft (5) moves up and down freely.

Note: If it is necessary to remove the plunger shaft (5), unscrew the plug (8) from underneath and withdraw the plunger shaft.

Check that the diameter of plastic plunger is .5335" (13,55 mm). Replace the plunger or reduce its diameter if required.

Installation

The height of the cold start solenoid above the control unit housing governs the operation of the cold start device. It is essential that it be carefully adjusted or serious damage may occur to the control unit.

Fit the plunger shaft (5) and the plug (8) in reverse order of removal.

Install the solenoid (1) and lock the nut (2) to same solenoid height "H" as previously measured.

Connect the plunger shaft (5) to the solenoid with the clevis pin (4). Then install the cotter key (3).

To adjust solenoid height "B" a .7490"(19 mm) dummy thermostat (tool no. A.4.0159) has to be installed.

Measure the clearance "A" between the pin (6) on the lever actuated by the solenoid and the arm (7) which it actuates. Refer to the figures. Clearance must be .008" - .012". Screw the solenoid out to decrease the clearance and screw in to increase clearance.

Tighten solenoid lock nut (2) and install inspection plates.

Assemble pump to engine as described in D 1.

D 6 TESTING THE INJECTORS

Since the operating conditions of the injectors are not so heavy (being located in the air intake ports and therefore not subject to the high pressures and temperatures of the combustion chamber) and since the life of the injectors is expected to be the same as that of the car, they should undergo a test only when the cause for malfunctions is unquestionably attributed to the injectors themselves.

To test the injectors use a handpump like that for testing Diesel injectors but supplied with gasoline and provided with a pressure gage whose top dial reading is 700 - 1000 psi (50 ÷ 70 kg/cm^2). Use Bosch EFEFP 345 or equivalent.

The procedure for checking the spray shape, injection pressure and leaks is as follows:

- connect the test pump pipe to the injector inlet fitting which has a 12 x 1.5 mm metric thread;

- pump quickly to prime pump and injector;

- pump slowly until injector nozzle opens; this must take place at 360 - 400 psi (25 ÷ 28 kg/cm^2) for new injectors and at no less than 260 psi (18 kg/cm^2) for used injectors;

- again pumping slowly, bring the pressure to 15-30 psi (1÷2 kg/cm^2) below the rating pressure taken as directed above and make sure that there is no drip from the nozzle within five seconds;

- pump quickly and check that the spray is narrow, deeply plunging and has good vaporization even at minimum delivery. At a distance of 4" (100 mm) from the nozzle orifice the spray cone diameter should be about .8" (20 mm). If the injector does not meet these requirements, replace it with a new one;

- the injectors must be tightened in place with a torque of 20.2 - 23.1 lb-ft (2.8 ÷ 3.2 kgm).

N.B. - To remove the injectors use the wrench tool no. A.5.0165.

D7 REPLACING THE ALTITUDE COMPENSATOR (in-car)

Proper adjustment of the barometric capsule is critical for proper operation of the pump.

In order to make the adjustment you must have an accurate barometer in your shop which has been set to compensate for your elevation above sea level. Your barometer will have directions for doing this and it is essential that they are followed.

Proceed as detailed below after having removed in this sequence:

- The air cleaner;

- The relay crank-control unit rod;

- The rear inspection cover from the control unit;

- The altitude compensator with its mounting flange.

CAUTION: Do not move the control unit input lever (even better tape it in place) nor disturb the inside devices of control unit or serious damage and out-of-adjustment may result.

Measure the dimension "A" (see fig. 18) between the mounting flange face on which the spring rests and the top of bellows: such a dimension should fall between .35 and .41" (9 ÷ 10.5 mm) when the temperature setting lever is in "N" position.

Loosen the locknut and unscrew the capsule taking care not to rotate the setting lever with respect to the mounting flange.

Screw in the new capsule until the dimension previously taken is obtained; then slightly tighten the locknut

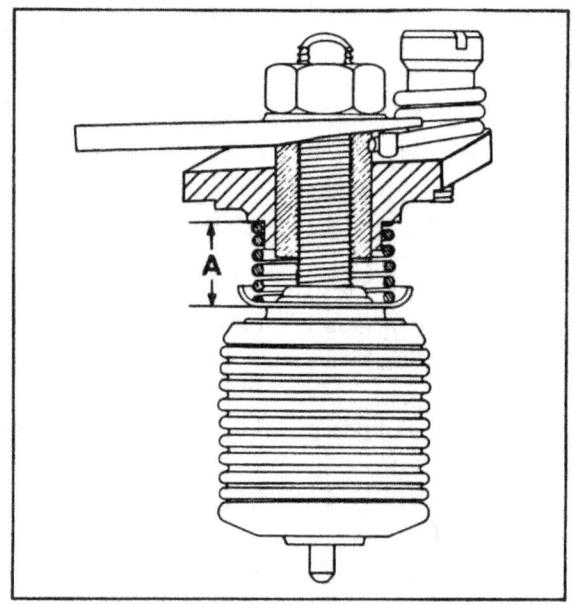

Fig. 18 - ALTITUDE COMPENSATOR

NOTE: If, because of any reason, the dimension "A" does not fall within the specified limits, screw in the new capsule to a dimension of .37" (9.5 mm) irrespective of the dimension previously read.

Install capsule and mounting flange assembly on the control unit making sure the setting lever spring is properly positioned and the setting lever itself is in "N" position.

Refit the rear inspection cover and the rod.

Start the engine and warm it up until the coolant has reached a temperature of no less than 158° F (70° C) then race the engine a few times up to 4,000 rpm and fully release the throttle pedal each time.

Stop the engine, again remove the rear inspection cover and (with the aid of a suitable mirror and a lamp to light the inside of control unit) see whether the wire at the end of link engages the notch corresponding to the actual atmospheric pressure as listed below (notches to be counted starting from the top of the notched lever):

- atmospheric pressure falling between 29.9 - 30.7 in Hg: the wire should engage the 7th notch;

- pressure falling between 29.1 - 29.9 in Hg: the wire should engage the 8th notch;

- pressure between 28.3 - 29.1 in Hg: the wire should engage the 9th notch;

- pressure between 27.6 - 28.3 in Hg: the wire should engage the 10th notch.

Fig. 19 - ENGAGING WIRE AND NOTCHED LEVER

If the above conditions are not fulfilled, adjust the position of the capsule so that, when the engine is started again (before that refit the rear inspection cover on control unit) and the warming up procedure (racing the engine followed by a complete release of accelerator) is repeated, the wire positions itself correctly: screw in the capsule to cause the wire to engage notches of higher numbers and unscrew the capsule to engage notches of lower numbers. Keep in mind that a rotation of about 150 degrees corresponds to one notch.

Tighten securely the locknut on the capsule, place the temperature setting lever in the position corresponding to the ambient conditions and reinstall the air cleaner.

D 8 CHECK THE RELATIONSHIP BETWEEN THROTTLE ANGLES AND CONTROL UNIT LEVER ANGLES

Perform this check when the engine is cold; the air cleaner must then be removed from engine (see under "Replace the air cleaner elements"), the procedure for disconnecting the rods (5) and (6) (see fig. 10) must be repeated as well as the removal of thermostatic actuator (taking care not to distort excessively the small pipe).

At this point check the positioning of linkage at idle and full throttle setting with the special tool no. A.4.0121 and fit the dum my actuator, tool no. A.4.0120. Reconnect the rod and check for a clearance "A" of .012 to .024" (the closer to .019" the better) between the control unit lever and its reference screw (if necessary, adjust the rod length by acting on the threaded clevis).

> **WARNING**
>
> Never tamper with the seal on the reference screw of control unit input lever as this will result in loss of any benefit under warranty.

Fit the fixed protractor tool no. C.6.0140 onto rear end of control unit, using the cover attaching screws, and the pointer tool no. C.6.0141 aligned with the zero on the scale (see fig. 20); to take readings use the suitable built-in light mirror.

Reconnect the rod (5) and check for a proper closure of throttles as directed under "Check the positioning of throttle/control unit linkage".

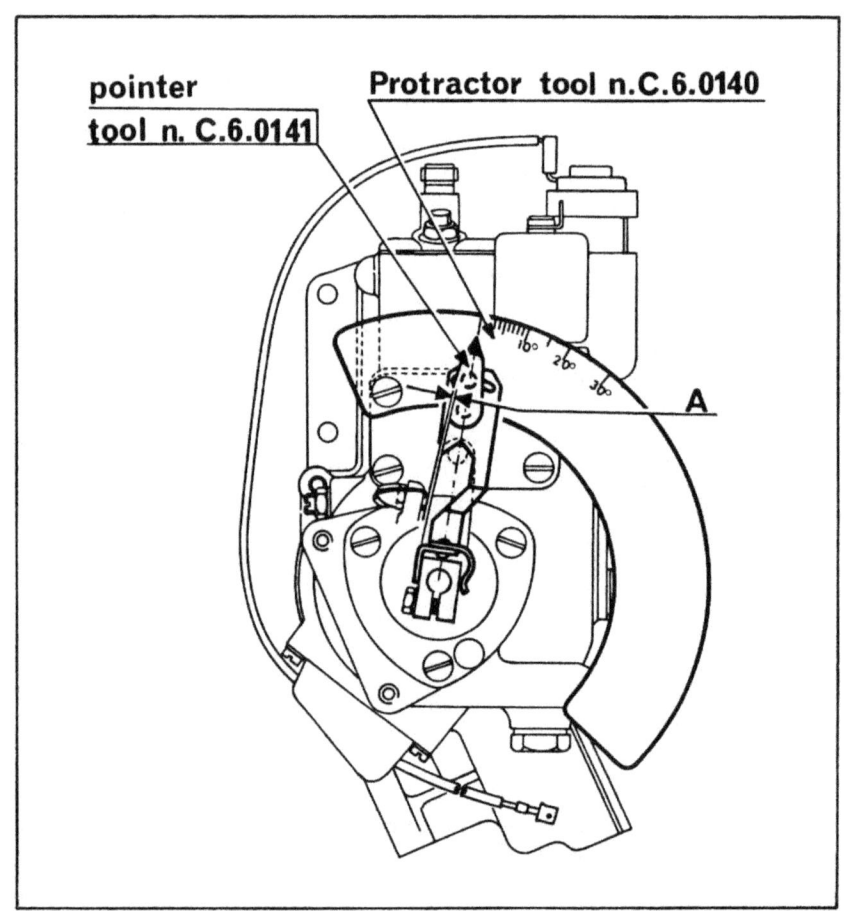

Fig. 20 - CHECKING THE CONTROL UNIT LEVER ANGLE

Place the movable protractor tool no. C.6.0142 on the spindle of rear throttle valve pair and set to zero in correspondence of the pointer tool no. C.6.0143 (see fig. 21).

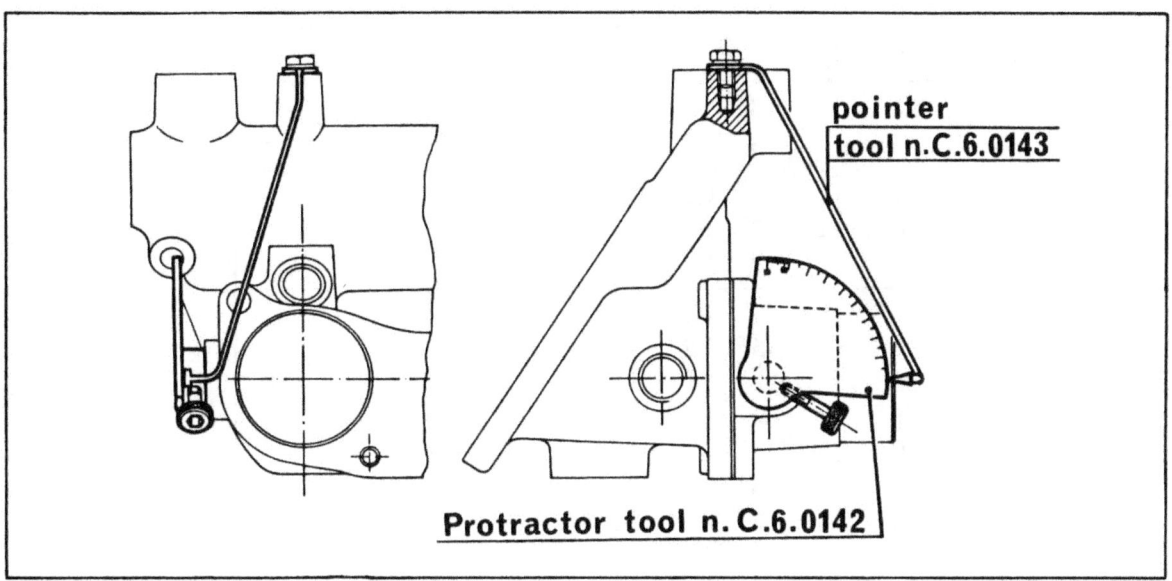

Fig. 21 - CHECKING THE THROTTLE OPENING ANGLES

Install the tool no. A.2.0181 using the cable sheath clips and gradually rotate the relay crank by acting on the adjuster (See fig. 22).

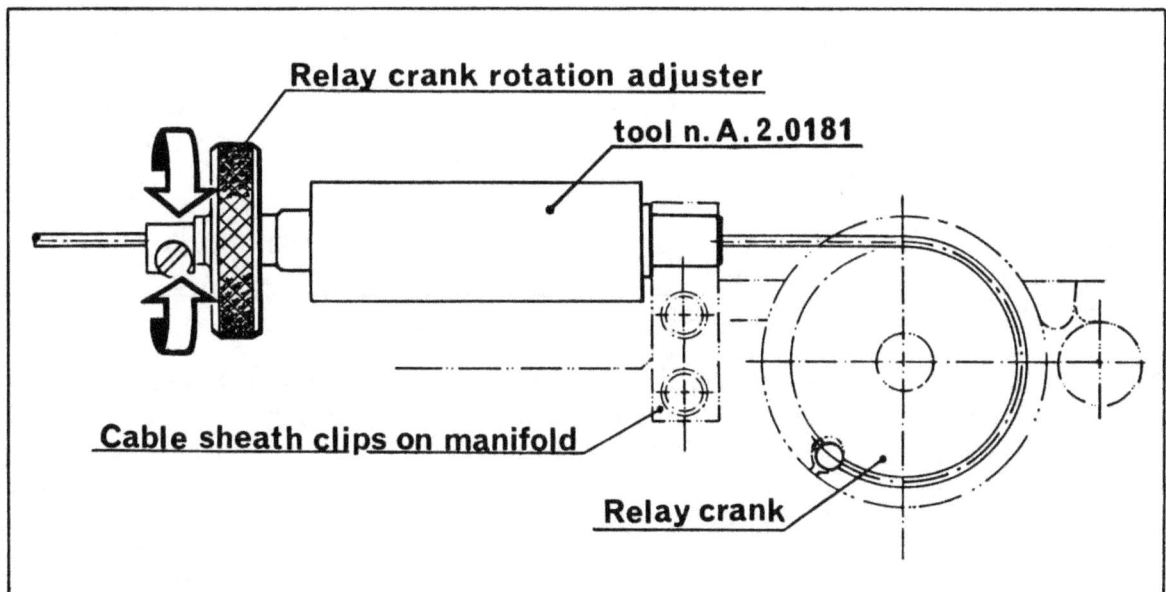

Fig. 22 - ADJUSTING THE RELAY CRANK

Open the throttle valves to predetermined angles (2, 4, 6 degrees - see table) and read the corresponding rotations of control unit lever.

Throttle angles - control unit lever angles relationship table

α	β	Tolerance on β
0°	0°	
2°	8° 13'	± 20'
4°	14° 40'	
6°	20° 09'	
10°	29° 30'	± 1°
15°	39° 20'	
20°	47° 54'	
25°	55° 33'	
30°	62° 30'	
35°	68° 51'	
40°	74° 41'	± 2°
50°	84° 55'	
60°	93° 25'	
70°	100° 12'	
82°	106° 08'	

α = throttle rotation angle
β = control unit lever rotation angle

In the event the throttle angles and control unit lever angles are out of the specified relation, it is likely that checking procedure has not been perfectly accomplished; therefore, try once more; if again it will not satisfy, inspect carefully any component of control linkage, or parts directly affecting it, replace any defective part and repeat the procedure.

When the above checks are over, lengthen the rod (6) until there is a clearance of .035 to .051" (0.9 ÷ 1.3 mm) or 1° to 1° 30' between the control unit lever and the reference screw.

On completion of adjustment, reinstall the standard thermostatic actuator and check for a clearance of .012 to .024" (.3 to .6 mm) with a hot engine (coolant temperature above 158° F - 70°C) between the control unit lever and its reference screw; if necessary, adjust the length of rod (6) by acting on the clevis thread.

D 9 REPLACING THE ROTATING SEAL AND THE MOTOR OF THE ELECTRIC PUMP
(See fig. 23)

Remove the electric pump unit from the car. Loosen the screws (1) securing the motor to the pump assembly and remove the motor. Take

the seal (3) out of pump body. Lubricate the seal housing and install
a new seal (3) with the aid of the suitable tool (no. A.3.0476); to
do this, position a thin strip of foil (no more than 0.05 mm thick
and about 5 mm wide) over the drain hole so as to prevent damaging
the outer edge of the seal being installed; after the seal has been
fitted, the foil strip can be slipped off. Also replace the mating
face (7) and the "O" ring (6) on motor shaft with new ones.

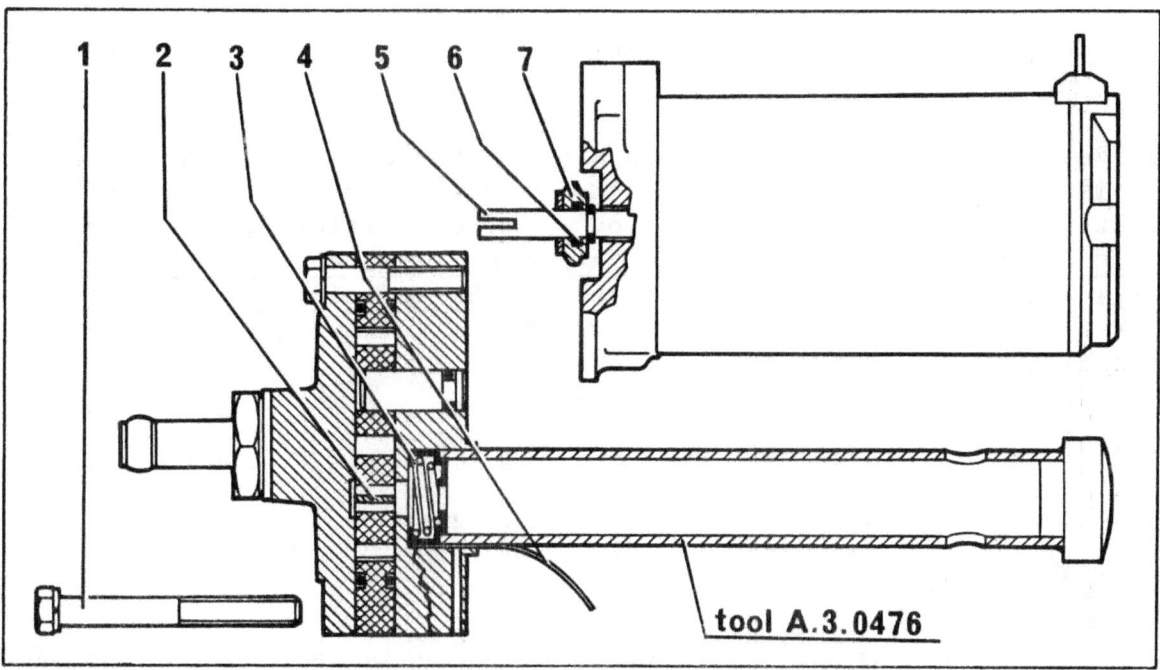

Fig. 23 - REPLACING THE ROTATING SEAL OF THE ELECTRIC PUMP

Re-assemble the motor to the pump body taking care that the coupling
at the shaft end properly engages the key in the gear.

WARNING - The rotating seal must be renewed whenever the pump is
overhauled and/or the pump motor is replaced with a new
one.

Re-install the pump and check whether the seal settled properly
within 20 minutes of pump operation; fuel ceasing to drip from the
drain hole indicates that the seal has settled down.

Should the fuel dripping fail to stop within the above mentioned
lapse of time, the seal must again be inspected.

E TROUBLE SHOOTING

The following chart lists several malfunctions, possible cause for each of them and remedies.

If deficiencies or malfunctions are experienced in the fuel system, it is absolutely essential to make sure they are not caused nor affected by the incorrect operation of the ignition system: <u>in fact it is impossible to distinguish "a priori" whether a failure of fuel or ignition system is the cause for the deficiencies</u>; therefore, first inspect the ignition system for the following and remedy, if necessary

- spark plugs for proper operation and type;

- contact-breaker points conditions and gap;

- ignition coil for continuity or leakage;

- ignition distributor for correct timing using a timing light; adjust timing or replace the ignition distributor, if necessary.

Should any of the troubles listed be experienced, it is recommended to clean thoroughly the affected areas of both engine and engine compartment with a suitable solvent; this to the purpose of <u>preventing any foreign matter from entering, on removal or reinstallation</u>, the mechanical components and specifically the fuel feed circuit.

Soon after cleaning, inspect the mechanical units for loose attaching or joining parts, the pipes for loose fittings and the brackets for sound conditions.

E 1 ALFA ROMEO SPICA PUMP POLICY

Injection pumps are not to be opened for any reason. An exchange pump service is available for complete pump units. Pumps that have been tampered with will forfeit any core valve.

Always before removing a pump consult your Alfa Romeo representative or zone office

E 2 TROUBLE CHART

TROUBLE	POSSIBLE CAUSE	REMEDY
Low fuel pressure warning light does not flash on when ignition key is turned	Fuse no. 6 blown Warning light bulb burnt out Pressure switch faulty (jammed open)	Replace fuse Replace bulb Check switch and replace, if necessary
Low fuel pressure warning light stays on (fuel pump operates properly)	Pressure switch faulty (jammed closed) Low fuel pump outlet pressure due to: - tank to pump lines clogged or air seeping thru them - tank fuel filter clogged - main fuel filter clogged - main filter pressure relief valve defective or stuck open Fuel pump delivery too low	Replace switch - Inspect fuel lines - Replace filter (See C3) - Clean filter and replace element (see C2) - Check relief valve and replace, if necessary Have fuel pump checked or replaced (See D9)
Low fuel pressure warning light stays on (fuel pump fails to operate)	Fuse blown (in the additional fuse box) Electric wires to pump disconnected Fuel pump faulty	Replace fuse Check and reconnect Have the pump checked or replaced (see D9)
Engine will not start from cold	Solenoid-actuated cold start device fails to operate	- check electric connections - have the device checked or replaced
Smoky exhaust after starting	Cold start solenoid plunger stuck	Have the plunger checked (see D 5)

TROUBLE	POSSIBLE CAUSE	REMEDY
Engine misfires; rough idle	One injector defective	Trace the cylinder by grounding each spark plug and replace the injector, if necessary
	Injection pipe fittings leaking	Tighten fittings
	Injection pipes cracked	Check and replace, if necessary
Idle too slow but even Idle CO too high (engine runs smoothly)	Too rich a mixture	Adjust idle as directed in C 14
Idle too slow and rough (engine runs unevenly)	One of the hoses connecting idle equalizer to throttle throats is obstructed (by buckling) cracked or disconnected from a fitting	Reconnect or replace the hose, if necessary and adjust idle as directed in C 14
Idle too fast and rough (engine runs unevenly; hunting also takes place)	Too lean a mixture due to air leaking through one of the hoses connecting idle equalizer to throttle throats or even to an idle equalizer improperly adjusted	Check the hoses for sound conditions and leaks and adjust idle as directed in C 14
Idle HC too high	Too rich or too lean a mixture Ignition system not in perfect working order. Heavy deposits in combustion chambers and spark plug fouling due to particular driving conditions such as short rides preventing proper warming up.	Adjust idle as directed in C 14. Check ignition system. With a hot engine, drive the car hard for a few miles using high revolutions and low gears to burn off any deposit

TROUBLE	POSSIBLE CAUSE	REMEDY
Too fast an idle and smoky exhaust	Faulty thermostatic actuator	Replace thermostatic actuator (see D 3)
Engine keeps running at idle but stops on accelerating	Altitude compensator faulty	Replace altitude compensator (see D 7)
Idle too fast	Accelerator linkage fails to return fully	Check: - flexible cable - linkage joints and pivot pins for free movement - pedal return spring for sound conditions - pedal and linkage limit stop for proper adjustment Clean linkage joints and pack with grease
Unsatisfactory drive ability; hesitations	Control linkage out of adjustment	Check throttle/control unit linkage (see C 12)
	Fuel pump outlet pressure too low (warning light comes on while running at high speed)	Check and replace, if necessary, tank fuel filter and/or main filter element
	Injector defective	Refer to remedies as under "Engine misfires; rough idle"
	Injection pump or control unit defective	Have them checked and replaced, if necessary, by an authorized workshop
	Temperature setting lever improperly positioned	Position the lever correctly

TROUBLE	POSSIBLE CAUSE	REMEDY
Unsatisfactory road performance	Temperature setting lever improperly positioned	Position the lever correctly
	Control linkage out of adjustment	Check throttle/control unit linkage (see C 12)
	Fuel pump outlet pressure too low (warning light comes on while running at high speed)	Check and replace, if necessary, tank fuel filter and/or main filter element
	Air induction clogged	Check and replace air cleaner elements, if necessary
	Injector defective	Refer to remedies as under "Engine misfires; rough idle"
	Injection pump or control unit/defective (defective carburation)	Have them checked and replaced, if necessary, by an authorized workshop
Excessive fuel consumption	Fuel feed circuit leaks	Check pipes, fittings, seals and replace defective parts
	Thermostatic actuator defective; also refer to causes as under "Too fast an idle"	Have the thermostatic actuator checked and replaced, if necessary, by an authorized workshop (see D 3)
	Defective carburation	Have the injection pump adjusted by an authorized workshop
Engine stalls in positions other than idle	Defective altitude compensator or excessive vibrations of injection pump and control unit	Have the altitude compensator checked (see D 7); also check injection pump and control unit brackets for sound conditions and firm attachment
Engine stalls flat	Injection pump driving belt broken	Replace belt (check for proper injection pump timing) (See D 2)

TROUBLE	POSSIBLE CAUSE	REMEDY
Engine does not slow down to idle on deceleration (fast idle)	Both throttles and control unit lever fail to return fully on deceleration	Check: - flexible cable - linkage joints and pivot pins for free movement - pedal and linkage return springs for sound conditions - pedal and linkage limit stops for proper adjustment - clean linkage joints and pack them with grease suitable for low temperatures
Detonations in the exhaust pipe on deceleration	Fuse no. 8 blown	Replace fuse
	Feed wire disconnected at fuel cut off solenoid	Re-connect wire
	Loose junction of fuel cut off device feed wire disconnected	Re-connect junction
	Defective fuel cut off solenoid	Have the fuel cut off solenoid checked and replaced, if necessary
	Defective fuel cut off device microswitch	Have the fuel cut off device checked by an authorized workshop
Engine stops: - wholly or occasionally on deceleration in neutral - occasionally or wholly when re-accelerating after a deceleration Engine fires again suddenly and with delay when reaccelerating after a deceleration	Fuel cut off solenoid stuck in cut off position or sluggish in backing up	Have the fuel cut off solenoid checked and replaced, if necessary

TROUBLE	POSSIBLE CAUSE	REMEDY
Noisy electric fuel pump	Line between pump and main filter distorted or forced in the rubber mounting or against the recovery pipe	Reset the line making certain it is centered in the rubber mountings without forcing against the recovery pipe
	Tank filter and hoses improperly fitted	Check that the filter is properly fitted and that hoses have a correct run

2000 Berlina
2000 GT Veloce
2000 Spider Veloce

FUEL INJECTION MODELS

U.S.A. VERSION

technical characteristics
and
principal inspection specifications

CONTENTS

TECHNICAL CHARACTERISTICS

Principal characteristic data	Page	1
Performance	"	2
Oil	"	2
Oil pressure	"	3
Fuel, coolant and tires pressures	"	3
Valve timing	"	4
Ignition	"	5
Spark plugs	"	5
Cooling system	"	6
Electrical equipment	"	9
Bulb's wattage	"	9
Tightening torque specifications	"	12

MAJOR INSPECTION SPECIFICATIONS

Camshafts	"	16
Valves and valve guides	"	16
Valve seats	"	17
Valve cups	"	18
Valve springs	"	18
Connecting rods	"	19
Piston pins	"	19
Piston and piston rings	"	20
Cylinder sleeves	"	21
Crankshaft	"	22
Clutch	"	23
Gearbox	"	24
Rear axle and suspension	"	25
Front suspension	"	27
Brake system	"	29
Wheel alignment	"	32

TECHNICAL CHARACTERISTICS

Principal characteristic data

Number of cylinders	4
Bore	84 mm
Stroke	3.48" (88.5 mm)
Total displacement	1962 cm^3
B.H.P. at 5,800 rpm	SAE 129 NET
Front track	52.1" (1324 mm)
Rear track	50.1" (1274 mm)
Wheelbase — Berlina	101.1" (2570 mm)
Wheelbase — GT Veloce	92.5" (2350 mm)
Wheelbase — Spider Veloce	88.6" (2250 mm)
Min. turning circle — Berlina	36.5 ft (5500 mm)
Min. turning circle — GT Veloce	34.8 ft (5300 mm)
Min. turning circle — Spider Veloce	34.5 ft (5250 mm)
Overall length — Berlina	172.7" (4390 mm)
Overall length — GT Veloce	161.6" (4100 mm)
Overall length — Spider Veloce	165.4" (4202 mm)
Overall width — Berlina	61.6" (1565 mm)
Overall width — GT Veloce	62.2" (1580 mm)
Overall width — Spider Veloce	64.1" (1630 mm)
Overall height (unladen) — Berlina	56.3" (1430 mm)
Overall height (unladen) — GT Veloce	51.8" (1315 mm)
Overall height (unladen) — Spider Veloce	50.8" (1290 mm)
Curb weight (full tank) — Berlina	2,442 lbs (1110 kg)
Curb weight (full tank) — GT Veloce – Spider Veloce	2,292 lbs (1040 Kg)
Number of seats — Berlina	4
Number of seats — GT Veloce	2
Number of seats — Spider Veloce	2
Tires 165 HR 14"	CEAT D2
	MICHELIN XAS
	PIRELLI Cinturato HR
	KLEBER COLOMBES V 10 GT
	FIRESTONE Cavallino Sport 200
	CONTINENTAL Conti TT 714

PERFORMANCE
(with 41 : 9 final drive)

DURING BREAKING IN	
Mileage	Max engine speed
Up to 600	3500 RPM
From 601 to 1900	4500 RPM

After breaking-in Max speed (mph)		
Gear	BERLINA	SPIDER GT VELOCE
1st	26	27
2nd	44	45
3rd	64	66
4th	86	88
5th	112	118
Rev.	28	29

OIL

Engine (pan and filter) { when full* .... abt. 7.1 qts
                          danger level .... abt. 4.75 qts
Transmission .... abt. 3.8 pts
Differential .... abt. 3.0 pts
Steering box .... abt. .8 pt

* This quantity is that needed for regular changing. The total amount of oil in the circuit (pan, filter and passages) is .... 7.8 qts

It is recommended to top up with the same type of oil as that in the engine.

LUBRICANTS

PART	Classification	Commercial equivalents		
		AGIP	ESSO	Shell
Engine	SAE 20 W/50 API MS	AGIP F.1 Woom SAE 20 W/50	UNIFLO Motor Oil 10 W - 20 W - 40	Super Shell Motor Oil 10 W/40
Transmission Steering box and differential	SAE 90 EP	AGIP F.1 Rotra MP 90	ESSO Gear Oil GX 90	SHELL Spirax HD 90
Drive shaft slip yoke	SAE NLGI 1	AGIP F.1 Grease 15	ESSO Multipurpose Grease « H »	SHELL Retinax G
Front wheel bearings (see maintenance schedule)	SAE NLGI 2/3	AGIP F.1 Grease 33 FD	ESSO Norva 275	SHELL Retinax AX

API - American Petroleum Institute
NLGI - National Lubricating Grease Institute
SAE - Society of Automotive Engineers

OIL PRESSURE

Oil pressures with hot engine - psi
- Engine running fast — minimum 50, maximum 65-70
- Engine idling — minimum 7

F U E L

Tank capacity . . . . abt. 14.3 gals
Reserve . . . . abt. 1.6-1.8 gals
Lead content (maximum) . . . . abt. 2.4 g/gals

IMPORTANT

Use of the correct fuel cannot be overemphasized. Recent changes in "Octane Ratings" can cause confusion. Below are the octane numbers required for your engine:

- Research method (RON) . . . . 91 minimum
- F.T.C. method * . . . . 87 minimum

* This rating number is required by the Federal Trade Commission to be posted on gasoline pumps in filling stations after March 15, 1972. While it is not an actual measure of an engine's requirement, its purpose is to approximate the actual octane requirement on the road.

C O O L A N T

ALFA ROMEO coolant mixture . . . . abt. 2.5 gals

T I R E S
Inflation pressure (cold) under all conditions

		BERLINA			GT VELOCE-SPIDER VELOCE			
		FRONT		REAR		FRONT		REAR	
		PSI	Kg/cm^2	PSI	Kg/cm^2	PSI	Kg/cm^2	PSI	Kg/cm^2
165 HR 14"	CEAT D2	24	1.7	26	1.8	24	1.7	26	1.8
	CONTINENTAL Conti TT 714	24	1.7	26	1.8	24	1.7	26	1.8
	FIRESTONE Cavallino Sport 200	24	1.7	26	1.8	24	1.7	26	1.8
	KLEBER COLOMBES V 10 GT	24	1.7	29	2	24	1.7	29	2
	MICHELIN XAS	24	1.7	26	1.8	21	1.5	26	1.8
	PIRELLI Cinturato HR . .	24	1.7	26	1.8	24	1.7	26	1.8

4

VALVE TIMING

Checking of valve opening and closing angles

Clearance (with cold engine) between the unlobed { intake .... .0187-.0197" (0.475/0.500 mm)
profile of cams and the valve cup ceiling   { exhaust .... .0206-.0216" (0.525/0.550 mm)

To facilitate this adjustment the pads are made available in a series of thicknesses ranging from .051" to .138" (1.3 to 3.5 mm) in increments of .001" (0.025 mm).

Opening of intake valve { lift of cup .... .008" (0.20 mm)
                        { corresponding to an angle (before TDC) .... 4° 16' ± 1° 30'

Closing of intake valve { lift of cup .... .008" (0.20 mm)
                        { corresponding to an angle (after BDC) .... 52° 16' ± 1° 30'

Opening of exhaust valve { lift of cup .... .006" (0.15 mm)
                         { corresponding to an angle (before BDC) .... 40° 16' ± 1° 30'

Closing of exhaust valve { lift of cup .... .006" (0.15 mm)
                         { corresponding to an angle (after TDC) .... 16° 16' ± 1° 30'

ANGLE VALUES OF THE ACTUAL DIAGRAM OF VALVE TIMING SYSTEM WITH COLD ENGINE

(clockwise rotation direction of the crankshaft as seen from the front side)

Opening of intake valve (before TDC) .... 21° 54'
Closing of intake valve (after BDC) .... 69° 54'

Opening of exhaust valve (before BDC) .... 51° 14'
Closing of exhaust valve (after TDC) .... 27° 14'

Induction stroke .... 271° 48'
Exhaust stroke .... 258° 28'

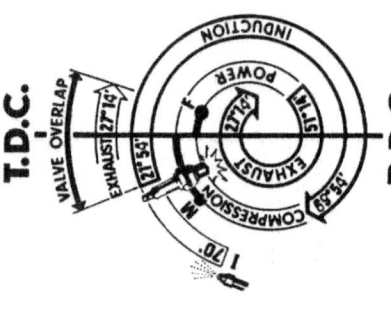

M IGNITION TIMING AT 5000 RPM
F IGNITION TIMING AT IDLE
I TIMING OF INJECTION START

IGNITION

Firing order: 1 - 3 - 4 - 2 (no. 1 cylinder is that at the fan side).

VALUES OF ADVANCE OF IGNITION DISTRIBUTOR

Opening of contact points of ignition distributor   S = .017-.019" (0.43-0.48 mm)

Dwell angle . . . . 57°/63°

Idle ignition	Maximum advance M Before T D C
5°/7° A T D C	27°/33° at 5000 rpm

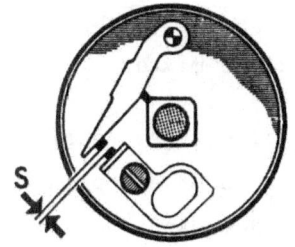

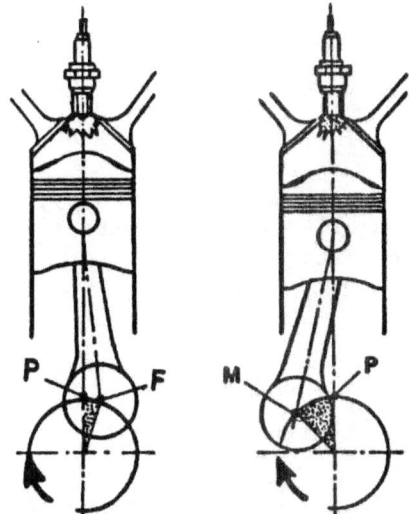

P = T.D.C.

F = Idle ignition

M = Maximum advance

Spark plugs

The standard plugs fitted to the engine are LODGE HL. A decal, giving the specifications for these plugs, is attached under the hood; here below, the text of the decal is repeated.

In order to comply with the Federal rule regarding the control of air pollution the engine is fitted with LODGE-HL spark plugs.

These plugs are completely adequate when the automobile is driven at speeds not exceeding the limits specified by speed regulations. If the automobile is driven at sustained speeds higher than the said speed limits, LODGE-2HL spark plugs must be used.

COOLING SYSTEM

The cooling circuit is provided with a compensating reservoir containing a special ALFA ROMEO Coolant Mixture which gives full protection against freezing down to - 22°F.

TO ENSURE THE EFFICIENT OPERATION OF THE COOLING SYSTEM THE FOLLOWING PROCEDURE SHOULD BE OBSERVED

Occasionally, check level of coolant in the reservoir: this should be done exclusively with a cold engine as with a hot engine the level may increase remarkably, even after stopping the engine.

The level of mixture in the reservoir should never fall below the "MIN" or exceed the "MAX".

To top up, use the specified Coolant Mixture to be added to the reservoir only.

If too frequent a topping up is required, check the cooling system for damage.

Should sudden and excessive leaks be experienced from the system, the use of fresh water is provisionally allowed. To replenish the circuit follow the directions given on next page.

W A R N I N G

Never remove radiator cap unless absolutely necessary; in any case, to avoid severe injuries, wait that the liquid is cooled down to outside temperature.

Changing the coolant mixture

Every 24,000 mi (or every two years whichever comes first) flush the circuit and renew the coolant mixture. (See next page).

W A R N I N G

In places where the temperature falls below - 22°F the antifreeze mixture can be strengthened by varying its concentration.

To this end, a certain amount of mixture should be drained off the circuit and replaced by the same quantity of "ALFA ROMEO Antifreeze" drawn from suitable containers.

The quantities of antifreeze to be added to radiator and reservoir depending on the lowest anticipated temperature are the following.

Temperature	Amount of ALFA ROMEO coolant Mixture to be replaced with an equal quantity of "ALFA ROMEO Antifreeze"		
°F	Radiator	Reservoir	Total
-24	400 cc	100 cc	500 cc
-33	800 cc	200 cc	1,000 cc
-38	1,200 cc	300 cc	1,500 cc

Draining and replenishing the system

Proceed as follows:

Draining

- Remove radiator filler cap "3".
- Unscrew the drain plug "7" and the bleed screw "1" on manifold.
- Turn on the heater valve "11".
- Turn on the drain plug "10" on crankcase; let liquid drain off and empty the reservoir "5" by detaching pipe "6". Then refit the drain plug "7", reconnect pipe "6" to reservoir and retighten drain plug "10".

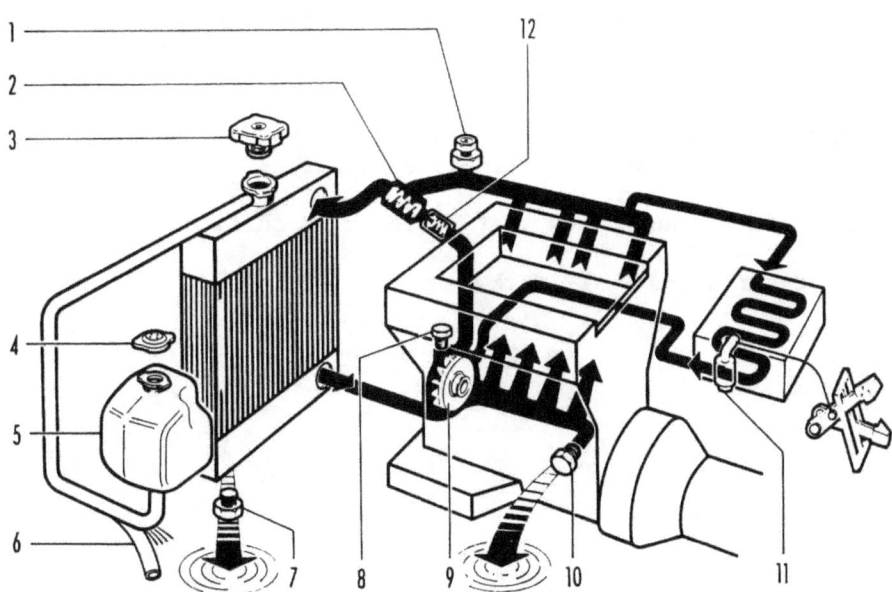

1. Air bleed screw on manifold
2. Thermostat
3. Radiator filler cap
4. Reservoir filler cap
5. Reservoir
6. Supply line from reservoir to radiator
7. Radiator drain plug
8. Air bleed screw on pump
9. Coolant pump
10. Drain plug on crankcase
11. Heater valve
12. By-pass control valve

Replenishing

- Remove radiator cap and reservoir filler cap and turn on the heater valve.
- Open the bleed screw "1" on manifold and "8" on pump.
- Pour coolant mixture through radiator filler port until coolant escapes from bleed screw "8"; then screw in the latter. Go on in adding mixture until it appears at the bleed screw "1" on manifold.
- With the bleed screw on manifold opened and no cap on filler port of radiator, start the engine and keep it running for a few seconds in order to bleed air completely.
- Close the bleed screw on manifold.
- Add mixture to radiator filler port until full.
- Add mixture also to reservoir until "MAX" level is reached.
- Refit reservoir and radiator caps.

Checking cooling system for proper operation after topping up

After the system has been fully replenished or even topped up owing to drainings for mixture change or for repair, it is advisable to check the system for proper operation as follows:

a) with the circuit closed and the heater valve opened, run the engine until the coolant mixture has reached a temperature of about 176-185°F (80-85°C) and keep on idling the engine; in this condition the thermostat opens thus allowing possible air bubbles trapped in the circuit to pass in the radiator and then in the reservoir.

b) let the engine cool down to room temperature in order to allow the mixture in the reservoir to compensate for the air bled off as said above.

c) remove the filler cap and check that radiator is full.

d) fill the reservoir up to "MAX" mark.

N.B. - If, when opening the filler cap as in c) above, the radiator is not full, repeat the procedure, keeping the engine running for a longer time at operating temperature (thermostat opened) to bleed all the air from the circuit.

Should the trouble persist, air instead of coolant from reservoir is likely to enter the circuit through some leaking component (radiator filler cap included) in this case, inspect the circuit accordingly, then again repeat the checking procedure.

ELECTRICAL EQUIPMENT

Voltage . . . . 12 V

Battery . . . . 60 Ah

Alternator { Bosch K1 14V 45 V 22
            { Motorola S.E.V. Marchal A.14.45/55.712 70 702

Regulator { Bosch AD 1 14 V
          { Motorola S.E.V. Marchal 14 V

Starter motor: Bosch EF (R) 12 V 0,7 PS

Coil: Marelli BZR 2000 D

Distributor { BERLINA: Marelli S.103 B
            { GT VELOCE - SPIDER VELOCE: Marelli S.103 B

Windshield wiper, two-speed for Berlina: W S 4927 AR 5 A (0)

Windshield wiper, two-speed for GT Veloce: W S 4928 AR 2 A (0)

Windshield wiper, two-speed for Spider Veloce: W S 4912 AR 2 A (1)

Bulb's wattage

2000 Berlina

Engine compartment light	5 W
Front direction indicators-emergency flashers and parking lights .	5/21 W
Headlamp Hi/Low	Sealed beam
Headlamp Hi	Sealed beam
Side marker lights	3 W
Instrument lights	3 W
Fuel reserve warning light	1,2 W
Direction indicators warning light	1,2 W
Warning light for fluid level, service brake pressure and parking brake	1,2 W
Blower warning light (two brightness levels)	1,2 W
Low fuel pressure warning light	1,2 W
Alternator warning light	1,2 W
Parking light warning	1,2 W
High beam warning light	1,2 W
Hand throttle warning light	1,2 W
Low oil pressure warning light	1,2 W
FASTEN SEAT BELTS light	1,2 W
Glove compartment light	5 W

10

Heater control panel light	1,2 W
HAZARD light	1,2 W
Emergency flashers pushbutton warning light	1,2 W
Heated rear window pushbutton warning light	1,2 W
DEF light	1,2 W
WIPE light	1,2 W
Courtesy light	5 W
Trunk light	5 W
Rear direction indicators and emergency flashers	21 W
Rear parking and stop lights	5/21 W
Back-up lights	21 W
License plate lights	5 W

2000 GT Veloce

Engine compartment light	5 W
Front direction indicators-emergency flasher and parking lights	5/21 W
Headlamp Hi/Low	Sealed beam
Fog lamp	Sealed beam
Side marker lights	3 W
Instrument lights	3 W
Fuel reserve warning light	3 W
Hand throttle warning light	3 W
Direction indicators warning light	3 W
Alternator warning light	3 W
Low fuel pressure warning light	3 W
Blower warning light (two brightness levels)	3 W
High beam warning light	3 W
Warning light for fluid level, service brake pressure and parking brake	3 W
Low oil pressure warning light	3 W
Parking light warning	3 W
Glove compartment light	5 W
FASTEN SEAT BELTS light	1,2 W
Heater control panel light	1,2 W
Emergency flashers pushbutton warning light	1,2 W
HAZARD light	1,2 W
Heated rear window pushbutton warning light	1,2 W
DEF light	1,2 W
WIPE light	1,2 W

Courtesy light	5 W
Trunk light	5 W
Rear direction indicators and emergency flashers	21 W
Rear parking and stop lights	5/21 W
Back-up lights	21 W
License plate lights	5 W

2000 Spider Veloce

Engine compartment light	5 W
Front direction indicators-emergency flasher and parking lights . .	5/21 W
Headlamp Hi/Low	Sealed beam
Side marker lights	3 W
Glove compartment light	5 W
Low oil pressure warning light	1,2 W
High beam warning light	1,2 W
Low fuel pressure warning light	1,2 W
Parking light warning	1,2 W
Instrument lights	3 W
Fuel reserve warning light	3 W
Blower warning light (two brightness levels)	3 W
Alternator warning light	3 W
Direction indicators warning light	1,2 W
Warning light for fluid level, service brake pressure and parking brake	1,2 W
Hand throttle warning light	1,2 W
FASTEN SEAT BELTS light	1,2 W
HAZARD light	1,2 W
Emergency flasher pushbutton warning light	1,2 W
Heater control panel light	1,2 W
DEF light	1,2 W
WIPE light	1,2 W
Ash tray light	5 W
Courtesy light	5 W
Trunk light	5 W
Rear direction indicators and emergency flashers	21 W
Parking and stop lights	5/21 W
Back-up lights	21 W
License plate lights	5 W

TIGHTENING TORQUE SPECIFICATIONS

ENGINE - GEARBOX UNIT

		lb-ft	Kgm	Manner of tightening
Cylinder head nuts *	Inspection — when cold	57.1/58.5	7.9/8.1	Slacken, in proper sequence, the nuts by one and one half turn and torque with lube between washer and nut.
	Inspection — when hot	60.7/61.4	8.4/8.5	Warm up the engine and when hot retighten without unscrewing.
	After repairing — when cold	57.1/58.5	7.9/8.1	Retighten with lube
	After repairing — when hot	60.7/61.4	8.4/8.5	Warm up the engine by actually driving the car and when hot retighten without unscrewing.
	when cold	57.1/58.5	7.9/8.1	After tested the car, slacken, when cold and in proper sequence, the nuts by one and one half turn and torque with lube between washer and nut.
Spark plugs		18.1/25.3	2.5/3.5	With graphite grease, when cold
Nuts of the camshaft caps		14.5/16.2	2 / 2.25	in oil
Bolts of the connecting rod caps		36.2/38.3	5/5.3	" "
Nuts of main bearing caps		34.0/36.1	4.7/5	" "
Palnuts of main bearing caps		7.9/9.4	1.1/1.3	" "
Bolts securing flywheel to crankshaft		81.1/83.1	11.2/11.5	" "
Injectors		20.2/23.1	2.8/3.2	dry

* **WARNING:** In case of any repair work involving the removal of cylinder head, the gasket must be renewed at all times.

	lb-ft	Kgm	Manner of tightening
Pulley on crankshaft	138/144	19/20	in oil
Oil drain plug on pan	50.6/57.8	7/8	dry
Thermostat on manifold	25.3/28.9	3.5/4	"
Screws securing clutch to engine	14.75/18.23	2.040/2.520	"
Nut of alternator pulley	25.3/26	3.5/3.6	"
Nut of clutch shaft	68.7/75.9	9.5 / 10.5	"
Nut of gearbox main shaft yoke	68.7/75.9	9.5 / 10.5	"
Nut of gearbox layshaft	68.7/75.9	9.5 / 10.5	"
Nuts and bolts of gearbox half-casings	12.3/13.7	1.7/1.9	"
Gearbox filler & drain plugs	34.3/37.9	4.75/5.25	"
Bolts joining output shaft yoke to prop shaft yoke	39.8/41.2	5.5/5.7	"
Nut of gear lever swivel to bracket	23.5/26.4	3.25/3.65	"
Nuts of pedal housing to brake booster	8.7 / 10.8	1.2/1.5	"
Nut securing flange to prop shaft front section	72.3/101.2	10/14	"
Bolts joining drive shaft sections	27.5/28.9	3.8/4	"
REAR FRAME			
Screws securing ring gear to differential case	43.4/47.7	6/6.6	"
Ringnut securing yoke on final drive pinion shaft	57.9/101.2	8 / 14	"
Nuts securing caliper bracket to bearing housing	34.7/39.7	4.8/5.5	"
Bolts securing trailing arms to body	58.6/72.3	8.1 / 10	"
Bolts securing trailing arms to rear axle tubes	79.6/98.7	11 / 13.65	"
Screws securing T-arm to body	31.8/39.4	4.4 / 5.45	"
Nut securing T-arm to differential carrier	73.7/91.1	10.2/12.6	"
Nut securing stabilizer rod to rear axle	23.9/25.3	3.3/3.5	"

	lb/ft	Kgm	Manner of tightening
Screw securing rear brake caliper to support	39.8/47.0	5.5/6.5	dry
Nuts securing wheels	43.4/57.8	6/8	"
Bolts joining differential yoke to drive shaft yoke	27.5/28.9	3.8/4	"
Bolts for rebound strap butt joints	3.6	0.5	"
Nuts securing rear axle tubes to differential carrier . . .	17.3	2.4	"
Nuts securing shock absorbers to body	17.3/21.3	2.4/2.95	"
Differential filler and drain plugs	10.9/13.0	1.5/1.8	"
FRONT FRAME			
Nut securing steering wheel to column	36.2/39.7	5/5.5	"
Screws securing Burman steering box cover	16.6/18.0	2.3/2.5	"
Bolts securing steering box to body	37/39.4	5.12/5.45	"
Bolts securing crank bracket & steering lock to body . . .	31.8/39.4	4.4/5.45	"
Nuts of steering linkage ball joints	34.7/39.7	4.8/5.5	"
Nut securing steering arm to box	90.4/101.2	12.5/14	"
Screws securing upper wishbone front arm to body	15.9/19.8	2.2/2.75	"
Nut securing upper wishbone front arm to rear arm	27.5/33.9	3.8/4.7	"
Nut securing upper wishbone rear arm to body	79.6/98.7	11/13.65	"
Bolts securing lower wishbone shaft to cross-member . . . . (to tighten these nuts use tool A.5.0161 and torque to 5.2/5.5 Kgm)	40.5/42.6	5.6/5.9	"
Nuts securing steering arm to steering knuckle	28.9/32.5	4/4.5	"
Nut securing upper wishbone rear arm to steering knuckle .	54.2/61.4	7.5/8.5	"
Nut securing lower ball joint to wishbone	59.3/66.5	8.2/9.2	"

	lb-ft	Kgm	Manner of tightening
Nut securing lower ball joint to steering knuckle	54.2/61.4	7.5/8.5	dry
Nuts securing caliper support to steering knuckle	54.2/61.4	7.5/8.5	"
Nuts securing splash shields to steering knuckle	5.8/7.2	0.8/1	"
Nuts securing wheels and brake discs	43.4/57.8	6/8	"
Bolt securing steering column to bracket	11.7/13.8	1.62/1.91	"
Nut securing shock absorber to lower arms	54.2/61.4	7.5/8.5	"
Bleed screw	1.45/2.53	0.2/0.35	"
Caliper joining bolt	21/24.5	2.9/3.4	"
Inlet fitting to caliper { with gasket	5.8/7.9	0.8/1.1	"
without gasket	7.2/10.8	1/1.5	

A T E B R A K E S

MAJOR INSPECTION SPECIFICATIONS
All dimensions, unless otherwise stated, are in millimeters

Camshafts

Diameter of journals .... A =	26.959/26.980
Diameter of journal bearings .... B =	27.000/27.033
Clearance between journals and bearings ...... B-A =	0.020/0.074
End play of camshaft in thrust bearing .... C =	0.065/0.182

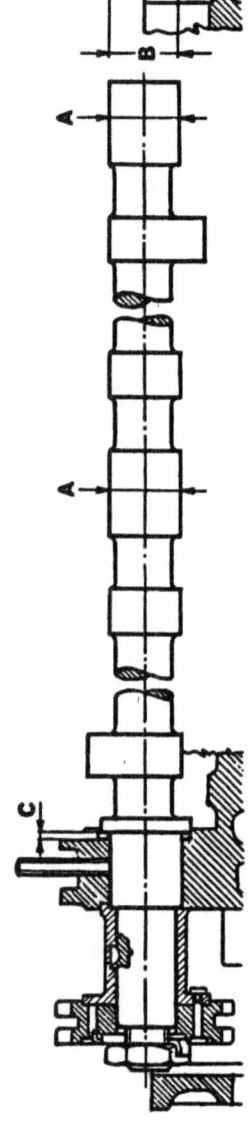

Valves and valve guides

	Intake		Exhaust (sodium cooled)	
	LIVIA H	ATE	ATE	LIVIA C
Diameter of valve poppet ..... O	44.000/44.150	44.000/44.150	40.000/40.150	40.000/40.150
Diameter of valve stem ...... M	8.972/8.987	8.972/8.987	8.935/8.960	8.935/8.960
Total length L	104.96	104.96	104.71/104.96	104.53 / 105

N.B. - ATE - LIVIA valves are alternative supply.

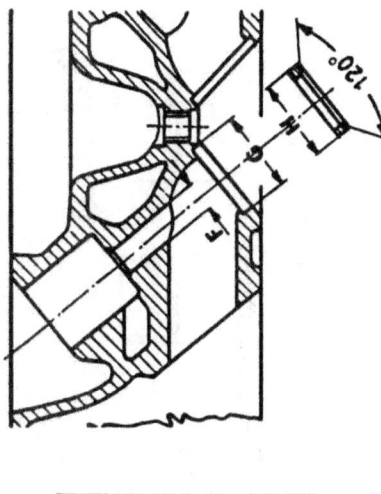

Valve guide	Outside diameter with guide removed .... E =	14.033/14.044
	Inside diameter with guide assembled in cylinder head .... D =	9.000/9.015

Protrusion of intake valve guides from their recesses in cylinder head ...	13.300/13.500
Protrusion of exhaust valve guides from their recesses in cylinder head ..	16.300/16.500
Clearance between guide assembled in cylinder head and valve stem intake	0.013/0.043
exhaust	0.040/0.080
Height of cylinder head when new	111.913/112.000
Minimum grinding limit of cylinder head	111.500
Tolerance on flatness of head surface (block side)	0.05

Valve seats

Diameter of valve guide seat in cylinder head .... F = 13.990/14.018
Interference between seat and valve guide 0.054/0.015

		Intake	Exhaust
Outside diameter of the valve seat insert .... H =	standard	45.065/45.100	41.065/41.100
	oversized	45.365/45.400	41.365/41.400
Diameter of recesses in the cylinder head for valve seat insert .. G =	standard	45.000/45.025	41.000/41.025
	oversized	45.300/45.325	41.300/41.325

Interference between valve seat insert and recesses in cylinder head ... 0.040/0.100

Valve cups

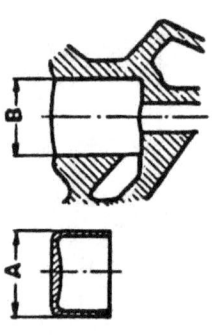

Diameter of cup A = standard 34.973/34.989
                    oversized 35.173/35.189

Diameter of cup seat in cylinder head B = standard 35.000/35.025
                                          oversized 35.200/35.225

Clearance between seat and cup 0.011/0.052

Valve springs

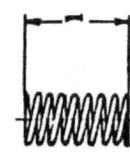 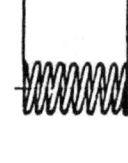

 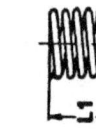

	Length		Test load
	Free	Under test load	
Inner spring .... l =	47	l1 = 26	Kg. 22.24/23.16
Outer spring .... L =	49.6	L1 = 27	Kg. 38.7/40.3

Connecting rods

Length between ₵ of big end and ₵ of small end of connecting rod . . . . D		156.950/157.050
Inside diameter of the big end of connecting rod . . . . . . E		53.695/53.708
Inside diameter of bushing in the small end of rod C		22.005/22.015
Thickness of connecting rod bearings F *	A - Red	1.831/1.837
	B - Blue	1.837/1.843
Radial clearance between crankpins and bearing for big end of connecting rod	A - Red	0.023/0.058
	B - Blue	0.021/0.056
Maximum out of parallelism between ₵ of big end hole and ₵ of small end hole		0.078
Offset of big end & rod ₵ with respect to small end ₵ . . . . M		1.5
Tolerance in weight between con. rod assemblies of the same engine		2 gr

* Note: Markings A or B and the relevant colour are on bearing edge.

Piston pins

O.D. of pin I	Black color	21.994/21.997
	White color	21.997/22.000
Clearance between piston pin and small end hole	Black color	0.008/0.021
	White color	0.005/0.018

Piston pin hole

	Black mark	White mark
BORGO piston . . . . H	22.000/22.0025	22.0025/22.005

End play of the connecting rods on the crankpins . . . . . . G   0.2/0.3

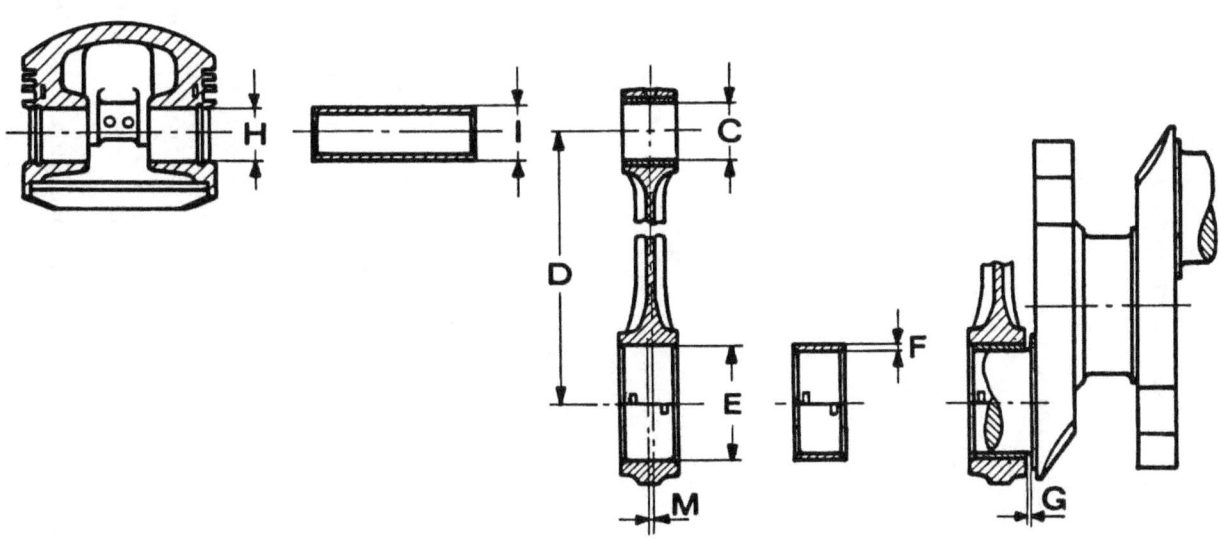

Pistons and piston rings

Diameter of pistons to be measured at right angle to the hole for piston pin and at a distance of L = 17 mm from the lower border of skirt.

	Class A (Blue)	Class B (Pink)	Class C (Green)
BORGO piston diameter	83.935/83.945	83.945/83.955	83.955/83.965

N.B. — On reassembly, make sure the arrow marked on piston is pointing toward the rotation direction of crankshaft (i.e. toward exhaust side).

Height of grooves for piston rings
- chromium-plated compression ring . . . . M = 1.525/1.545
- oil scraper ring . . . . N = 1.775/1.795
- oil control ring . . . . P = 4.515/4.535

Thickness of rings
- chromium-plated compression ring . . . . R = 1.478/1.490
- oil scraper ring . . . . S = 1.728/1.740
- oil control ring . . . . T = 4.478/4.490

End play of rings in grooves
- chromium-plated compression ring 0.035/0.067
- oil scraper ring 0.035/0.067
- oil control ring 0.025/0.057

Gap of compression ring and oil scraper ring (to be inspected in ring gauge or in cylinder sleeves) . . U = 0.30/0.45

Gap of oil control ring (to be inspected in ring gauge or in cylinder sleeves) . . . . V = 0.25/0.40

Tolerance in weight between piston assemblies of the same engine . . . . 2 gr

Cylinder sleeves

For cylinder classification purpose, use the minimum diameter recorded.

	Blue - A	Pink - B	Green - C
Cylinder sleeve diameter	83.985/83.994	83.995/84.004	84.005/84.014

Clearance between cylinder sleeve and piston 0.040/0.059

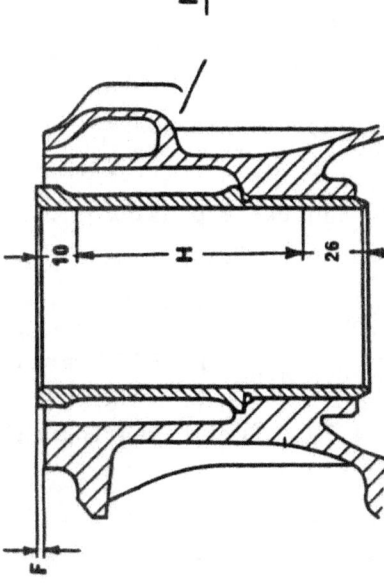

H = Area of measurement

Protrusion of sleeves from cylinder block* .... F = 0.01/0.06

Surface roughness .... R = 0.5/1 μ

Elongation and taper of sleeves 0.01

*Note: To check the protrusion of cylinder sleeves use tool C.6.0148 as directed in Tool Bulletin no. 144.

CRANKSHAFT

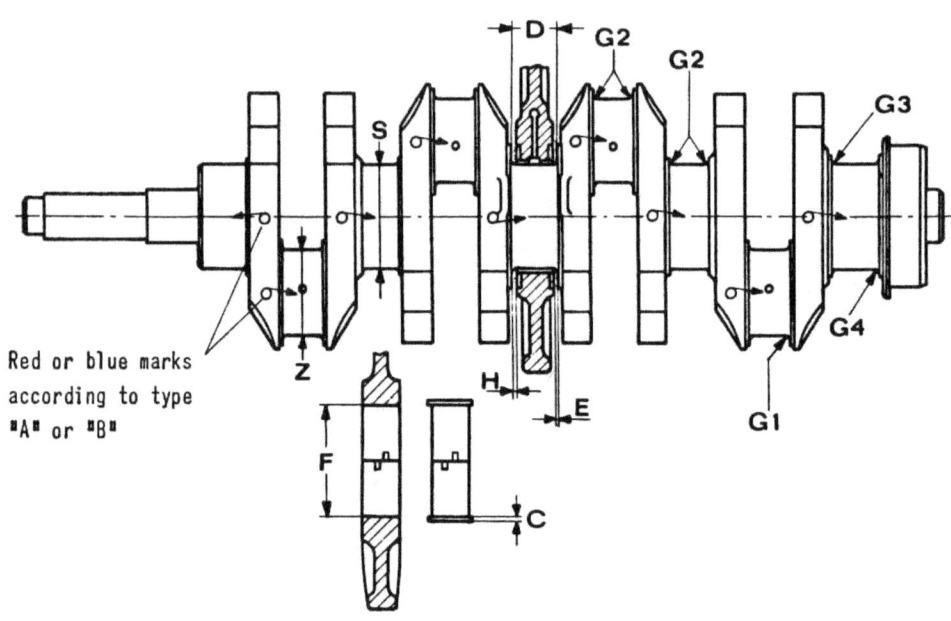

Diameter of main journals S	A - Red		59.961/59.971
	B - Blue		59.951/59.961
Diameter of crankpins Z	A - Red		49.988/49.998
	B - Blue		49.978/49.988
Thickness of main bearings C	A - Red	SFCM	1.824/1.830
		CLEVITE	1.829/1.835
	B - Blue	SFCM	1.830/1.836
		CLEVITE	1.835/1.841

Diameter of seat for main bearings in crankcase . . . . F = 63.657/63.676
Length of central journal . . . . D = 30.000/30.035
Thickness of thrust rings for central journal . . . . E = 2.310/2.360
End play of crankshaft . . . . H = 0.080/0.265

Clearance between journals and main bearings	A - Red	SFCM bearing	0.026/0.067
		CLEVITE bearing	0.016/0.057
	B - Blue	SFCM bearing	0.024/0.065
		CLEVITE bearing	0.014/0.055

Note: Clearance = main bearing ID - (twice bearing thickness - jou̲rnal OD)

Fillet radii	no. 4 crankpin, flywheel side . . . . G1 =		2.7/3.1
	main journals and crankpins . . . . G2 =		1.7/2.1
	rear main	crank side . . . . G3 =	3.7/4.1
	journal	flywheel side . . . . G4 =	1.50/1.75

Main journals & crankpins surface roughness . . . . Ra = 0.16 بر
Maximum elongation of main journals and crankpins 0.007
Maximum taper of main journals and crankpins as measured on their full length 0.01
Maximum error of parallelism of main journals and crankpins as mea̲sured on their full length 0.015
Maximum misalignment allowed between main journals 0.01
Maximum misalignment between ₵ of the two pairs of crankpins and ₵ of main journals 0.300

CLUTCH

The clutch is of the self-adjusting, hydraulically-operated single-plate dry type. The clutch pedal acts on a master cylinder supplied by the fluid reservoir "2". When the clutch pedal is depressed, the fluid under pressure actuates the piston in the cylinder "4" connected to the clutch release lever "6".
The driven plate "9" is controlled by means of diaphragm spring "8".
This type of clutch has the throwout bearing constantly in contact with the diaphragm spring. Thus, no more clearance exists and the wear is automatically taken up.
No regular adjustment of the play is required.

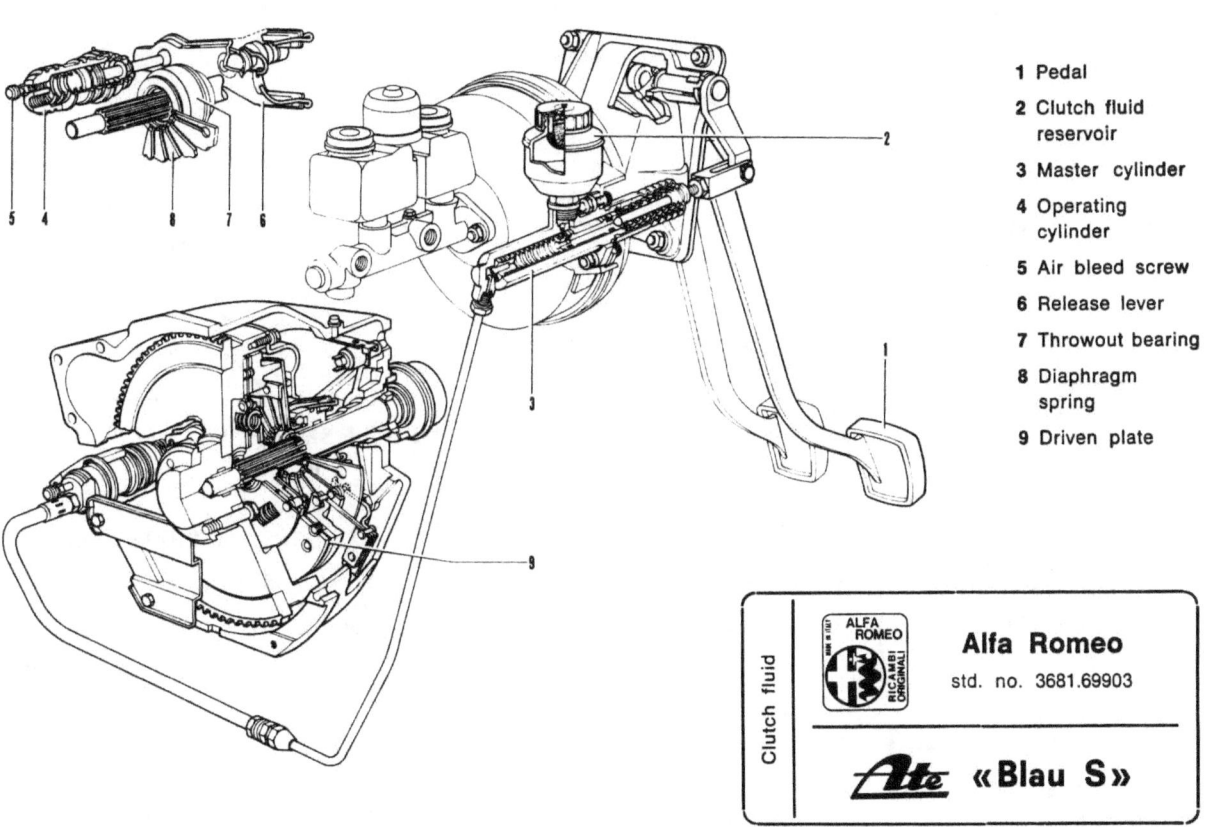

1 Pedal
2 Clutch fluid reservoir
3 Master cylinder
4 Operating cylinder
5 Air bleed screw
6 Release lever
7 Throwout bearing
8 Diaphragm spring
9 Driven plate

Clutch fluid — Alfa Romeo std. no. 3681.69903 — Ate «Blau S»

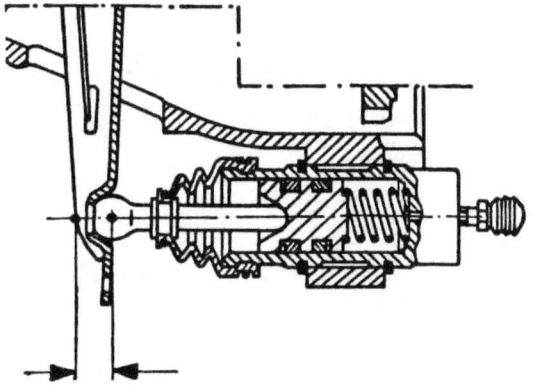

11 to 12 mm   Release travel

If necessary, check that, when the clutch pedal is depressed fully the push rod of cylinder "4" moves through a total travel of 11 to 12 mm.

If adjustment is needed, proceed as follows:

- slacken the locknut on master cylinder push rod.

- screw in or unscrew the push rod to increase or diminish its travel until the travel of the rod of cylinder "4" falls within the above specified limits. In this conditions, the travel of master cylinder rod shall in turn be 27 $\pm$ 1.5 mm.

GEARBOX

Transmission ratios
- 1st gear . . . . 3.30 : 1
- 2nd gear . . . . 1.99 : 1
- 3rd gear . . . . 1.35 : 1
- 4th gear . . . . 1 : 1
- 5th gear . . . . 0.79 : 1
- Rev. . . . . 3.01 : 1

Maximum eccentricity of main shaft at the working areas of 1st, 2nd, 3rd and 5th speed gears and at the working areas of roller bearing 0.01

End play between forks and sleeves
- assembly . . .150/.340 mm (.006/.013")
- wear limit . .850 mm (.033")

Calibration of spring for striking rod balls
- free length . . . . . 35.8 mm (1.41")
- length under test load 17.2 mm (.69")
- test load . . . . . . 7.680/8.320 kg (16.97/18.3 lbs)

Maximum end play of mainshaft gears
- 1st speed gear . . . . . . .170/.245 mm (.0067/.0096")
- 2nd & 3rd speed gears . . . .130/.205 mm (.0052/.0081")
- 5th speed gear . . . . . . .160/.220 mm (.0063/.0087")
- Reverse gear . . . . .160/.220 mm (.0063/.0087")

Radial clearance between gear bushings and main shaft
- 1st speed gear . . . . .125/.170 mm (.0049/.0067")
- 2nd & 3rd speed gears . .095/.140 mm (.0038/.0055")
- 5th speed gear . . . . .065/.107 mm (.0026/.0041")

Distance between outer planes of the engaging teeth of 3rd and 4th gears . . . . 42.000/42.200 mm (1.65/1.66")

Distance, in neutral, of the rear band (drive shaft side) of 5th speed sleeve from the rear edge of gear engaging teeth . . . . 12.9 mm (.508")

REAR AXLE AND SUSPENSION

Overall ratios with 41:9 final drive
- 1st gear . . . . 15.049 : 1
- 2nd gear . . . . 9.055 : 1
- 3rd gear . . . . 6.172 : 1
- 4th gear . . . . 4.555 : 1
- 5th gear . . . . 3.603 : 1
- Rev. . . . . 13.710 : 1

Maximum eccentricity of axle shafts	.10 mm (.004")
Play between teeth of planetary gears	.05 mm (.002")
Play between teeth of final drive	.05/.10 mm (.002/.004")
Reference dimension on tool C.6.0101 for pinion-to-ring gear fitting	70 ± .0025 mm (2.7559 ± .0001")
Maximum end play between T-arm and attachment to body	1 mm (.04")
Pre-load on pinion bearing	11.5/15.5 Kgcm (10/13.5 in. lbs)
Total pre-load on final drive bearings	16.5/24.5 Kgcm (14.4/21.3 in. lbs)

Checking of shock absorbers on test bench - Calibration data (when cold)

	BIANCHI - SPICA	
	Extension	Compression
High speed	135/190 Kgs (298/418 lbs)	50/80 Kgs (111/176 lbs)
Low speed	19/55 Kgs (42/121 lbs)	9/22 Kgs (20/48 lbs)

CHECKING OF SUSPENSION SPRINGS

Berlina L.H.D.

Free length mm	Length under test load mm	Test load lb	Test load Kg	Identification number
467	252	769.4/779.3	349/353.5	39
		781.5/792.5	354.5/359.5	40
		794.7/805.7	360.5/365.5	41
		808/817.9	366.5/371	42

GT Veloce L.H.D.

Free length mm	Length under test load mm	Test load lb	Test load Kg	Identification number
445	252	617.3/628.3	280/285	18
		631.5/643.7	286/292	48
		645.9/656.9	293/298	49

Spider Veloce L.H.D.

Free length mm	Length under test load mm	Test load lb	Test load Kg	Identification number
437	252	593/604	269/274	16
		606.2/617.2	275/280	17
		619.5/628.3	281/285	18

FRONT SUSPENSION

Adjustment of clearance in wheel bearings

When performing regular servicing or whenever the removal of wheel hubs is required, adjust the bearing clearance as follows:

- Pre-load the bearings by applying a torque of 2 to 2.5 Kgm to the castellated nut; at the same time rotate the hub to set the bearings properly and to prevent the rollers from brinelling the races.
- Slacken the nut and tighten it again to 0.5 - 1 Kgm with a torque wrench.
- Back up the nut by a quarter turn and insert the split pin; if the slot in the castellated nut and the hole in the axle are not aligned, screw in the nut of the minimum required to line up the hole and the next slot.
  Lightly tap on the stub axle end with a mallet.
- Make sure the bearing retainer plate is not blocked by inserting the tip of a screwdriver in the plate holes; the plate should be easily rotated.
- If the plate is locked, unscrew the nut by one slot and tap slightly on the stub axle end with a mallet.

Wheel bearing lubricating instructions

The quantity of lubricating grease should be about 65 grammes (2½ ozs) for each hub; do not exceed such a quantity to avoid bearing overheating, grease leakage, etc.
The grease should be well distributed inside the bearings and into side recesses. Subsequently, at the regular schedule, remove the hub cover and pack the outboard bearing.

Ball joints

End play of lower ball joint in its socket . . . . 1 mm (.04")

Note- Ball joints require no regular lubrication being provided with special grease seals which retain the grease packed in by factory on assembly.

Checking of shock absorbers on test bench
Calibration data (when cold)

	ALLINQUANT - SPICA	
	Extension	Compression
High speed	150/190 Kgs (331/418 lbs)	55/80 Kgs (121/176 lbs)
Low speed	25/55 Kgs (56 / 121 lbs)	9 / 22 Kgs (20/48 lbs)

Checking of suspension springs

Berlina L.H.D.

Right spring				
Free length mm	Length under test load mm	Test load lb	Test load Kg	Identification number
345	214	1988.6/2010.6 2012.8/2034.8 2037.1/2059.1 2061.3/2085.6 2087.8/2112.0	902/912 913/923 924/934 935/946 947/958	29 30 31 32 33

Left spring				
Free length mm	Length under test load mm	Test load lb	Test load Kg	Identification number
355	214	2138.5/2162.7 2165.0/2189.2 2191.2/2215.6 2217.8/2242.0 2244.3/2270.9	970/981 982/993 994/1005 1006/1017 1018/1030	34 35 36 37 38

GT Veloce L.H.D.

Free length mm	Length under test load mm	Test load lb	Test load Kg	Identification number
320.5	200	2114.2/2136.3	959/969	54

Spider Veloce L.H.D.

Free length mm	Length under test load mm	Test load lb	Test load Kg	Identification number
318	214	1608.3/1627.0 1629.2/1646.8 1649.0/1666.7 1668.9/1688.7 1691.9/1707.5	729.5/738 739/747 748/756 757/766 767/774.5	19 20 21 22 23

Note: On GT Veloce a 7 mm thick spacer is fitted together with the springs.

On Spider Veloce a 4.5 mm thick spacer is fitted together with the springs.

BRAKE SYSTEM

The brake unit consists of a dual power braking system.
Each one of the separate circuits, front and rear, is servo assisted and controlled by a tandem master cylinder, with one cylinder operating the front brakes and the other cylinder the rear brakes.
The friction pads of the front and rear brakes are directly actuated by the cylinders integral with the calipers.
The brakes are self-adjusting.
A valve, inserted in the rear brake circuit, regulates the pressure between front and rear brakes to provide balanced braking action.

WARNING: the pressure regulator must never be tampered with; specifically, do not attempt to act on the adjusting nut as it is factory sealed.

The stop light switch is directly operated by the brake pedal.
The two brake reservoirs have suitable markings for maximum and minimum levels; the reservoirs are provided with a baffle, which prevents fluid from interflowing between each other; however, the reservoirs are replenished thru a single filler port common to both.
Two microswitches, located at the top of reservoirs, light up a red warning light on instrument panel when the level of fluid in the reservoirs is too low.
This warning light serves also as a warning for a drop in service brake pressure and for the parking brake when applied.
Therefore, should the warning light come on, first make certain the parking brake is fully released; if the warning light still remains on, stop the car and check the fluid level in the service brake reservoirs; if the level is too low, check the relevant circuit for possible failure.
To check the operation of the warning light pull the parking brake lever.

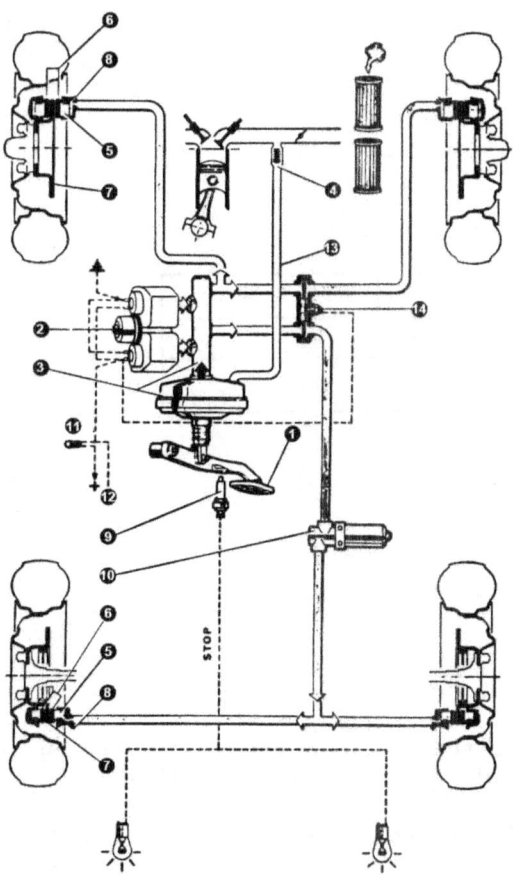

1 - Brake pedal
2 - Fluid reservoirs (with warning light switches)
3 - Power cylinder
4 - Suction port
5 - Pistons
6 - Friction pads
7 - Discs
8 - Bleed screws
9 - Stop light switch
10 - Pressure regulator
11 - Warning light for fluid level, service brake pressure and parking brake
12 - Connection for the switch of parking brake
13 - Vacuum connection for booster
14 - Pressure switch unit for brake pressure warning light

ATE BRAKES

Disc

When a brake disc is replaced it is necessary to check it for run-out after installation:

- use a dial indicator and the special tool A.2.0151 which is mounted to the caliper by means of the pad retaining pins.

Maximum permissible run out as measured at the swept surface should not exceed .22 mm (.0086").

Note - Run-out readings can be misleading if bearing clearance is not as specified; therefore, check and adjust if necessary, according to factory instructions.

If the disc is scored, see I.S. 22.70.2.1; the grinding of the surfaces is allowed providing not to exceed an under size of 1 mm (.0394"), equalized on both faces, i.e. .5 mm (.0197") each face; disc grinding limit: front 11.5 mm (.452") rear 8.5 mm (.335") thick.

WARNING: the discs must be renewed when worn down to the following wear limits: front: 10.7 mm (.421"); rear 7.5 mm (.295").

Inspection specifications after regrinding of disc surfaces:

- Max. out of parallelism with disc mounting plane: .05 mm (.0020");
- Max. out of flat: .025 mm (.0010") and max. difference in thickness: .038 mm (.0015") as measured along any radial line;
- Max. out of flat: .025 mm (.0010") and max. difference in thickness: .015 mm (.0006") as measured along any circular line;
- The surface should show no sign of scoring or porosity.

The surface roughness should be:

- 32 microinches as measured circularly;
- 50 microinches as measured radially.

Friction pads

	Front	Rear
Thickness when new	15 mm (.590")	
Wear limit	8 mm (.315")	7 mm (.275")

Calipers

On replacement of disc or caliper, measure the running clearance between caliper and disc on each side; the difference should not exceed .5 mm (.0197").

To centralize the caliper about the disc, insert shims between caliper and mounting flange as required.

Parking brake

It is mechanically operated and acts on the rear wheels through suitable shoes which spread apart against a drum machined in the disc casting.

For a brief description and repair and maintenance instructions refer to:

ATE DISC BRAKES (Publication no. 1202)

N o t e - When reassembling the operating levers, a slight quantity of grease AGIP F1 Gr SM or SHELL Retinax AM is to be applied to the pivot points and rubbing surfaces of levers.

Bleeding the brake system

The bleeding should be performed with the greatest care and following these instructions:

- Fill the reservoirs, if necessary, with the genuine fluid freshly drawn from sealed containers; during bleeding operations pay attention that fluid level does not drop below the full by more than a quarter.

- Jack up a side of the car and remove both wheels.
  Push rubber pipes over the bleed screws of a front and a rear caliper (either the two at right side or the two at left side); the other end will lead to glass containers half full of fluid.

- Loosen the bleed screws of front and rear caliper at the same time; depress the brake pedal several times allowing it to return slowly and waiting a few moment before depressing it again.

  This sequence must be repeated until the pipes discharge fluid free from air bubbles.

- Then, hold the pedal down, tighten the bleed screws and remove the pipes.

- Proceed the same way for the other two wheels; then, top up fluid in reservoirs.

If the bleeding has been carefully performed, it will be found that, when brake pedal is depressed, direct action on the fluid can be felt, free of resilience, immediately at the end of the free travel. If not, repeat the procedure.

WHEEL ALIGNMENT

Checking of wheel angles and car "trim" under static load

Put the car under static load, with shock absorbers and stabilizer rods disconnected, with full tank or equivalent with spare wheel, tool kit and the tires inflated as specified.

Before checking, slightly move the car up and down so as to settle the suspensions.

Berlina

Front seats { 1 weight of 45 Kgs (100 lbs) on each seat
2 weights of 25 Kgs (55 lbs) on flooring where feet rest

Rear seats { 2 weights of 45 Kgs (100 lbs) on seat
2 weights of 25 Kgs (55 lbs) on flooring where feet rest

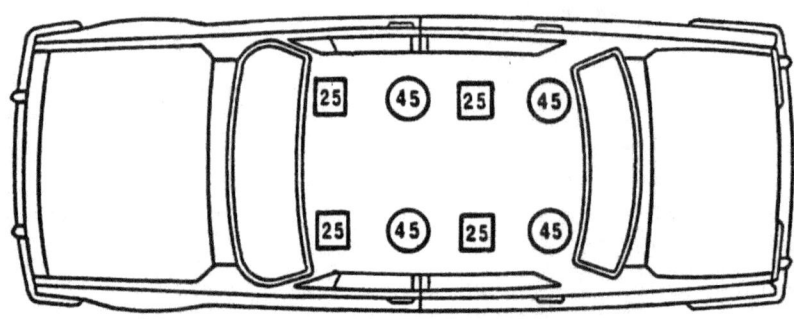

G.T. Veloce & Spider Veloce

Static load { 2 weights of 45 Kgs (100 lbs) on front seats
2 weights of 25 Kgs (55 lbs) on flooring where feet rest

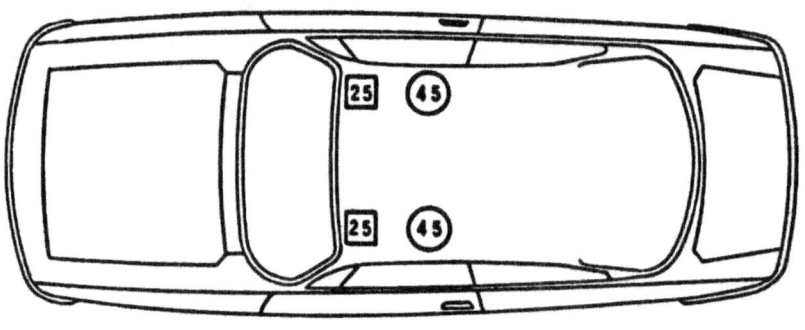

Distance of lower arms of front suspension from a reference level

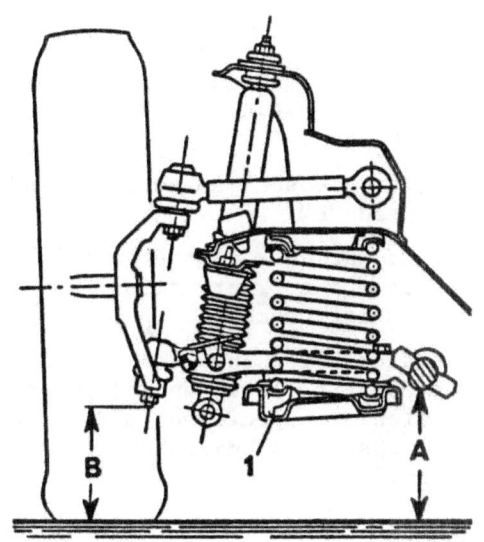

Berlina: A - B = 34 ± 5 mm (1.34 ± .20")
GT Veloce: A-B = 49 ± 5 mm (1.929 ± .20")
Spider Veloce: A-B = 24 ± 5 mm (.94 ± .20")

Dimension "A" must be measured in correspondence of the lower line of shaft as shown.

To adjust add shims in "1".

Shims are available in the following thicknesses:

3.5 mm (.14") - 7 mm (.28") - 10.5 mm (.42")

Distance of rear axle from rubber buffers

Berlina   C = 36 ± 5 mm (1.42 ± .20")
GT Veloce   C = 41 ± 5 mm (1.62 ± .2")
Spider Veloce   C = 33 ± 5 mm (1.30 ± .2")

Note - To adjust, remove the seat "3" and add shims in "2" as shown.

Shims are available in the following thicknesses:

6.5 mm (.26")
11.5 mm (.45")
16.5 mm (.65")
21.5 mm (.85")

In the condition as specified check the wheel angles.

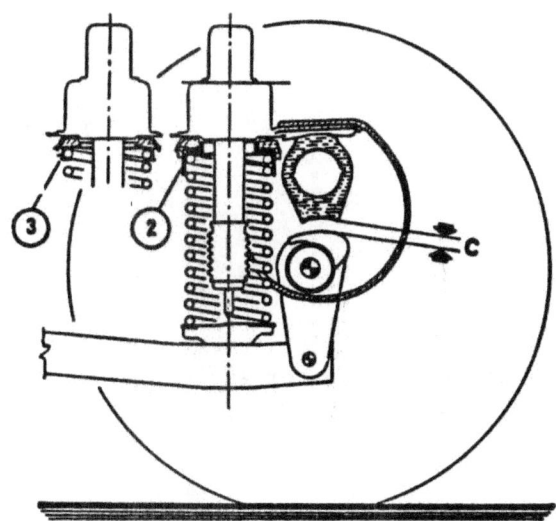

Caster angle: $\alpha = 1°\ 30' \pm 30'$

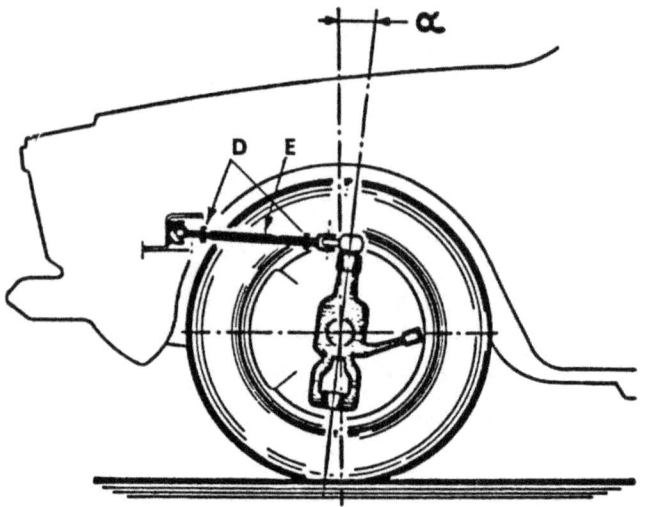

The difference in caster angle between R.H. and L.H. wheel must not exceed 0° 20'.

To adjust, loosen jam nuts "D" and rotate rod "E".

Small adjustments of the caster angle allow to correct slight drift tendency of the car.

The caster angle should be checked under static load and alignment conditions as specified and with shock absorbers disconnected at one end.

N.B. - Before checking the caster angle shake the front end of car in order to allow the rubber bushing on the front slanting arm to set properly.

Front wheel camber

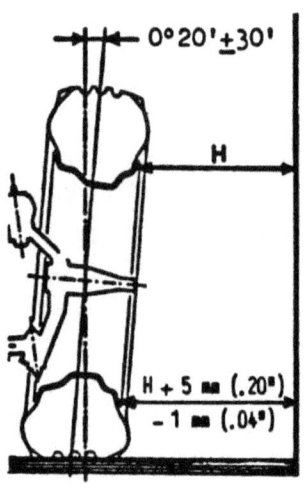

Difference in camber angle between R.H. and L.H. wheel = 0° 40'

Note - Not adjustable. Check the chassis and suspension arms if necessary.

FRONT WHEEL TOE-IN

Lock steering wheel in the central position i.e. with the spokes symmetrically disposed in relation to the vertical.

Starting with the rod "1" on the steering box side, place the corresponding wheel so that the toe-in is .06" (1.5 mm).

Measure the length thus obtained of the rod and adjust the rod "2" on the other side to a length .20" (5 mm) shorter.

Bring the first wheel to a .06" (1.5 mm) toe-in by adjusting the center track rod "3".

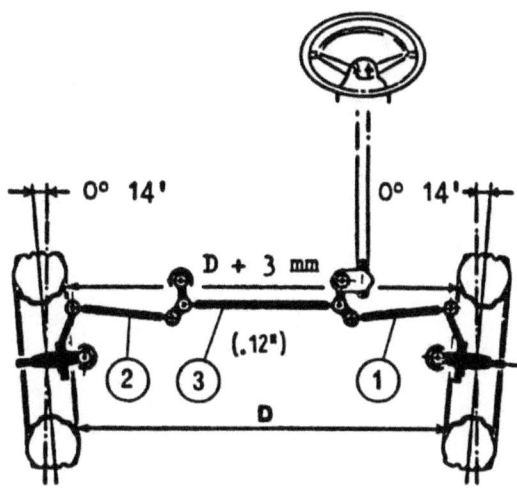

Rod length:

    side . . . . 264 to 280 mm (10.4 to 11")

    track . . . . 530 to 550 mm (20.86 to 21.65")

With the toe-in as specified, the length of rods as measured between ball joint centers should fall within the limits shown. If these values cannot be restored, the cause will probably be attributable to distortion of the body resulting from a collision.

NOTES

Direzione Assistenza

MAINTENANCE MANUAL

FOR ALFA ROMEO 2000 AND ALFETTA

FUEL INJECTION MODEL

U.S.A. VERSION

1975 MODEL YEAR

CONTENTS

IMPORTANT NOTE . . . . Page 1

A - FUEL INJECTION SYSTEM

    A1 General . . . . " 2
    A2 Fuel feed system . . . . " 2
    A3a Air induction system . . . . " 2
    A3b Air intake temperature control system . . . . " 3
    A4 Injection pump . . . . " 3
    A5 Cold start device . . . . " 3
    A6 Initial running device . . . . " 4
    A7 Crankcase ventilating system . . . . " 4
    A8 Fuel vapor recovery system and tank ventilation . . . . " 4
    A9 Air injection system . . . . " 5

B - RECOMMENDATIONS ON THE USE

    B1 Starting the engine . . . . " 6
    B2 Deceleration . . . . " 6

C - REGULAR SERVICING

    C1 Schedule of regular servicing required to keep the exhaust emission level within limits
       prescribed by U.S. regulations . . . . " 7
    C2 Replacing the air filter elements . . . . " 7
    C3 Replacing the main fuel filter element . . . . " 7
    C4 Checking the spark plugs and replacing . . . . " 8
    C5 Checking the alternator and fan driving belt . . . . " 9
    C6 Checking the valve timing chain tension . . . . " 9
    C7a Checking the distributor and the ignition timing . . . . " 9
      - Automatic advance graph and specifications of Marelli S 103 B or S 103 BA distributor . " 10
      - Condenser capacity test . . . . " 10
      - Ignition timing . . . . " 11
      - Timing adjustment . . . . " 12
    C7b Replacing the distributor . . . . " 12
    C8 Checking the valve clearance and valve timing diagram . . . . " 13
    C9 Replacing the tank fuel filter . . . . " 13
    C10 Cleaning the throttle valve throats . . . . " 14
    C11 Replacing the injection pump oil filter . . . . " 14
    C12 Checking the positioning of throttle-control unit linkage . . . . " 15
    C13 Checking the positioning and alignment of throttles . . . . " 17
    C14 Idle adjustment-mixture and exhaust emissions adjustment . . . . " 18
      - First step: preliminary idle adjustment . . . . " 19
      - Second step: road test and operating mixture adjustment . . . . " 20
                    adjusting the fuel mixture . . . . " 20
      - Third step: idle speed and CO adjustment, HC emission checking . . . . " 21
    C15 Checking the injection pump timing . . . . " 22
    C16 Checking the air intake temperature control system . . . . " 22

D - INJECTION PUMP REPAIRS

    D1 Removal of the injection pump . . . . " 24
    D2 Reinstallation of the injection pump . . . . " 25
    D3 Replacement of thermostatic actuator . . . . " 27
    D4 Replacing the fuel cut off solenoid . . . . " 28
    D5 Replacement of cold start solenoid and plunger removal . . . . " 29
    D6 Testing the injectors . . . . " 31
    D7 Replacing the altitude compensator . . . . " 32
    D8 Check the relationship between throttle angles and control unit lever angles . . . . " 33

E - TROUBLE SHOOTING

    E1 Alfa Romeo Spica pump policy . . . . " 37
    E2 Trouble chart . . . . " 38

F - TOOL LIST . . . . " 43

IMPORTANT NOTE

The fuel injection system for the 2000 and Alfetta models has been designed not only to attain high performance and low fuel consumption but also to keep the exhaust emissions below the levels allowed by U.S.A. regulations.

The low exhaust emissions have been obtained by improving the fuel distribution and combustion and providing devices to burn the unburned gases downstream of the exhaust valves.

Simple and efficient systems for controlling crankcase and evaporative emissions are fitted.

Of course, even with the mentioned systems fitted to the Alfa 2000 and Alfetta the emissions will not continue to meet Federal and State regulations unless the owner himself provides to have the prescribed servicing, carried out by authorized Alfa Romeo Dealers and provided that, when remedying troubles or performing any maintenance work on the engine or fuel feed system, the factory prescribed procedures are strictly followed.

Alfa Romeo warrants to the ultimate purchaser and each subsequent purchaser that the vehicle is designed, built, and equipped so as to conform at the time of sale with all U.S. emission standards applicable at the time of manufacture and that is free from defects in materials and workmanship which would cause it not to meet these standards within the period of 5 years or 50,000 miles, whichever occurs first. Failures, other than those resulting from defects in material or workmanship, which arise solely as a result of owner abuse and/or lack of proper maintenance are not covered by the warranty.

To obtain this service the owner must submit written receipts or routine maintenance book for services obtained that will verify the vehicle has been maintained according to the written instructions issued to assure proper functioning of emission control devices and systems on the vehicle.

This warranty is the only warranty in addition to the standard Alfa Romeo warranty in the routine maintenance booklet or owner's manual applicable to the vehicle and is expressly in lieu of any warranty or conditions implied in law pertaining to emissions or emission control systems.

The remedies under this warranty shall be the only remedies available to the owner of the vehicle or any other person, and neither Alfa Romeo S.p.A. or A.R. Inc. nor the authorized selling dealer assumes any other obligation or responsibility with respect to the condition of the vehicle, and neither assumes nor authorizes anyone to assume for any of them, any additional liability.

Federal Law prohibits manufactures and dealers from knowingly removing or rendering an emission control system inoperative or ineffective after sale and delivery to an ultimate purchaser.

NOTES

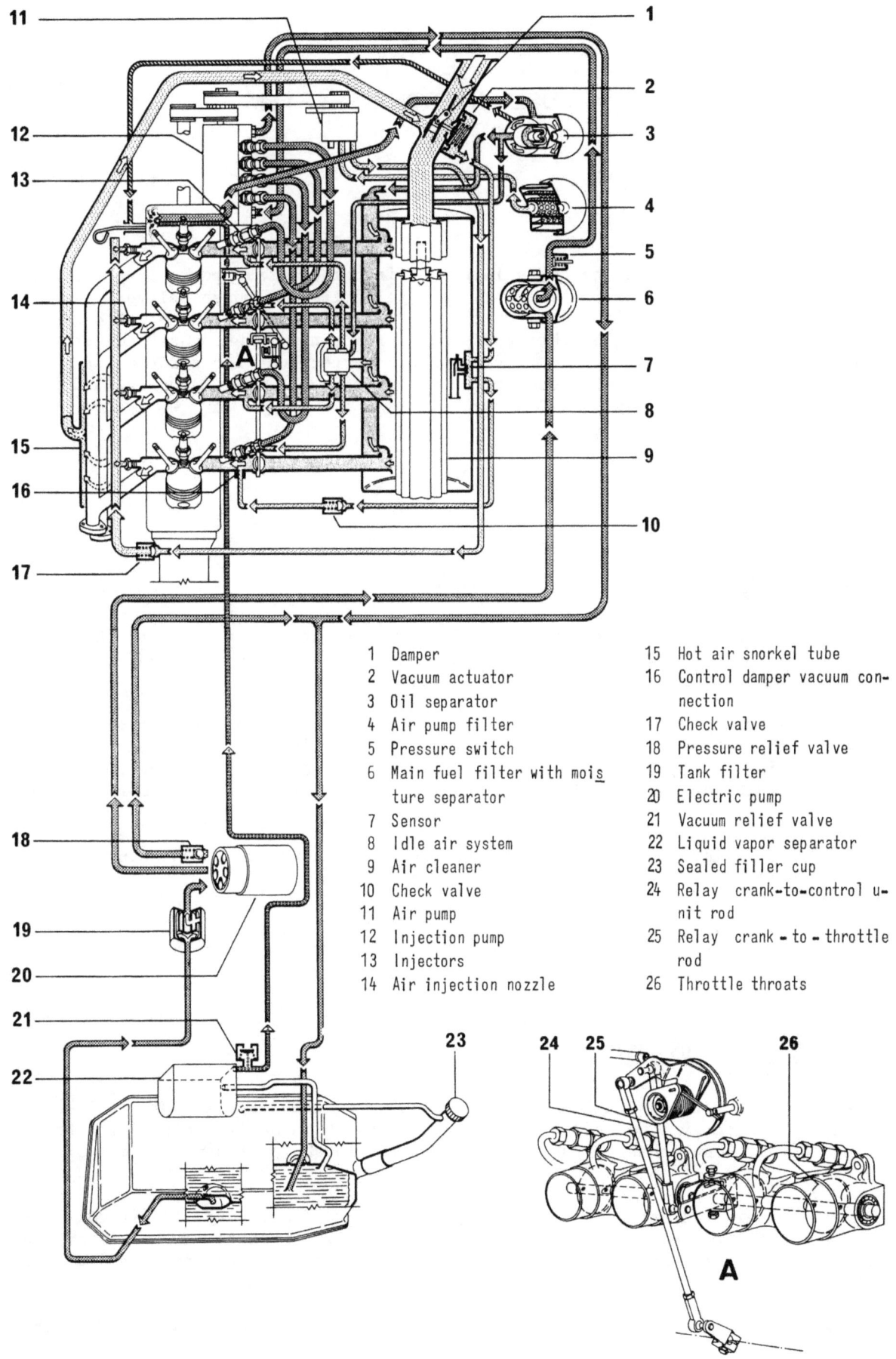

1 Damper
2 Vacuum actuator
3 Oil separator
4 Air pump filter
5 Pressure switch
6 Main fuel filter with moisture separator
7 Sensor
8 Idle air system
9 Air cleaner
10 Check valve
11 Air pump
12 Injection pump
13 Injectors
14 Air injection nozzle
15 Hot air snorkel tube
16 Control damper vacuum connection
17 Check valve
18 Pressure relief valve
19 Tank filter
20 Electric pump
21 Vacuum relief valve
22 Liquid vapor separator
23 Sealed filler cup
24 Relay crank-to-control unit rod
25 Relay crank-to-throttle rod
26 Throttle throats

A   FUEL INJECTION SYSTEM

A 1   GENERAL

Fuel is supplied to the engine by injection into the intake port of each cylinder by means of four pumping elements (one per cylinder) whose delivery is controlled by a control unit. A cam in the control unit provides a "base" delivery according to the opening of throttles and to rpm range; the "base" delivery is varied by compensating devices giving proper corrections for atmospheric pressure, engine and ambient temperature, cold starting, initial running and fuel cut off on deceleration.

A 2   FUEL FEED SYSTEM

Inserting the key in the ignition switch and rotating clockwise to the first click will operate the electric pump. The gasoline flows from the tank thru tank filter and main filter and feeds the injection pump.

The excess fuel, acting also as a coolant for the injection pump, before returning to the tank, passes thru a calibrated orifice which regulates the fuel pressure within the injection pump. A pressure switch inserted in the delivery pipe will switch on the warning light on dashboard if a pressure drop occurs in fuel lines.

A pressure relief valve limits the fuel pump outlet pressure bypassing fuel to the recovery pipe.

A 3a   AIR INDUCTION SYSTEM

The air induction system consists of the housing incorporating two filtering elements, directly connected to the intake ducts which deliver air to the throttles; an air hose connects the housing to a ram intake port at the front of the car.

The idling air (throttle valves closed) is fed thru a separate circuit consisting of a filtered air supply pipe, an adjuster ring fitted to the equalizer and four small hoses connecting the equalizer to the intake ducts downstream of the throttles.

The accelerator pedal is mechanically linked thru a relay crank to both the throttle lever and the control unit lever. Therefore, any position of accelerator pedal corresponds to an exact position of throttle and control unit levers.

A 3b AIR INTAKE TEMPERATURE CONTROL SYSTEM

The system is designed to maintain the intake air temperature entering the engine at approximately 40°C (104°F). The sensor element a bimetallic bleed unit, is modulating the vacuum from the engine, and controlling the position of the damper in the intake snorkel tube. The position of the damper controls the amount of hot air entering the inlet manifold, maintaining the correct air temperature under all engine temperature and driving conditions.

A 4 INJECTION PUMP

The injection pump, (SPICA AIBB. 4C.S.75), has four variable displacement plungers controlled by the control unit thru a rack. The plungers are actuated by conn. rods driven by a crankshaft revolving at half engine speed. The pump is lubricated with the engine oil drawn from the main gallery just after the main filter.

The lubricating oil, filtered further by a filter in the injection pump mount, seeps past the plungers, lubricates the various moving parts then returns to the pan thru a suitable port in the pump mount itself.

A 5 COLD START DEVICE

The cold start device incorporates a solenoid which, energized when the engine is started, enriches the mixture by increasing the injection pump delivery thru an additional movement of control unit rack.

The cold start device cuts off gradually, according to engine temperature, when the ignition key is released from cranking position.

A 6   INITIAL RUNNING DEVICE

This device provides for a smooth operation of the engine soon after a cold start; it consists of a thermostat which, sensing engine coolant temperatures, acts thru a linkage on the control unit rack so as to increase the injection pump delivery in accord with the decrease in temperature and at the same time, thru rods and outside the control unit, opens the throttles so that the engine can be properly fed.

The device cuts off automatically and progressively as the engine warms up to operating temperature thus restoring the standard idling conditions.

A 7   CRANKCASE VENTILATING SYSTEM

The exhaust gases and the oil vapors developed during engine operation and gas vapors from the fuel tank are sucked thru the camshaft cover in the combustion chambers and burned.

The crankcase ventilating system controls gases both at high engine rpms and at idling speed when the throttles are closed.

The gases and vapors flow from camshaft cover to the oil separator thru the hose, then enter either the main or secondary crankcase ventilating system according to the opening of throttles:

when throttles are fully opened, the vapors are delivered from the oil separator, thru the main system hose, to the manifold gallery, communicating directly with the four intake ducts and, from here, to the throttle throats; when the throttles are instead closed or partially opened, the oil vapors are delivered from the oil separator, via the secondary system hose, to the equalizer, where they are suitably mixed with fresh air and thence, thru four hoses they are delivered to the intake ducts downstream of the throttles.

The oil collected in the oil separator returns to the pan via the hose.

A 8   FUEL VAPOR RECOVERY SYSTEM AND TANK VENTILATION

Gas vapors, emanating from fuel tank both during engine operation and hot soak period after engine shutdown, are collected in the expansion tank which acts also as a vapor liquid separator returning the condensate to the fuel tank via the pipe located at the bottom of expansion tank.

The pipe serves to make a proper connection between the fuel tank, when fully replenished, and the expansion tank.

To prevent gas vapors from escaping in the open air, a sealed filler cap is provided.

Gas vapors coming to the expansion tank flow out of the separator from the top and, passing thru the pipes, enter the cylinder head, then, via the pipe which extends into the cylinder head, get into the crankcase: during the hot soak period, the crankcase is used as a storage volume while during engine operation the crankcase is purged of vapors by the action of the ventilation system.

In the event that, after engine shut down, the pressure in the vapor separator tends to diminish as a consequence of drop in temperature, gas vapors will flow back thru pipes thus keeping the fuel tank and expansion tank at atmospheric pressure.

A valve on the pipe allows to keep a constant supply of fuel to the engine even if an obstruction should occur in the pipe itself.

A 9 AIR INJECTION SYSTEM

The system has been designed to inject air into the exhaust manifold so as to obtain a combustion of the exhaust gas. The air is supplied by a vane type pump, through a check valve, to an air manifold that distributes the air to four injection nozzles located near the exhaust ports. The non return valve is provided in the system to stop gas flowing back into the air pump when air pressure drops for any reason, such as drive belt failure.

B RECOMMENDATIONS ON THE USE

B 1 STARTING THE ENGINE

1) <u>Under normal conditions</u>:

   Insert the key in the ignition switch and turn it clockwise to the first click; wait a few seconds to make sure the low fuel pressure warning light goes off.

   WARNING: if the warning light does not flash on or stays on, this is an indication of failure of the indicating device or fuel feed system; therefore have them checked as soon as possible.

   Turn the ignition key further clockwise to operate the starter.

   As soon as the engine fires release the key.

   NOTE: automatic devices act as a standard choke usually does, namely, facilitate the initial running of engine after a cold start until the proper operating temperature is reached.

2) <u>As an aid in starting from cold</u>, proceed as per 1) above taking care to depress slightly the accelerator pedal as soon as cranking motor starts operating (at the second "click"). After a cold start and particularly when the ambient temperature is below freezing point, wait a fairly long time before getting away so as to warm up properly all engine parts and allow the oil to reach all points requiring lubrication.

   Top performance must never be demanded of the car until coolant temperature is about 70°C (158°F).

3) <u>When the engine is already hot</u> or with very high ambient temperatures (above 25°C - 77°F) proceed as per 1) above taking care to depress slightly the accelerator pedal as soon as cranking motor starts operating (at the second "click").

   CAUTION: owing to the special construction of the injection pump the pump plungers must on no account be operated directly with a lever or any other tool.

B 2 DECELERATION

On deceleration, the injection pump delivery is automatically cut off by means of an electromagnetic device fed thru a microswitch which, being actuated by a particular profile suitably shaped in the control unit cam, closes when the accelerator pedal is released; this not only eliminates the unburned gases in a condition which is critical for the emission levels, but also favorably affects the fuel consumption.

As the engine speed reaches about 1,300 rpm, the fuel delivery restores to prevent stopping the engine. Of course, the fuel delivery restores even if the engine is re-accelerated before it slows down to 1,300 rpm.

C REGULAR SERVICING

C 1 SCHEDULE OF REGULAR SERVICING REQUIRED TO KEEP THE EXHAUST EMISSION LEVEL WITHIN LIMITS PRESCRIBED BY U.S. REGULATIONS

In order to maintain the fuel injection system in good operating conditions and the exhaust emissions below the limits specified by Federal regulations, the servicing operations listed in the Owner's Manual and in the Routine Maintenance Program Booklet must be performed at the prescribed period.
On the following pages, each operation specifically related to the injection system will be set out in details particularly those requiring the special tools and facilities the authorized workshops are equipped with.

C 2 REPLACING THE AIR FILTER ELEMENTS

To provide room for subsequent operations, the air filter elements shall be removed as a whole; to do so disconnect the hot air snorkel tube, remove the pipe; detach the two upper anchoring straps at manifold side; loosen at the engine side the four clamps on the intake hoses; free the crankcase ventilation hose from the oil separator; disconnect the idle hose from the idling air equalizer; disconnect the hoses from thermal sensor.

Then the cover of filter housing can be removed and the elements replaced after having cleaned the inside of air filter housing.

Do not reinstall the air filter on engine at this point.

C 3 REPLACING THE MAIN FUEL FILTER ELEMENT

This operation, to be performed after the previous one has already been accomplished, should be carried out as follows:

disconnect the battery negative terminal, disconnect the starter positive cable if necessary.

CAUTION: first of all clean carefully the outside of filter body to make sure no foreign matter could enter the filter on reassembly.

1 - Screw
2 - Copper washer
3 - Sealing ring
4 - Top gasket
5 - Bottom gasket
6 - Housing

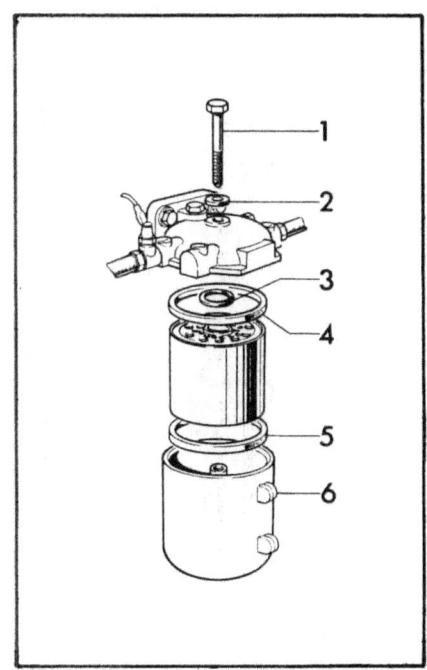

Fig. 2 - MAIN FUEL FILTER ELEMENT

slacken the bolt securing the filter to its bracket and remove the filter,

withdraw the filter element,

get rid of foreign matter that may have collected in the housing and fit a new element; also replace the housing gasket if damaged and the sealing ring on bolt.

WARNING: extreme cleanliness is required in the area of the main fuel filter.

C 4 CHECKING THE SPARK PLUGS (Lodge HL) AND REPLACING

The spark plugs are of the surface gap type with four points and a central electrode. The only maintenance required is occasional cleaning with a brush of the central electrode and points. No routine adjustment is necessary of the gap between the electrode and points.

If the ceramic insulator is cracked or the electrodes are excessively worn away, the spark plugs must be replaced.

The spark plugs should be tightened when cold to a torque of 2.5 to 3.5 kgm (18-25.3 lb-ft); lubricate the threads with graphite grease before fitting.

The standard plugs fitted to the engine are LODGE HL. A decal, giving the specifications for these plugs, is attached under the hood; here below, the text of the decal is repeated.

In order to comply with the Federal rule regarding the control of air pollution the engine is fitted with LODGE-HL spark plugs.

These plugs are completely adequate when the automobile is driven at speeds not exceeding the limits specified by speed regulations. If the automobile is driven at sustained speeds higher than the said speed limits, LODGE - 2HL spark plugs must be used.

Under no condition can substitute spark plugs be used, unless they are specifically advised and approved by Alfa Romeo. Use of other plugs can promote serious engine damage, as well as alter emission levels.

C 5   CHECKING THE ALTERNATOR AND FAN DRIVING BELT

The belt should be tightened enough to drive the fan and alternator pulley without slipping and without overloading the bearings.

The tension is correct when, on pressing the belt down, the sag is about 10 - 15 mm (1/2").

To tighten the belt unscrew the nut on the adjusting arm and move the alternator outwards.

C 6   CHECKING THE VALVE TIMING CHAIN TENSION

Run engine at idling speed; while performing the following adjustment any revving up of the engine must be absolutely avoided; with wrench A.5. 0189 (for A/C equipped cars) slacken off the set screw securing the chain tensioner; wait a few minutes to allow the tensioner to tighten the chain, then lock the chain tensioner setscrew firmly.

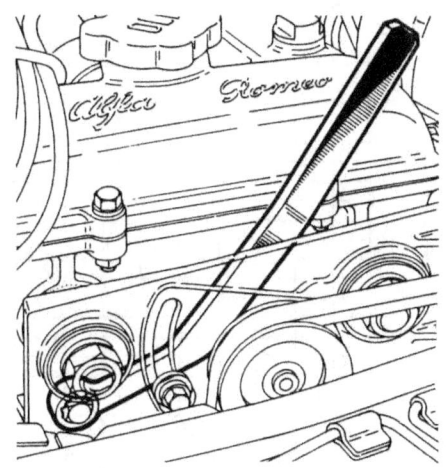

On refitting the camshaft cover, make sure the gasket is in sound conditions or replace, if necessary. Moderately tighten the cover retaining nuts in diagonal order.

C 7a   CHECKING THE DISTRIBUTOR (Marelli S 103 B or S 103 BA) AND THE IGNITION TIMING

Dwell meter should read 60° $\pm$ 3°, with new points closed, corresponding to .43 to .48 mm (.017 to .019") gap.

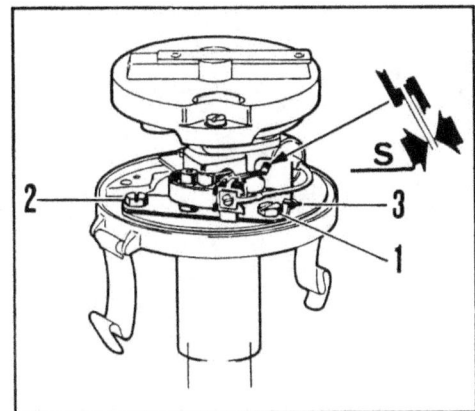

To adjust, loosen the screws (1) and (2), insert a screwdriver in the adjustment slot (3) and pry the stationary-point plate.

S = .017 - .019 in.

Fig. 3 - DISTRIBUTOR POINTS GAP CHECK

Automatic advance graph and specifications of Marelli S 103 B or S 103 BA distributor

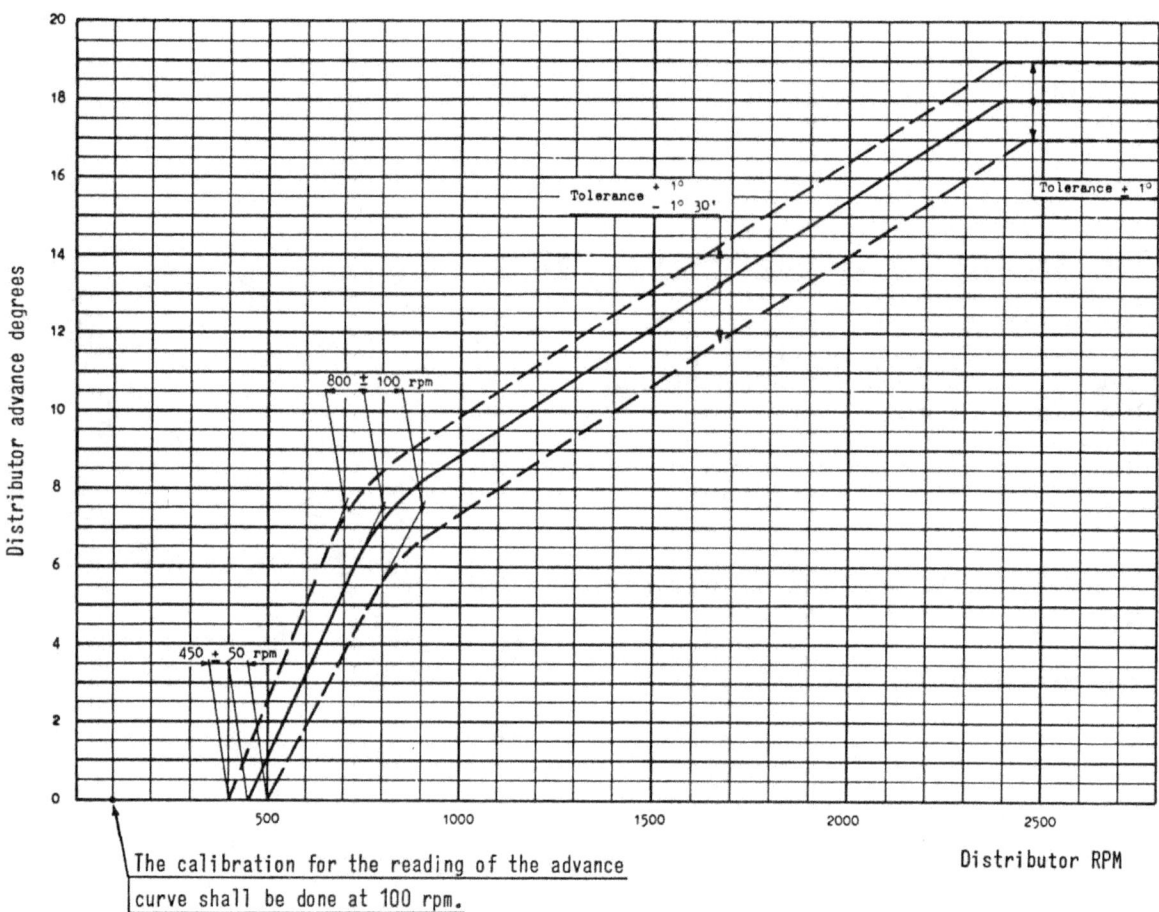

Fig. 4 - DISTRIBUTOR CENTRIFUGAL ADVANCE CURVE

Contact gap . . . . .017 - .019"

Contact opening angle . . . . 30° ± 3°

Dwell angle . . . . 60° ± 3°

Contact pressure . . . . 18 - 21 oz

Condenser capacity test

Should an excessive wear of breaker points be experienced, check that the condenser capacity is not lower than 0.20 µF i.e. over 20% less than its rated capacity (0.25 µF) marked on the condenser body.

Smear the distributor cam with grease. Check the inside of distributor cap for any sign of moisture, carbon deposits or cracks and the central power electrode for free movement in its seat and for effective spring action. Finally, check cap terminals for good conditions.

IGNITION TIMING

The ignition timing should be checked when the engine is warmed up to operating temperature (coolant exceeding 70°C; 158°F) by using a timing light.

At idle speed the timing should be 6° ± 1° ATDC, that is the mark "F" on the pulley should be in line with the pointer.

With the engine running with no load at 5,000 rpm, the ignition advance should be 30° ± 3°, that is the mark "M" on the pulley should be in line with the pointer or 3 mm (.12") apart either side.

Timing at idle speed must be adjusted with special care as it affects the emission levels greatly.

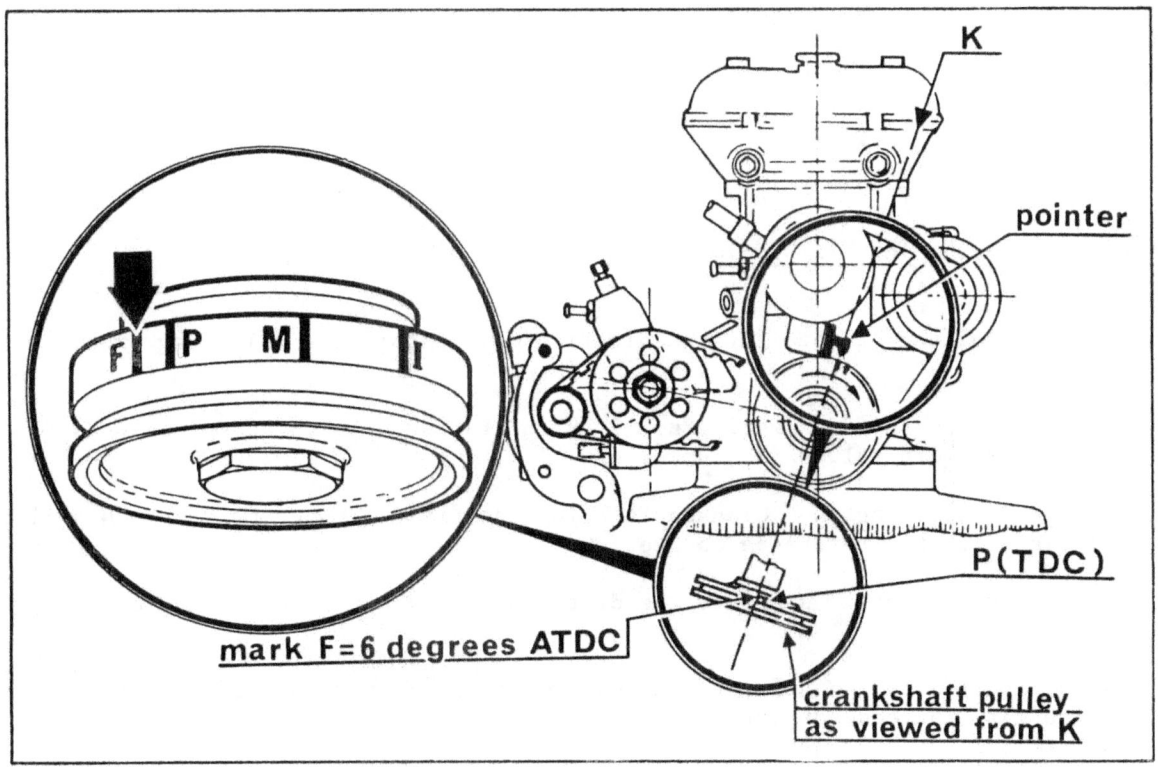

Fig. 5 - IGNITION TIMING

Timing adjustment (maximum accuracy required)

If the timing requires adjustment, proceed as follows:

with the wrench A.5.0213 unscrew the distributor securing nut (1) on the stud so as to allow the distributor to be rotated together with its supporting clamp, then rotate the distributor body counterclockwise or clockwise according to whether it is necessary to respectively advance "A" or retard "R" the ignition setting;

retighten the nut (1), taking care not to move the distributor body;

recheck timing.

In the event of reinstallation or renewal of the distributor, refer to the directions given on paragraph C7b.

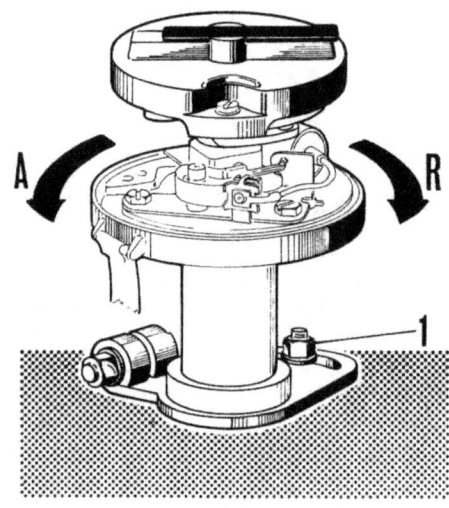

Fig. 6 - IGNITION TIMING ADJUSTMENT

C 7b REPLACING THE DISTRIBUTOR

When reinstalling or renewing the distributor, perform the following procedure:

rotate the crankshaft to bring no. 1 cylinder piston to the compression stroke that is with both valves closed;

by slightly rotating the crankshaft bring the fixed advance mark "F" on pulley into line with the reference pointer;

fit the supporting clamp into the distributor body and tighten the clamp just snug;

remove distributor cap and rotate the drive shaft by hand to bring the rotor arm in line with the contact for no. 1 cylinder;

as a trial installation place the distributor on engine and move the supporting clamp so that the stud is centered in the clamp slot when the contact-breaker points are about to open for no. 1 cylinder;

then, remove the distributor with its supporting clamp, taking care not to disturb the distributor body/clamp setting and lock the clamp in place;

reinstall the distributor and adjust timing as directed on paragraph C7a.

C 8   CHECKING THE VALVE CLEARANCE - VALVE TIMING DIAGRAM

The V-mounted overhead valves are directly operated by two camshafts acting thru oil bath cups.

When the engine is cold, carefully measure the clearance "G" with a feeler gage. If the clearance is not as specified, remove camshafts and valve cups; measure the thickness "S" of the adjusting pad on each valve stem and replace it with another of proper thickness so that the clearance is the correct one shown in the figure 8.

To facilitate this adjustment the pads are made available in a series of thicknesses ranging from 1,3 to 3,5 mm (.05 to .014") in increments of .025 mm (.001").

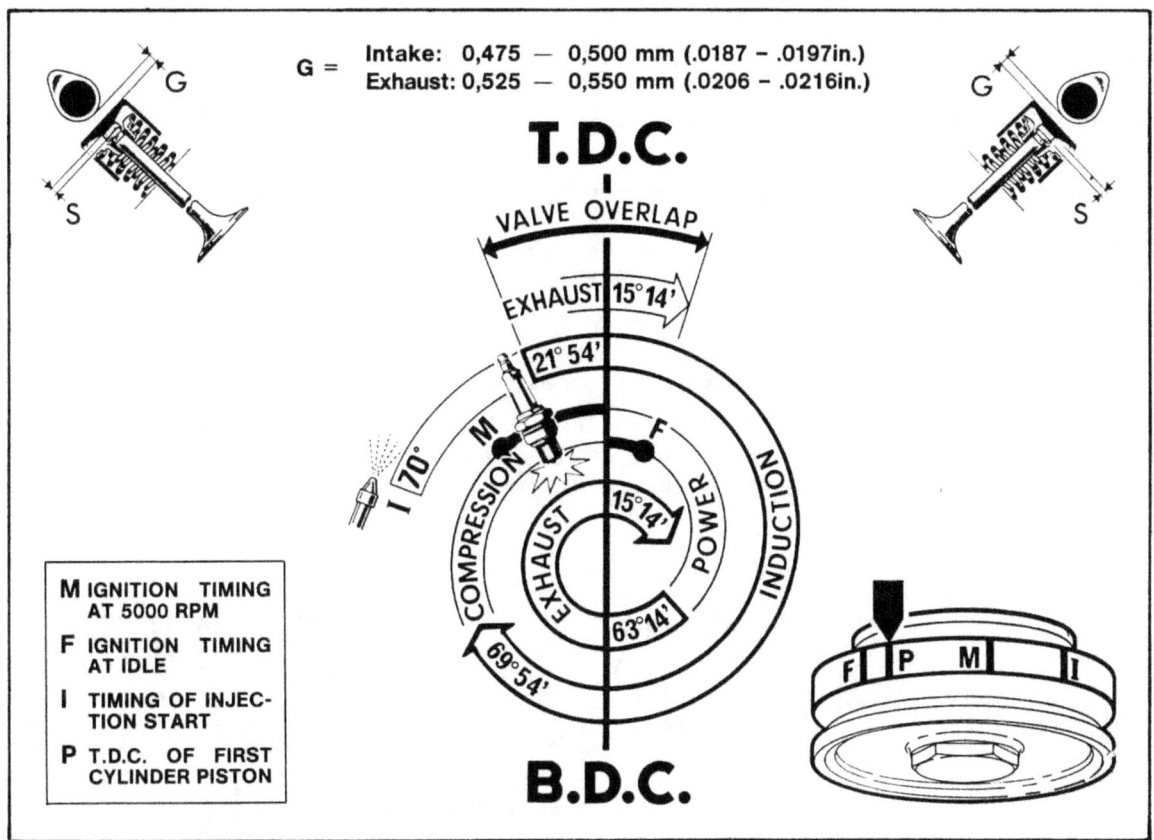

Fig. 7 - VALVE CLEARANCE AND VALVE TIMING DIAGRAM

C 9   REPLACING THE TANK FUEL FILTER

To replace the tank fuel filter (throw-away type) (see 2, fig. 1), located on the rear underbody of car, proceed as follows:

- slacken the bolt on the clamp securing the filter to the underbody;
- loosen the clamps securing the hoses to the filter inlet and outlet adapters; it is advisable to stop the pipe from fuel tank provisionally.

Remove the filter and replace it with a new one by proceeding in reverse order of removal. Make sure the hoses are properly positioned.

C 10 CLEANING THE THROTTLE VALVE THROATS

Clean the valve throats especially at the areas of contact of throttle valve edges and throat by holding the throttles in full open position and using a brush soaked in gasoline; the cleaning can be completed by rubbing repeatedly the affected areas with a lint-free cloth.

Then, clean in a similar way the throttle valve edges taking care not to strain the spindles.

C 11 REPLACING THE INJECTION PUMP OIL FILTER

On Berlina and GT remove the air pump prior to proceed as follows.

Clean very carefully the filter housing cover and the surrounding areas to prevent any foreign matter from entering the filter housing.

Remove the cover and withdraw the element; wash thoroughly the filter housing with gasoline, then insert the new element in such a way that the spring faces the cover; renew the cover gasket, if necessary.

To facilitate the air bleed and the quick filling up of filter housing with oil, slightly tighten the two upper cover retaining nuts, crank the engine a few seconds (even by means of the starter) until the oil just oozes out; then lock the nuts fully.

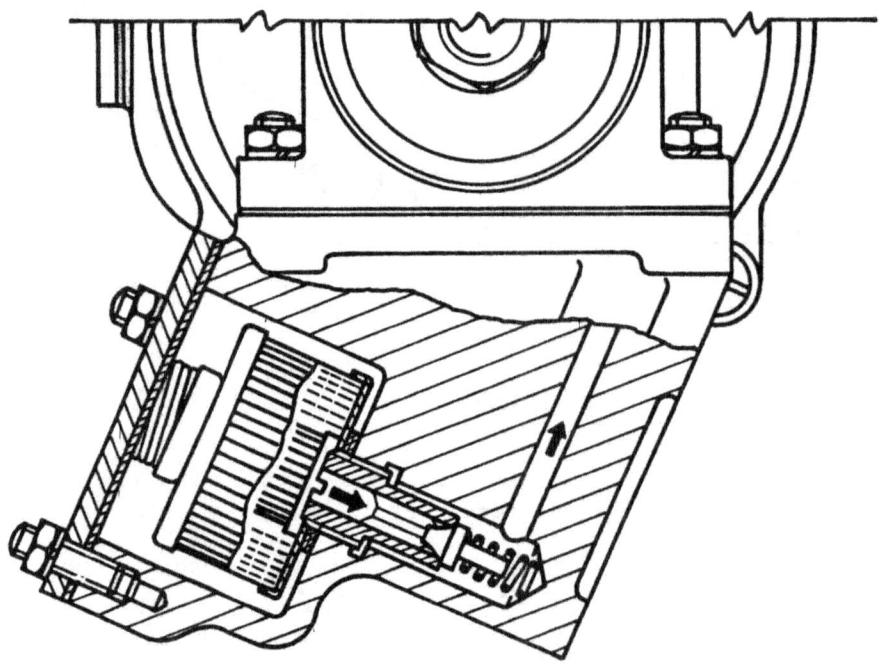

Fig. 8 - INJECTION PUMP OIL FILTER ARRANGEMENT

C 12 CHECKING THE POSITIONING OF THROTTLE-CONTROL UNIT LINKAGE

Proceed as follows:

Disconnect the push-pull rods (5) and (6) (see fig. 10), the cable from the relay crank sheave and the battery negative terminal.

Fit tool A.4.0121 to cable clamps studs (see fig.11), then adjust idle stop screw until ball joint just touches reference plane of tool and lock in position.

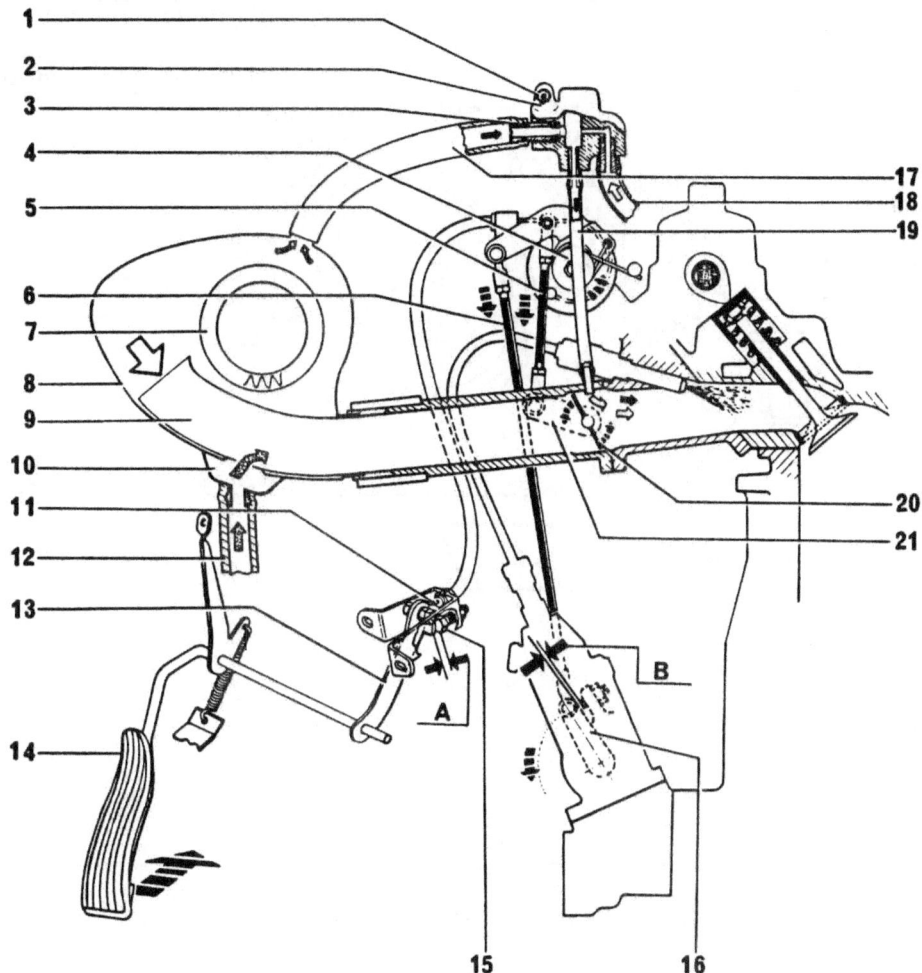

Fig. 9 - THROTTLE-CONTROL UNIT LINKAGE ADJUSTMENT

1 Lockscrew
2 Idle air adjuster and equalizer
3 Adjuster
4 Relay crank
5 Relay crank-to-throttle rod
6 Relay crank-to-control unit rod
7 Filter element
8 Filter housing
9 Intake duct
10 Manifold gallery
11 Throttle cable
12 Main crankcase ventilating system hose
13 Accelerator arm
14 Accelerator pedal
15 Limit screw
16 Control unit lever
17 Idle air supply pipe
18 Secondary crankcase ventilating system hose
19 Idle air hose
20 Throttles
21 Throttle lever

Also adjust the full throttle stop screw in the same manner. Now, remove tool and refit throttle cable. Apply grease to cable and pulley.

Check that clearance (see "A" fig. 10) between accelerator arm (13) and limit screw is .040 - .060" as pressure is applied to the pedal while the relay crank is prevented from rotating. Adjust screw if necessary.

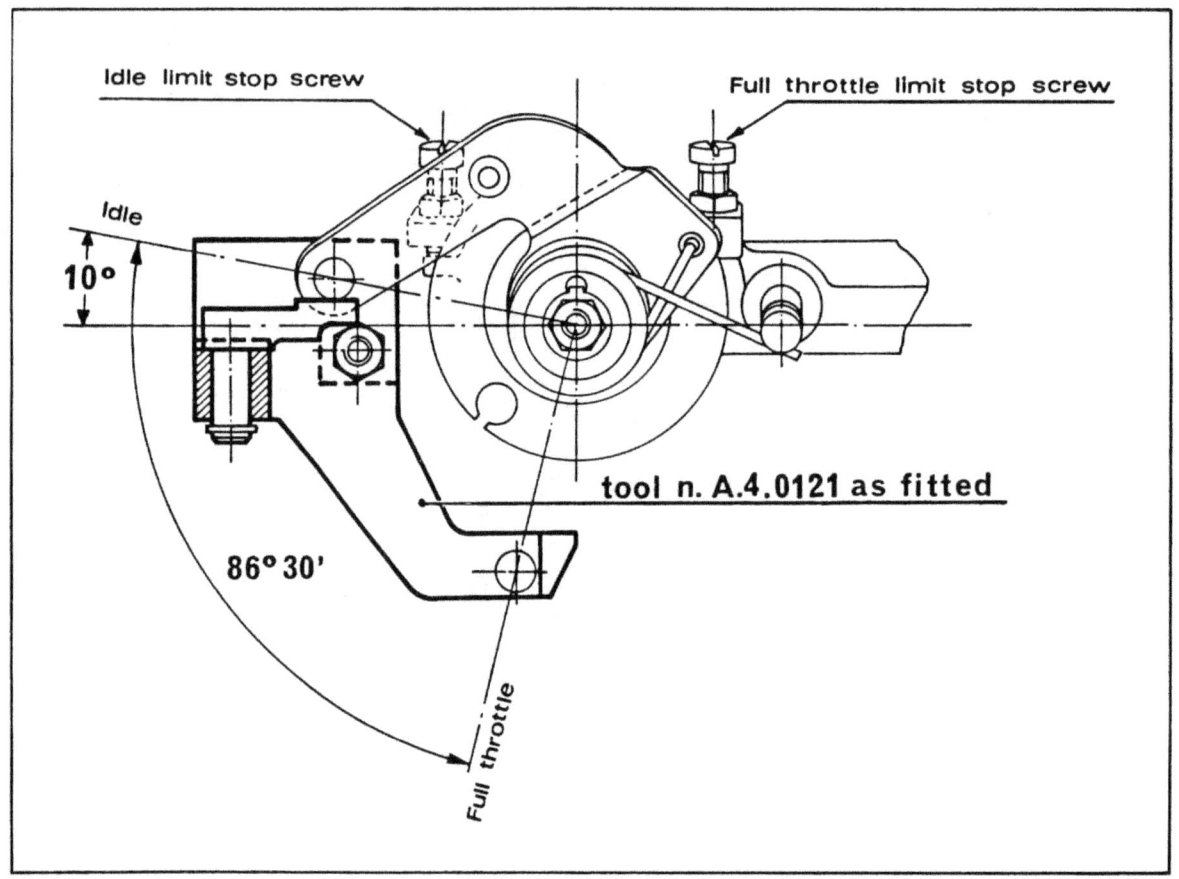

Fig. 10 - POSITIONING OF RELAY CRANK

Depress the accelerator pedal to the floor and check that the clearance between the relay crank lug and full throttle limit stop screw is .080". Adjust the pedal stop screw on floor as required.

Reconnect relay crank-to-throttle rod (5) (see fig. 10) and adjust its length so that throttle are just closed when the relay crank is resting on the idle limit stop screw. "Just closed" can be verified by opening and closing the throttles by hand with the relay crank very slowly. The throttle plates will be felt touching their bores as they close.

When the relay crank is opened slightly and allowed to close under its return spring pressure there will be a click as the crank hits the limit stop screw.

Reconnect the relay crank-to-control unit rod (6), the battery cable start the engine and warm it up to 77°C (170°F).

Check that clearance (free travel, see "B" fig.10) between control unit arm and its reference screw is 0.3 - 0.6 mm (.012 - .024") (the closer to 0.5 mm .019" the better).

WARNING: Never tamper with the sealed reference screw on control unit.

Adjust the length of the rod as required. Twisting the rod ends up to 30° off a common plane is permitted to obtain desired clearance.

C 13 CHECKING THE POSITIONING AND ALIGNMENT OF THROTTLES

To perform this check, the air cleaner body and hoses shall be removed from the engine and the four adapters of tool no.C.2.0012 connected to the idle fittings on the throttle valve throats after having removed the four idle pipes from the fittings; the other end of these adapters shall be connected to the four columns of mercury gage (tool no. C.2.0014) (see fig. 12).

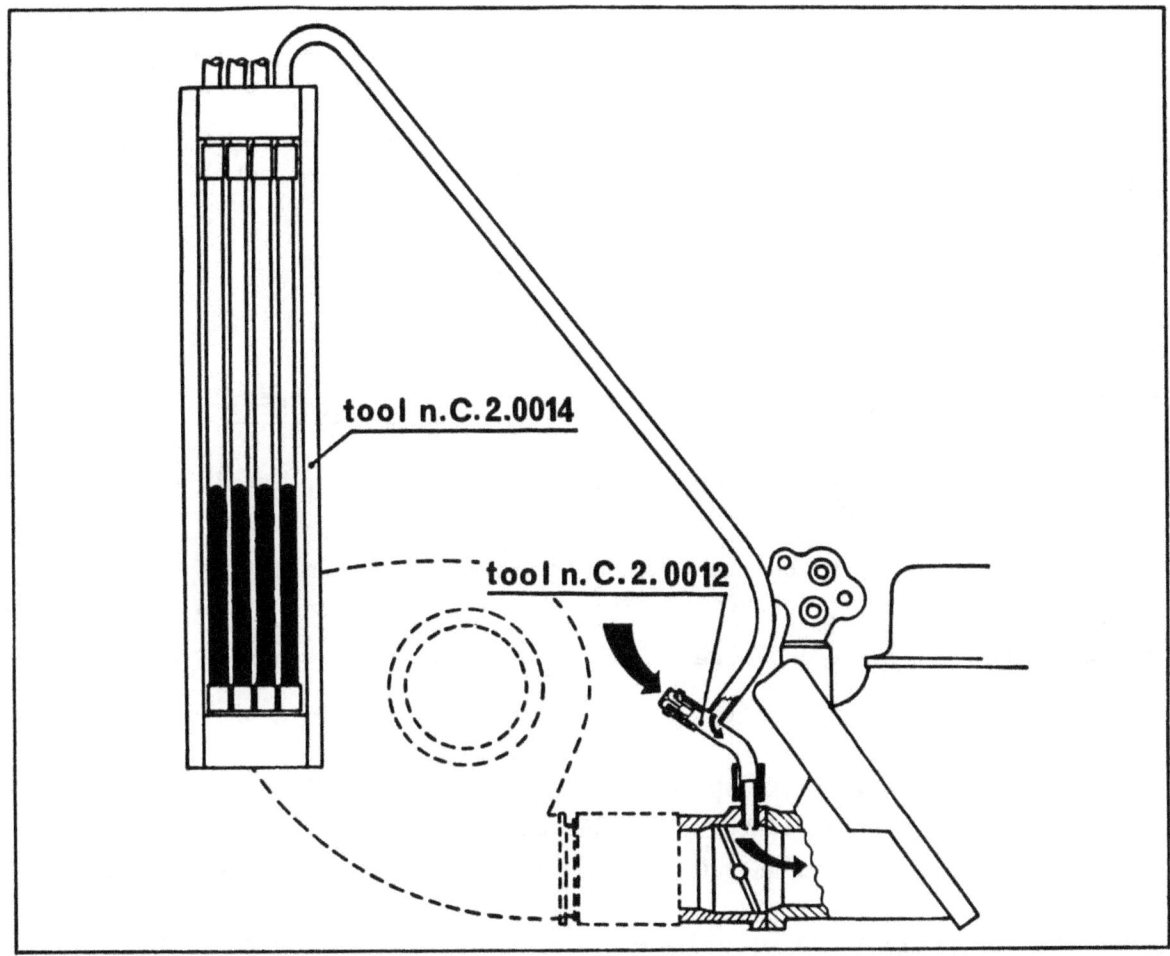

Fig. 11 - THROTTLES ALIGNMENT CHECKING

Start the engine and warm it up until the coolant temperature is at least 70° C (158°F); first check that the clearance between control unit lever and its reference screw is .012 to .024" (the closer to .019" the better) with hot engine and thermostat actuator fitted.

Now, check that readings on mercury gage columns are much the same (maximum difference: 10 mm - .4"); if this is not the case, proceed as follows:

- if readings show that vacuum in front pair of cylinders is higher than in the rear, unscrew the throttle coupling adjusting screw so as to close the rear pair of throttles;

- if vacuum in front pair of cylinders is lower than that in rear pair, disconnect the relay crank-to-throttle rod and set the throttle coupling adjusting screw in such a way as to close the front pair of throttles (screw in the adjusting screw); then, reconnect the relay crank-to-throttle rod and adjust its length so that the throttle valves are in the "just closed" condition as outlined in the paragraph: "Check the positioning of throttle/control unit linkage".

If, before commencing the above adjustments, the engine would run unevenly (lean mixture), make sure the throttle valves are in the "just closed" position; if not the relay crank-to-throttle rod must be shortened.

CAUTION: avoid sudden revving up of the engine or too great a vacuum could take place and the mercury might be sucked out of gage columns.

Disconnect adapters and install air cleaner, crankcase ventilation tube, four idle air tubes, fuel vapor tube and air cleaner-to-equalizer tube.

C 14   IDLE ADJUSTMENT - MIXTURE AND EXHAUST EMISSIONS ADJUSTMENT

To insure control of exhaust emissions and proper driveability it is necessary to adjust the idle and operating mixture correctly.

To obtain proper Carbon Monoxide (CO) percentage and HC emissions at idle, the operating mixture must be properly set.

Operating mixture can only be set with a road test or on a chassis dyno.

For this reason the steps to follow in adjusting idle and mixture are three.

- First   the idle speed is roughly set
- Second   the operating mixture is adjusted
- Third   the idle speed and CO are set accurately, HC emissions are checked

NOTE: On cars where it is known that the operating mixture is correct the second step can be eliminated.

FIRST STEP

Preliminary idle adjustment

The adjustment procedure is as follows:

Warm the engine up to 77° C (170° F).

Remove the air cleaner-to-equalizer block hose and loosen adjuster lock screw. (1).

Connect accurate electronic tachometer. Act on the adjuster (2) until the engine is idling at as fast a speed as possible, yet with no roughness or hunting (in any case not slower than 600 rpm).

Note: Screw in adjuster to reduce speed; screw out adjuster to increase speed; use tool A.2.0183.

Tighten lock screw (1) and replace hose.

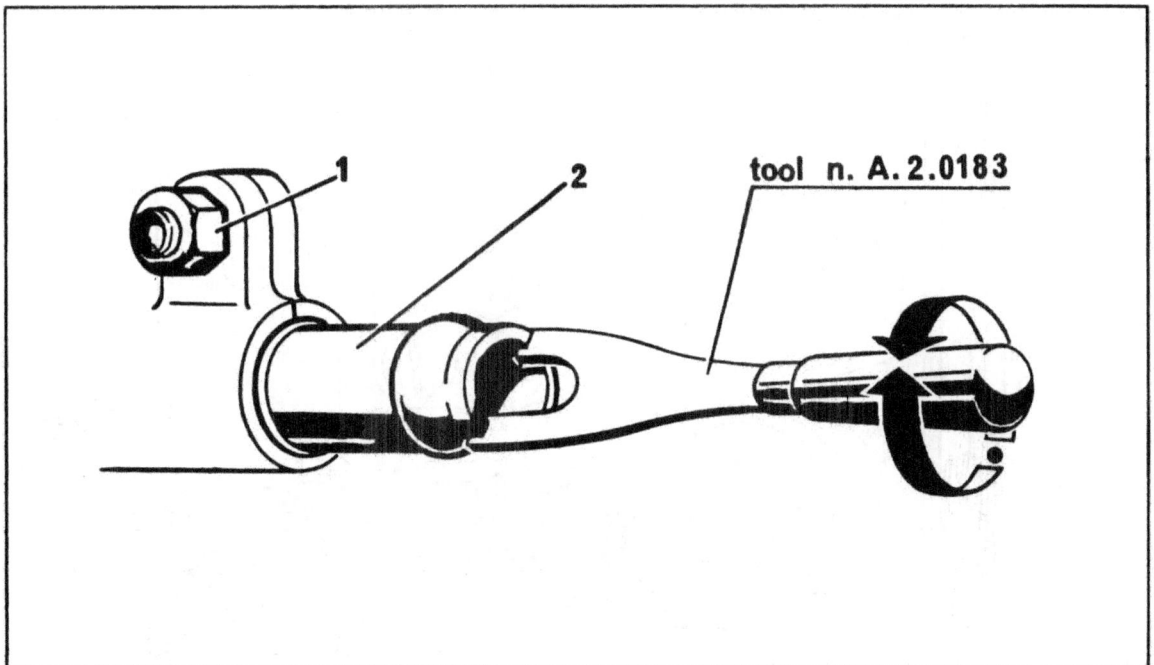

Fig. 12 - IDLE AIR ADJUSTMENT

SECOND STEP

Road test and operating mixture adjustment

With engine at operating temperature drive the car hard for a few miles using high revs and low gears to burn off any deposits from the spark plugs.

Drive the car at a constant speeds of 20-25-30 MPH in third gear and accelerate very slowly to 40-45 MPH. If any hesitation is felt the mixture is too lean and the fuel cut off solenoid must be unscrewed to obtain a richer mixture.

If, instead, during the road test the acceleration is sluggish and the car shows other signs of an over rich mixture such as dirty spark plugs or poor mileage, then the cutoff solenoid must be screwed in until a lean condition is experienced. Then proceed to screw out the solenoid only until the lean hesitation disappears.

Adjusting the fuel mixture

Looking down at the top of the fuel cut-off solenoid there are 8 notches around the top edge.

Fig. 13 - MIXTURE ADJUSTMENT

Mark one of the notches with respect to a fixed point on the control unit housing for a reference.

Disconnect the solenoid feed wire.

Loosen the ring nut at bottom of solenoid (tool A.5.0177) taking care not to rotate the solenoid.

Move the solenoid only one notch (1/8 of a turn), in or out, depending on whether mixture is rich or lean.

Retighten ring nut and connect feed wire. Check reference marks to insure that solenoid has been moved one notch.

Install air cleaner, idle air tubes, crankcase breather tubes, air inlet and road test.

THIRD STEP

Idle speed and CO adjustment, HC emission checking

This operation must be done with an accurate electronic tachometer with engine at normal operating temperature immediately after the road test.

The readings of values of carbon monoxide (CO) and unburned hydro-carbons (HC) at the exhaust must be taken exclusively with NDIR instrumentation.

Following manufacturer's instructions install and calibrate the NDIR analyzer; attach the tachometer.

> Idle speed must not be lower than 600 RPM (it is recommended not to exceed 700 RPM

> CO percentage must be 0,4 to 1,2%

If adjustments are necessary remove the air cleaner-to-equalizer block hose, loosen the adjuster lock screw (1) (see fig. 13) and adjust the equalizer adjuster accordingly:

  screw in to decrease RPM and increase CO

  screw out to increase RPM and decrease CO

Tighten lock screw and replace hose

> Check idle HC emissions that must not exceed 300 ppm.

N.B.: Should higher levels of HC emissions be experienced after having performed the idle adjustment as above directed, the cause may be found in an improperly operating ignition system component (spark plugs, breaker points, condenser, terminals, etc.) or in the formation of deposits in the combustion chambers (particularly those fouling the spark plugs).

To burn off such deposits, drive the car hard for a few miles using high revs and low gears.

C 15 CHECKING THE INJECTION PUMP TIMING

To check the injection pump timing, proceed as follows:

- unscrew the attaching nuts and remove the pump drive belt cover;

- turn the crankshaft over (by shifting into a top gear and pushing the car slowly) and inspect the belt throughout its length for sound conditions;

- turn the crankshaft over again so as to bring the reference mark I in line with the pointer; remove the spark plug from cylinder no.1 and check that the exhaust valve is still open (if closed, turn the crankshaft over by one more revolution);

- check that the reference mark on the splined pulley and the pointer on the pump body are aligned.

NOTE: reference mark and pointer can be out of alignment within a tolerance of about ± 5 mm (0.2") corresponding to half pitch of the pulley splines.

I = mark on pulley 70° BTDC of the induction stroke

If the pump is out of timing:

- take the drive belt off the pump pulley

- line up the reference marks of the injection pump and refit the drive belt by rotating the pulley in either direction to engage the nearest spline.

On completion of the timing procedure, re-install the drive belt cover.

C 16 CHECKING THE AIR INTAKE TEMPERATURE CONTROL SYSTEM

DAMPER DOOR

Remove the vacuum hose from the diaphragm motor connector and apply a separate hose from a vacuum source of about 9 in. Hg. The door should easily open and fully close off the cold air passage. If the valve momentarily opens and then starts to close, vacuum leaks are likely. Replace if necessary.

THERMAL SENSOR

Disconnect from the thermal sensor the hose to the inlet manifold and apply a separate hose from a vacuum source of about 9 in. Hg. The valve should open and maintain a fully open position. If the valve fails to open check the damper door as shown above, and if the diaphragm operates correctly, a failure of the sensor is likely.

CHECKING THE PUMP

Disconnect from the non return valve the hose to the air pump. Start engine and check for air delivery from the pump. If the pump supplies no air, it should be replaced.

CHECKING THE NON RETURN-VALVE

Disconnect from the valve the hose to the air pump. Unscrew the valve from the air manifold and orally blow through the same valve from each side. Air should only pass from air pump side to air manifold side. Replace if necessary.

CHECKING THE INJECTOR NOZZLES

Unscrew the nuts attaching the four injector pipe to the exhaust manifold. Start engine and check for air delivery from all tubes. Remove obstructions if necessary.

CLEANING AND REPLACING THE AIR FILTER ELEMENT

Unscrew the nut securing the cover to the cleaner housing. Remove the filter element and get rid of foreign matter that may have collected in the housing.

Clean the element and refit it inside the filter. Perform this operation every 5,000 miles. Replace the element with a new one every 15,000 miles.

To prevent dust particles from falling into the hose it is advisable when cleaning the inside of the housing, to remove the whole filter after loosening the clamps securing it to the body.

D INJECTION PUMP REPAIRS

Only the following repairs are permitted. For any other work the injection pump must be repaired by Alfa Romeo, Inc.

D 1 REMOVAL OF THE INJECTION PUMP

On Alfetta Berlina and GT remove the air pump prior to proceed as follows.

After having removed the air cleaner (see relevant directions) perform the following steps:

- disconnect the negative battery terminal;

- disconnect the lead from cold starting device solenoid and the loose junction on the wire feeding the microswitch of fuel cut-off solenoid;

- remove the two screws on the thermostat actuator mounting flange and the two screws clamping the actuator pipe anchoring grommet (do not remove the thermostat bulb); then withdraw the actuator from the control unit, taking care not to distort excessively the pipe;

- disconnect the fuel hoses from injection pump;

- detach the push-pull rod from the control unit.

Proceed by timing the injection pump with the engine (instant in which fuel injection starts); to do this, bring the no. 1 piston at 70°BTDC of the induction stroke by aligning the mark "I" cut in the crankshaft pulley with the pointer on crankcase front cover (doing so will facilitate the reinstallation on the injection pump to the engine).

Finally, unscrew the three attaching nuts and remove the drive belt cover (Spider only); then take the drive belt off the injection pump pulley.

Now, perform the removal of the injection pump proper as follows:

- fully slacken the injection pipe nuts on pump outlet fittings (use the wrench tool no. A.5.0164), without removing the pipes;

- unscrew the nuts on the two bolts attaching the pipe cluster plate and the injection pump slanting bracket;

- loosen the two screws attaching the control unit to its bracket at the engine mount;

- unscrew, from the underside of car, the four nuts (use tool A.5.0167 for the front ones) attaching the injection pump support to the engine front cover.

Withdraw the injection pump and its support as a unit by tilting it suitably.

D 2 REINSTALLATION OF THE INJECTION PUMP

To reinstall the injection pump, reverse the removal procedure.

The tightening torque of the injection pipe fittings is abt. 2,5 kgm (18 lb-ft). After re-tightening, check for leaks.

In case of injection pump renewal, the new injectors, supplied with the new pump, must be installed on the engine in place of the old ones. The new injectors bring a location number and must be installed accordingly.

The tightening torque of the injectors is 2,8 to 3,2 kgm (20.2-23.1 lb-ft).

Make sure the pump base-to-engine block gasket and O-ring are in place.

CAUTION: Owing to the special construction of the injection pump, the pump plungers must on no account be operated directly with a lever or any other tool.

If, for any reason, the crankshaft has been rotated or the injection pump drive belt needs replacement, follow this procedure to time the injection pump and reinstall the drive belt:

- Turn the crankshaft over (by shifting into fourth and pushing the car either forward or backward) so as to bring the no.1 piston to the T.D.C.; remove the spark plug from cylinder no. 1 to check that both valves, intake and exhaust, are in the open position (overlap stage). (If the valves are closed, turn the crankshaft over by one more revolution).

In this condition, the mark P on the crankshaft pulley shall line up with the pointer.

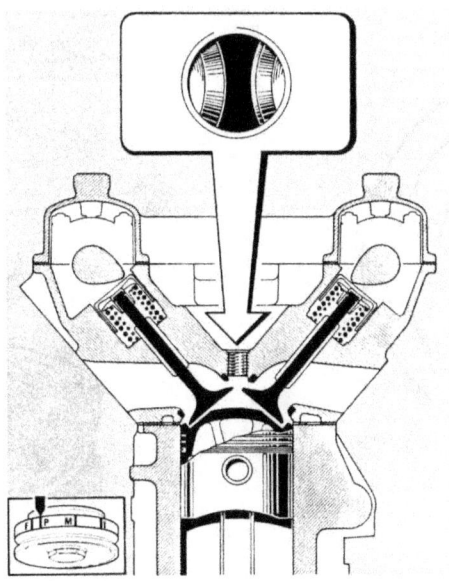

- Push the car slowly backward so as to rotate the crankshaft counterclockwise by 70 degrees, i.e. in such a way that mark I on crankshaft pulley and pointer line up.

    N.B.: Should the injection pump drive belt need replacement, loosen the bolt 1 and the nuts 2, move alternator toward the crankcase and take the alternator drive belt off. Replace the injection pump drive belt with a new one; to install the new drive belt, first mount it onto the crankshaft splined pulley.

- Then, rotate the injection pump splined pulley by hand to align the reference mark on the pulley with the pointer on pump body and mount the toothed belt onto the pump pulley; slightly turn the pulley in either direction to engage the nearest spline.

    N.B.: Reference mark and pointer can be out of alignment within a tolerance of about ± 5 mm (0.2") corresponding to half pitch of splines.

Refit:

- The spark plug.

- The alternator drive belt, if previously removed (and adjust tension).

- The pump drive belt cover.

- The air pump (for Alfetta Berlina and GT)

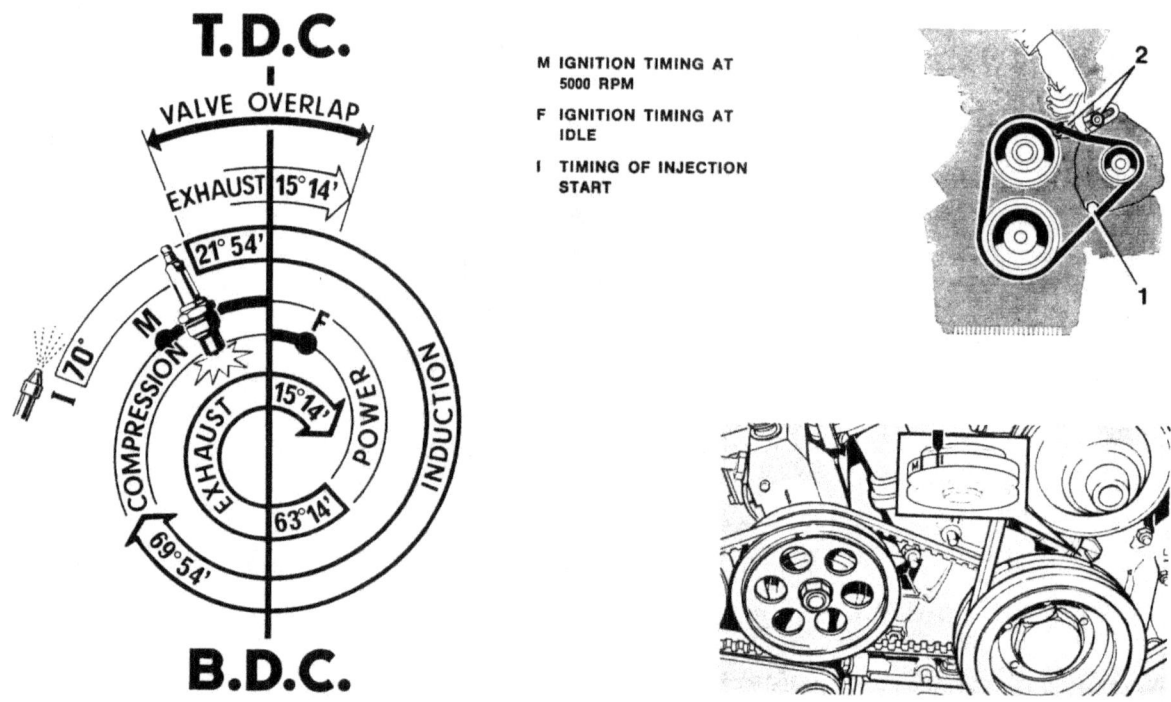

M IGNITION TIMING AT 5000 RPM

F IGNITION TIMING AT IDLE

I TIMING OF INJECTION START

After refitting, road test the car, adjust idle and test CO and HC emissions.

D 3 REPLACEMENT OF THERMOSTATIC ACTUATOR

1 - Remove air filter assembly
2 - Drain about one gallon of coolant from radiator
3 - Remove thermostatic actuator
4 - Disconnect the long rod from the control unit lever
5 - Install <u>27,8 mm</u> dummy thermostatic (A.4.0166)
6 - Check that the clearance between the control unit lever and its reference screw is

0,5 mm (.020")

If the clearance is <u>not</u> within this specification, the screw beneath the actuator, has been tampered with!

To recalibrate this setting see next paragraph. If the clearance is as required, proceed on to step 8 directly.

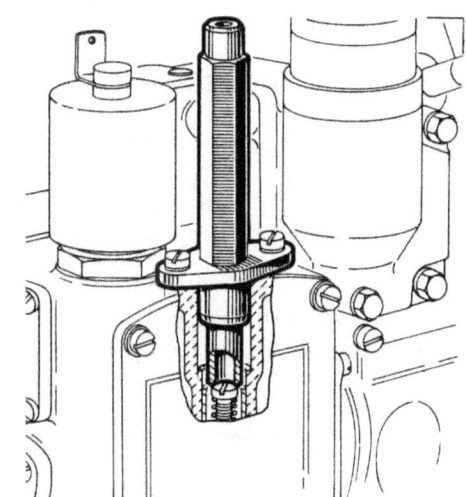

7 - If the calibration screw is to be reset to correct for tampering, do it only in this manner:

   a) if the tool (A.4.0166) is solid, remove it. If it has a hole, insert a small screwdriver and turn the calibration screw to obtain the 0,5 mm (.020") clearance at the control unit lever.

   If the dummy is solid, it must be reinstalled after each adjustment on the calibration screw until the specified clearance is obtained.

   b) Recheck the clearance and proceed to step 8.

8 - Remove dummy 27,8 mm actuator.

9 - Check the protrusion of the pin on the new actuator (or to check old actuators). The dimension from the end of the pin to the mounting flange surface should be 23 ± 1 mm tolerance. This measurement <u>must only be done after the actuator has stabilized</u> at a temperature of 20°C (68°F) for at least 15 minutes.

10 - Install new actuator, using new o'ring at inlet manifold (bulb end).

11 - Connect long link rod at control unit lever.

12 - Start engine and warm it until it reaches normal operating temperature. This is important! 80°C (176°F).

13 - Check the clearance between the reference screw and the control unit lever. It should be <u>0,3 + 0,6 mm (.012" - .024")</u> (the closer to 0,5 mm (.019") the better). If it is not, the clearance is achieved by adjusting the length of the long link rod. Minor rod length changes can be obtained by turning only the upper and lower ball joint rod ends. These ends can be turned up to 30° from their common place.

14 - Refir air cleaner.

D 4 REPLACING THE FUEL CUT OFF SOLENOID

To renew the solenoid, proceed as follows:

Remove the air cleaner.

Disconnect the terminal of solenoid feed wire.

Keep a record of the projection "A" of solenoid body from the ring nut top.

Slacken the ring nut with the special tool no. A.5.0177 taking care not to cock the solenoid.

Unscrew the solenoid by hand and take it away.

Test the solenoid by energizing it with a 12 Volt D.C. supply.

When energized, the solenoid plunger must protrude by 4,9 to 5,2 mm (.193 - .205"); when the solenoid is de-energized, the plunger must back up fully with no sluggishness.

Repeat the test several times, each time rotating the plunger to make certain it moves freely in any position.

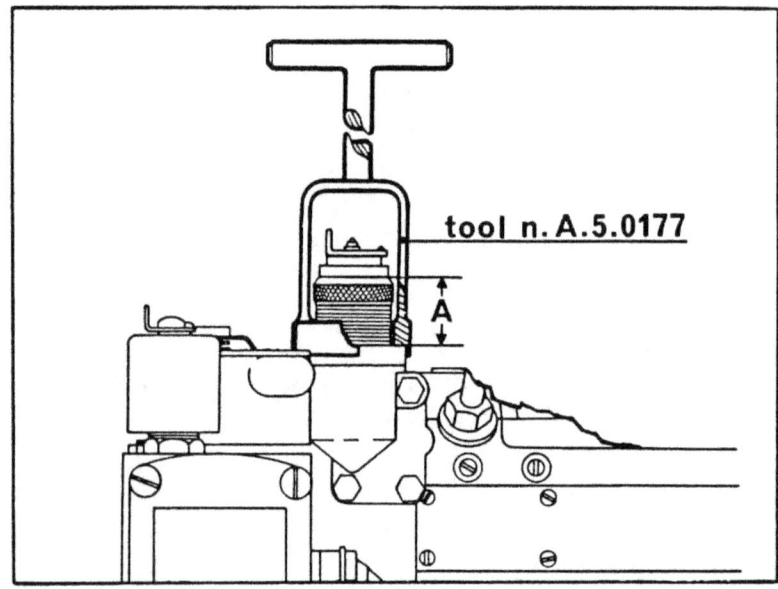

1 - If the solenoid is operating properly, screw it in again to the projection previously recorded (tighten the ring nut before checking for correct dimension "A").

2 - If the solenoid is not operating properly, change it with a new one and screw it in until projection "A" (ring nut tightened) is 25,4 mm (1 inch).

- Reconnect the feed wire

- Refit the air cleaner

Road test the car to check that driveability is satisfactory:

> 1 - If the solenoid has not been renewed and the driveability is not completely satisfactory, this may be due to a slight misalignment of the solenoid on reinstallation; in this case, merely unscrew the solenoid by one eighth of a turn (one reference notch as suitably provided).
>
> 2 - If the solenoid has been renewed and the driveability is not satisfactory, unscrew the solenoid by one notch at a time until the appropriate carburation is obtained.
>
> 3 - If the solenoid has been renewed and if the driveability is satisfactory, screw in the solenoid by one notch at a time until slight hesitations take place: at this point unscrew the solenoid by one notch so as to put it back into the next former setting giving good driveability.

CAUTION: When tightening or slackening the ring nut, take care not to rotate the solenoid or it will go out of correct setting.

Reset idle speed and CO as described in C 14/3.

D 5 REPLACEMENT OF COLD START SOLENOID AND PLUNGER REMOVAL

Removal

Remove the injection pump as described in D1. Remove the side and rear inspection plates from the control unit. Then remove the cotter key (3) and the clevis pin (4) attaching the solenoid to the plunger shaft (5). Measure the distance "H" from bottom of solenoid to control unit.

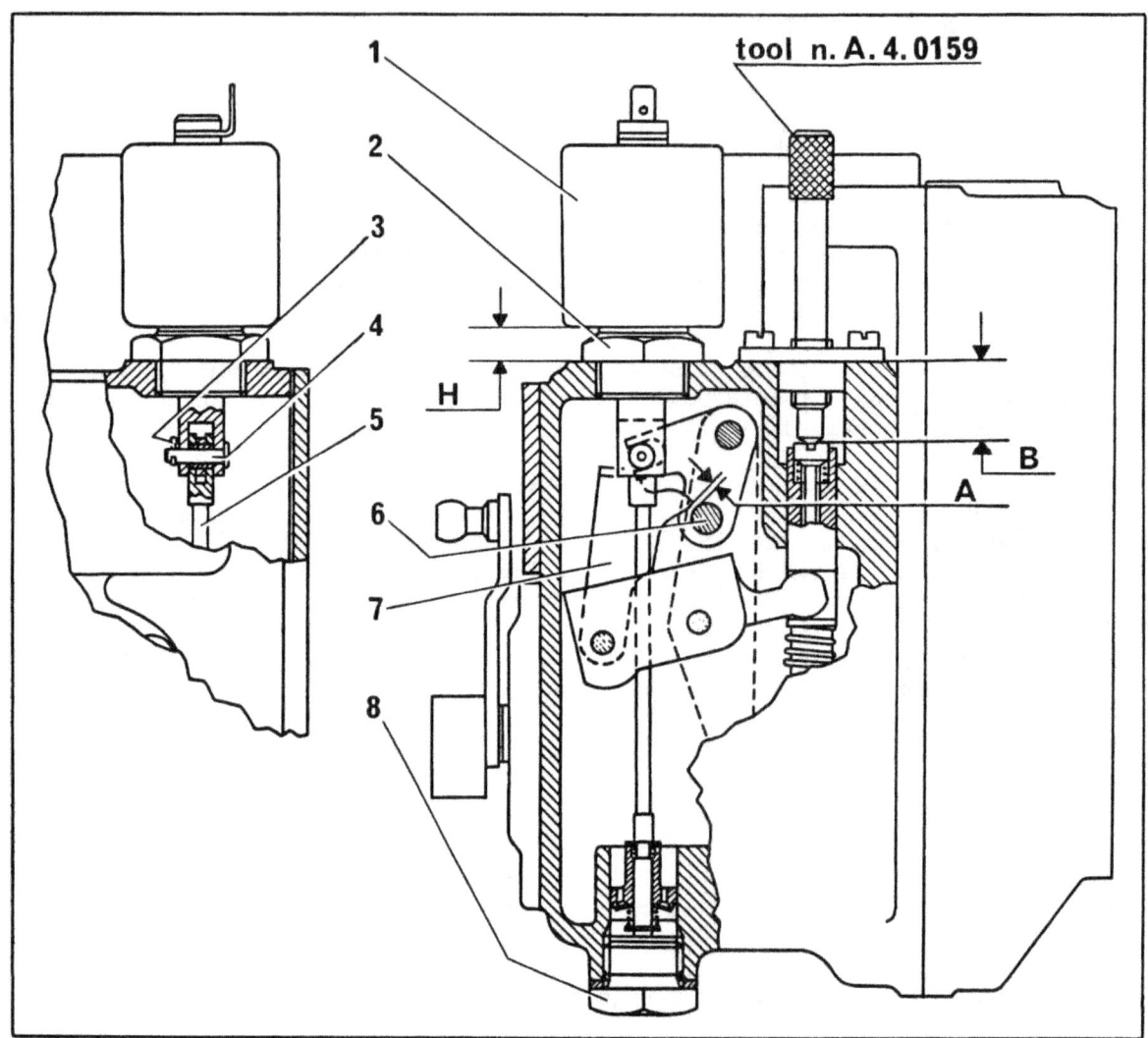

Fig. 16 - COLD START DEVICE AND ITS PLUNGER

Loosen the solenoid lock nut (2) and unscrew the solenoid (1). Then check that the plunger shaft (5) moves up and down freely.

Note: If it is necessary to remove the plunger shaft (5), unscrew the plug (8) from underneath and withdraw the plunger shaft.

Check that the diameter of plastic plunger is 13,55 mm (.5335"). Replace the plunger or reduce its diameter if required.

Installation

The height of the cold start solenoid above the control unit housing governs the operation of the cold start device. It is essential that it be carefully adjusted or serious damage may occur to the control unit.

Fit the plunger shaft (5) and the plug (8) in reverse order of removal.

Install the solenoid (1) and lock the nut (2) to same solenoid height "H" as previously measured.

Connect the plunger shaft (5) to the solenoid with the clevis pin (4). Then install the cotter key (3).

To adjust solenoid height "B" a 19 mm (.7490") dummy thermostat (tool no. A.4.0159) has to be installed.

Measure the clearance "A" between the pin (6) on the lever actuated by the solenoid and the arm (7) which it actuates. Refer to the figures. Clearance must be A = 1,15 to 1,25 mm (.045" - .049"). Screw the solenoid out to decrease the clearance and screw in to increase clearance.

Tighten solenoid lock nut (2) and install inspection plates.

Assemble pump to engine as described in D 1.

D 6 TESTING THE INJECTORS

Since the operating conditions of the injectors are not so heavy (being located in the air intake ports and therefore not subject to the high pressures and temperatures of the combustion chamber) and since the life of the injectors is expected to be the same as that of the car, they should undergo a test only when the cause for malfunctions is unquestionably attributed to the injectors themselves.

To test the injectors use a handpump like that for testing Diesel injectors but supplied with gasoline and provided with a pressure gage whose top dial reading is 50 to 70 kg/cm^2 (700 - 1000 psi).

The procedure for checking the spray shape, injection pressure and leaks is as follows:

- connect the test pump pipe to the injector inlet fitting which has a 12 w 1,5 mm metric thread;

- pump quickly to prime pump and injector;

- pump slowly until injector nozzle opens; this must take place at 25 to 28 kg/cm^2 (360-400 psi) for new injectors and at no less than 18 kg/cm^2 (260 psi) for used injectors;

- again pumping slowly, bring the pressure to 1 to 2 kg/cm^2 (15 - 30 psi) below the rating pressure taken as directed above and make sure that there is no drip from the nozzle within five seconds;

- pump quickly and check that the spray is narrow, deeply plunging and has good vaporization even at minimum delivery. At a distance of 100 mm (4") from the nozzle orifice the spray cone diameter should be about 20 mm (.8"). If the injector does not meet these requirements, replace it with a new one;

- the injectors must be tightened in place with a torque of 2,8 to 3,2 kgm (20.2 - 23.1 lb-ft).

N.B. - To remove the injectors use the wrench tool no. A.5.0165.

D 7 REPLACING THE ALTITUDE COMPENSATOR (in-car)

Proper adjustment of the barometric capsule is critical for proper operation of the pump.

In order to make the adjustment you must have an accurate barometer in your shop which has been set to compensate for your elevation above sea level. Your barometer will have directions for doing this and it is essential that they are followed.

Proceed as detailed below after having removed in this sequence:

- The air cleaner;
- The relay crank-control unit rod;
- The rear inspection cover from the control unit;
- The altitude compensator with its mounting flange.

CAUTION: Do not move the control unit input lever (even better tape it in place) nor disturb the inside devices of control unit or serious damage and out-of-adjustment may result.

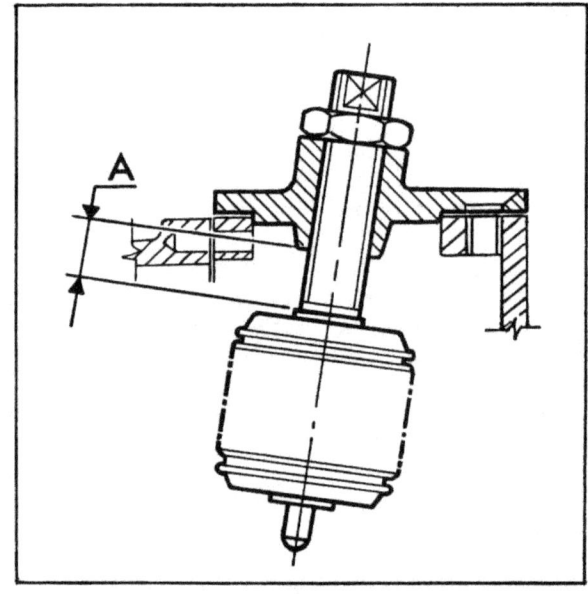

Measure the dimension "A" (see fig.18) between the mounting flange face on which the spring rests and the top of bellows: such a dimension should fall between 9,5 to 10,5 mm (.374" - .413").

Loosen the locknut and unscrew the capsule.

Screw in the new capsule until the dimension previously taken is obtained; then slightly tighten the locknut.

Fig. 17 - ALTITUDE COMPENSATOR

NOTE: If, because of any reason, the dimension "A" does not fall within the specified limits, screw in the new capsule to a dimension of 9,5 mm (.37") irrespective of the dimension previously read.

Install capsule and mounting flange assembly on the control unit.

Refit the rear inspection cover and the rod.

Start the engine and warm it up until the coolant has reached a temperature of no less than 70° C (158°F) then race the engine a few times up to 4,000 rpm and fully release the throttle pedal each time.

Stop the engine, again remove the rear inspection cover and (with the aid of a suitable mirror and a lamp to light the inside of control unit) see whether the wire at the end of link engages the notch corresponding to the actual atmospheric pressure as listed below (notches to be counted starting from the top of the notched lever):

- atmospheric pressure falling between 29.9 - 30.7 in Kg: the wire should engage the 7th notch;

- pressure falling between 29.1 - 29.9 in Hg: the wire should engage the 8th notch;

- pressure between 28.3 - 29.1 in Hg: the wire should engage the 9th notch;

- pressure between 27.6 - 28.3 in Hg: the wire should engage the 10th notch.

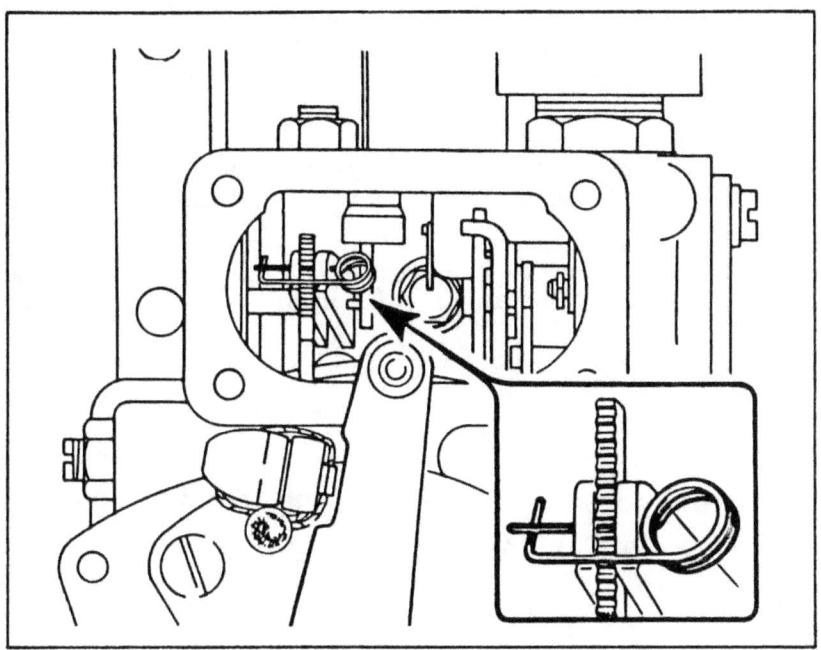

Fig. 18 - ENGAGING WIRE AND NOTCHED LEVER

If the above conditions are not fulfilled, adjust the position of the capsule so that, when the engine is started again (before that refit the rear inspection cover on control unit) and the warming up procedure (racing the engine followed by a complete release of accelerator) is repeated, the wire positions itself correctly: screw in the capsule to cause the wire to engage notches of higher numbers and unscrew the capsule to engage notches of lower numbers. Keep in mind that a rotation of about 150 degrees corresponds to one notch.

Tighten securely the locknut on the capsule and reinstall the air cleaner.

D 8 CHECK THE RELATIONSHIP BETWEEN THROTTLE ANGLES AND CONTROL UNIT LEVER ANGLES

Perform this check when the engine is cold; the air cleaner must then be removed from engine (see under "Replace the air cleaner elements"), the procedure for disconnecting the rods (5) and (6) (see fig.10) must be repeated as well as the removal of thermostatic actuator (taking care not to distort excessively the small pipe).

At this point check the positioning of linkage at idle and full throttle setting with the special tool no.A.4.0121 and fit the dummy actuator, tool no. A.4.0120. Reconnect the rod and check for a clearance "A" of .012 to .024" (the closer to .019" the better) between the control unit lever and its reference screw (if necessary, adjust the rod length by acting on the threaded clevis).

```
                            W A R N I N G
        NEVER TAMPER WITH THE CONTROL UNIT, IT IS PROHIBITED BY LAW
```

Fit the fixed protractor tool no. C.6.0140 onto rear and of control unit, using the cover attaching screws, and the pointer tool no. C.6.0141 aligned with the zero on the scale (see fig.20); to take readings use the suitable built-in light mirror.

Reconnect the rod (5) and check for a proper closure of throttles as directed under "Check the positioning of throttle/control unit linkage".

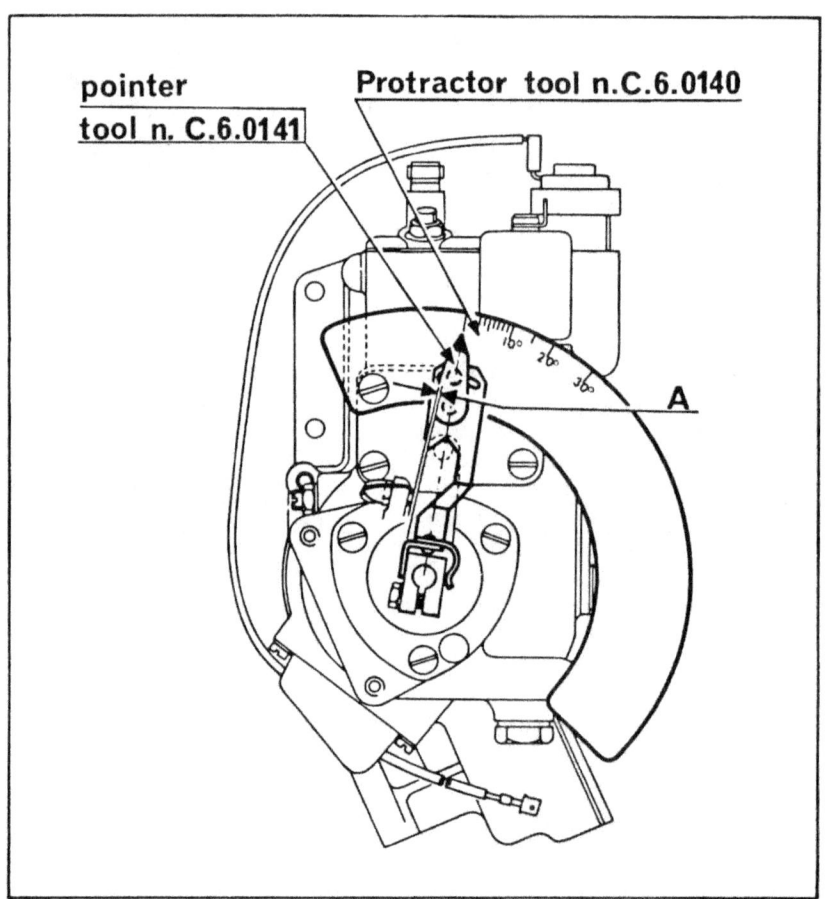

Fig. 19 - CHECKING THE CONTROL UNIT LEVER ANGLE

Place the movable protractor tool no. C.6.0142 on the spindle of rear throttle valve pair and set to zero in correspondence of the pointer tool no. C.6.0143 (see fig. 21).

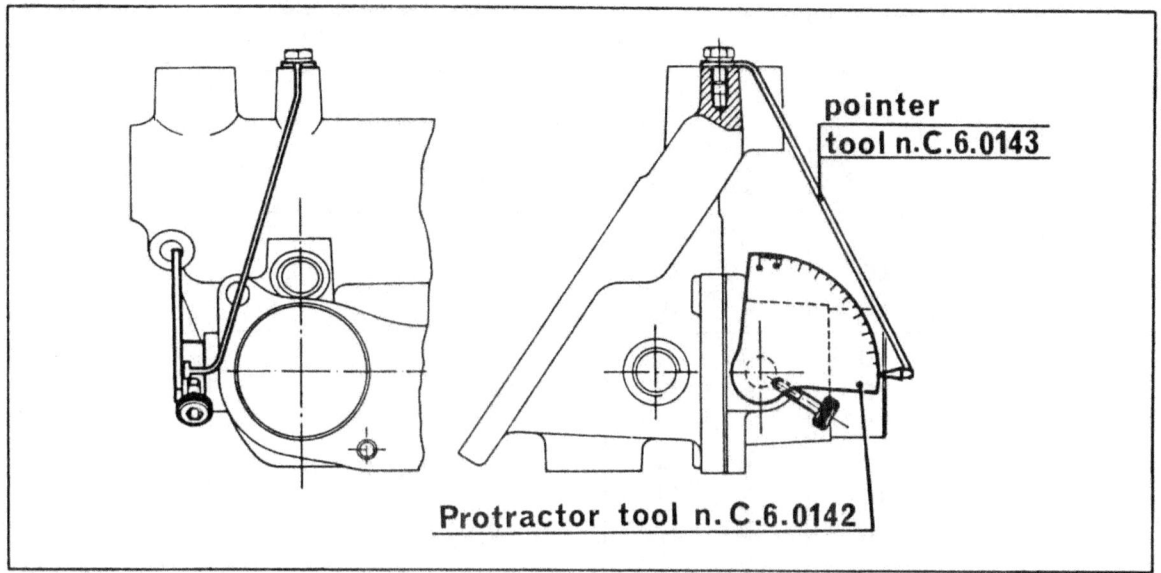

Fig. 20 - CHECKING THE THROTTLE OPENING ANGLES

Install the tool no. A.2.0181 using the cable sheath clips and gradually rotate the relay crank by acting on the adjuster (see fig. 22).

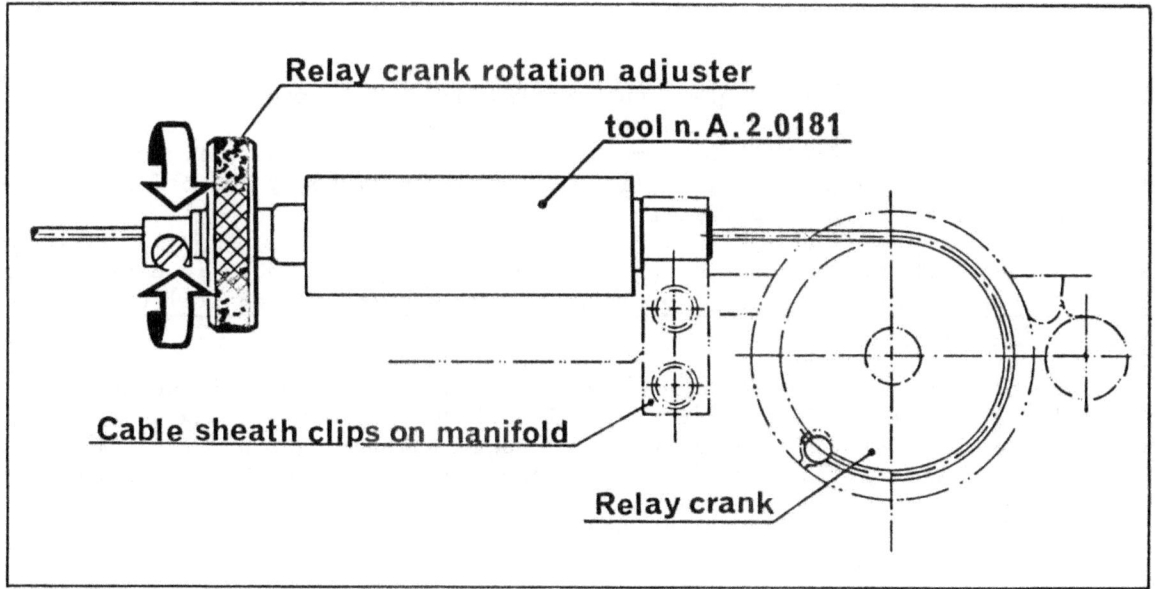

Fig. 21 - ADJUSTING THE RELAY CRANK

Open the throttle valves to predetermined angles (2, 4, 6 degrees - see table) and read the corresponding rotations of control unit lever.

Throttle angles - control unit lever angles relationship table

α	β	Tolerance on β
0°	0°	
2°	8° 13'	± 20'
4°	14° 40'	
6°	20° 09'	
10°	29° 30'	± 1°
15°	39° 20'	
20°	47° 54'	
25°	55° 33'	
30°	62° 30'	
35°	68° 51'	
40°	74° 41'	± 2°
50°	84° 55'	
60°	93° 25'	
70°	100° 12'	
82°	106° 08'	

α = throttle rotation angle

β = control unit lever rotation angle

In the event the throttle angles and control unit lever angles are out of the specified relation, it is likely that checking procedure has not been perfectly accomplished; therefore, try once more; if again it will not satisfy, inspect carefully any component of control linkage, or parts directly affecting it, replace any defective part and repeat the procedure.

When the above checks are over, lengthen the rod (6) until there is a clearance of 0.9 to 1.3 mm (.035 to .051") or 1° to 1° 30' between the control unit lever and the reference screw.

On completion of adjustment, reinstall the standard thermostatic actuator and check for a clearance of .3 to .6 mm (.012 to .024") with a hot engine (coolant temperature above 70°C (158°F) between the control unit lever and its reference screw; if necessary, adjust the length of rod (6) by acting on the clevis thread.

E TROUBLE SHOOTING

The following chart lists several malfunctions, possible cause for each of them and remedies.

If deficiencies or malfunctions are experienced in the fuel system, it is absolutely essential to make sure they are not caused nor affected by the incorrect operation of the ignition system: in fact it is impossible to distinguish "a priori" whether a failure of fuel or ignition system is the cause for the deficiencies; therefore, first inspect the ignition system for the following and remedy, if necessary

- spark plugs for proper operation and type;

- contact-breaker points conditions and gap;

- ignition coil for continuity or leakage;

- ignition distributor for correct timing using a timing light; adjust timing or replace the ignition distributor, if necessary.

Should any of the troubles listed be experienced, it is recommended to clean thoroughly the affected areas of both engine and engine compartment with a suitable solvent; this to the purpose of preventing any foreign matter from entering, on removal or reinstallation, the mechanical components and specifically the fuel feed circuit.

Soon after cleaning, inspect the mechanical units for loose attaching or joining parts, the pipes for loose fittings and the brackets for sound conditions.

E 1 ALFA ROMEO SPICA PUMP POLICY

Injection pumps are not to be opened for any reason. An exchange pump service is available for complete pump units. Pumps that have been tampered with will forfeit any core valve.

Always before removing a pump consult your Alfa Romeo representative or zone office.

E 2 TROUBLE CHART

TROUBLE	POSSIBLE CAUSE	REMEDY
Low fuel pressure warning light does not flash on when ignition key is turned	Fuse no. 7 blown	Replace fuse
	Warning light bulb burnt out	Replace bulb
	Pressure switch faulty (jammed open)	Check switch and replace, if necessary
Low fuel pressure warning light stays on (fuel pump operates properly)	Pressure switch faulty (jammed closed)	Replace switch
	Low fuel pump outlet pressure due to:	
	- tank to pump lines clogged or air seeping thru them	- Inspect fuel lines
	- tank fuel filter clogged	- Replace filter (See C3)
	- main fuel filter clogged	- Clean filter and replace element (see C2)
	- main filter pressure relief valve defective or stuck open	- Check relief valve and replace, if necessary
	Fuel pump delivery too low	Have fuel pump checked or replaced
Low fuel pressure warning light stays on (fuel pump fails to operate)	Fuse no. 8 blown	Replace fuse
	Electric wires to pump disconnected	Check and reconnect
	Fuel pump faulty	Have the pump checked or replaced
Engine will not start from cold	Solenoid-actuated cold start device fails to operate	- check electric connections - have the device checked or replaced
Smoky exhaust after starting	Cold start solenoid plunger stuck	Have the plunger checked (see D5)
Engine misfires; rough idle	One injector defective	Trace the cylinder by grounding each spark plug and replace the injector, if necessary
	Injection pipe fittings leaking	Tighten fittings
	Injection pipes cracked	Check and replace, if necessary

TROUBLE	POSSIBLE CAUSE	REMEDY
Idle too slow but even Idle CO too high (engine runs smoothly)	Too rich a mixture	Adjust idle as directed in C 14
Idle too slow and rough (engine runs unevenly)	One of the hoses connecting idle equalizer to throttle throats is obstructed (by buckling) cracked or disconnected from a fitting	Reconnect or replace the hose, if necessary and adjust idle as directed in C 14
Idle too fast and rough (engine runs unevenly; hunting also takes place)	Too lean a mixture due to air leaking through one of the hoses connecting idle equalizer to throttle throats er even to an idle equalizer improperly adjusted	Check the hoses for sound conditions and leaks and adjust idle as directed in C 14
Idle HC too high	Too rich or too lean a mixture Ignition system not in perfect working order Heavy deposits in combustion chambers and spark plug fouling due to particular driving conditions such as short rides preventing proper warming up	Adjust idle as directed in C 14 Check ignition system With a hot engine, drive the car hard for a few miles using high revolutions and low gears to burn off any deposit
Too fast an idle and smoky exhaust	Faulty thermostatic actuator	Replace thermostatic actuator (see D 3)
Engine keeps running at idle but stops on accelerating	Altitude compensator faulty	Replace altitude compensator (see D 7)
Idle too fast	Accelerator linkage fails to return fully	Check: - flexible cable - linkage joints and pivot pins for free movement - pedal return spring for sound conditions - pedal and linkage limit stop for proper adjustment Clean linkage joints and pack with grease.

TROUBLE	POSSIBLE CAUSE	REMEDY
Unsatisfactory driveability; hesitations	Control linkage out of adjustment	Check throttle/control unit linkage (see C 12)
	Fuel pump outlet pressure too low (warning light comes on while running at high speed)	Check and replace, if necessary, tank fuel filter and/or main filter element
	Injector defective	Refer to remedies as under "Engine misfires; rough idle"
	Injection pump or control unit defective	Have them checked and replaced, if necessary, by an authorized workshop
Unsatisfactory road performance	Control linkage out of adjustment	Check throttle/control unit linkage (see C 12)
	Fuel pump outlet pressure too low (warning light comes on while running at high speed)	Check and replace, if necessary, tank fuel filter and/or main filter element
	Air induction clogged	Check and replace air cleaner elements, if necessary
	Injector defective	Refer to remedies as under "Engine misfires; rough idle"
	Injection pump or control unit/defective (defective carburation)	Have them checked and replaced, if necessary, by an authorized workshop
Excessive fuel consumption	Fuel feed circuit leaks	Check pipes, fittings, seals and replace defective parts
	Thermostatic actuator defective; also refer to causes as under "Too fast an idle"	Have the thermostatic actuator checked and replaced, if necessary, by an authorized workshop (see D 3)
	Defective carburation	Have the injection pump adjusted by an authorized workshop
Engine stalls in positions other than idle	Defective altitude compensator or excessive vibrations of injection pump and control unit	Have the altitude compensator checked (see D 7); also check injection pump and control unit brackets for sound conditions and firm attachment

TROUBLE	POSSIBLE CAUSE	REMEDY
Engine stalls flat	Injection pump driving belt broken	Replace belt (check for proper injection pump timing) (See D 2)
Engine does not slow down to idle on deceleration (fast idle)	Both throttles and control unit lever fail to return fully on deceleration	Check: - flexible cable - linkage joints and pivot pins for free movement - pedal and linkage return springs for sound conditions - pedal and linkage limit stops for proper adjustment - clean linkage joints and pack them with grease suitable for low temperatures
Detonations in the exhaust pipe on deceleration	Fuse no. 8 blown	Replace fuse
	Feed wire disconnected at fuel cut off solenoid	Re-connect wire
	Loose junction of fuel cut off device feed wire disconnected	Re-connect junction
	Defective fuel cut off solenoid	Have the fuel cut off solenoid checked and replaced, if necessary
	Defective fuel cut off device microswitch	Have the fuel cut off device checked by an authorized workshop
Engine stops: - wholly or occasionally on deceleration in neutral - occasionally or wholly when re-accelerating after a deceleration	Fuel cut off solenoid stuck in cut off position or sluggish in backing up	Have the fuel cut off solenoid checked and replaced, if necessary

TROUBLE	POSSIBLE CAUSE	REMEDY
Engine fires again suddenly and with delay when reaccelerating after a deceleration		
Noisy electric fuel pump	Line between pump and main filter distorted or forced in the rubber mounting or against the recovery pipe	Reset the line making certain it is centered in the rubber mountings without forcing against the recovery pipe
	Tank filter and hoses improperly fitted	Check that the filter is properly fitted and that hoses have a correct run

F TOOL LIST

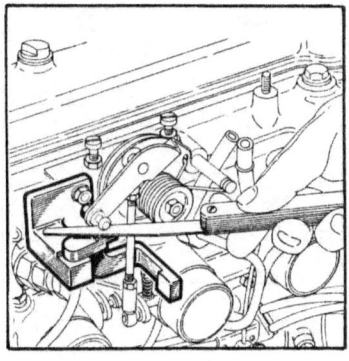

A.4.0121 Positioner, for throttle transmission lever minimum & maximum

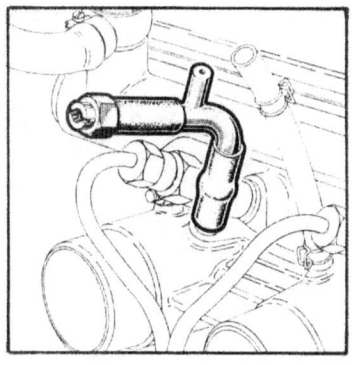

C.2.0012 Three-way union, for throttle alignment and minimum adjustment

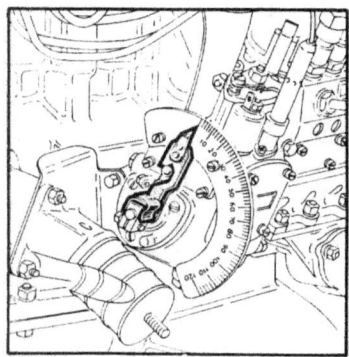

C.6.0141 Goniometer index, to fit on governor control

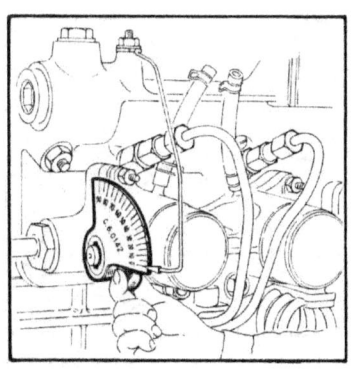

C.6.0142 Goniometer, for throttle shaft

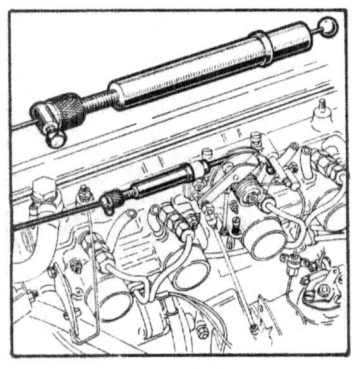

A.2.0181 Tool, throttle transmission hand driver

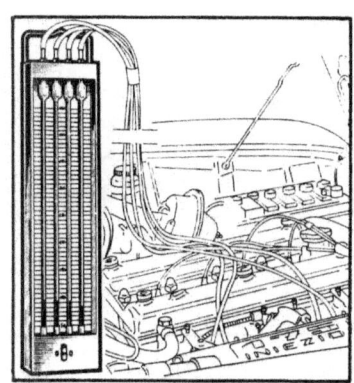

C.2.0014 Vacuometer, throttle alignment

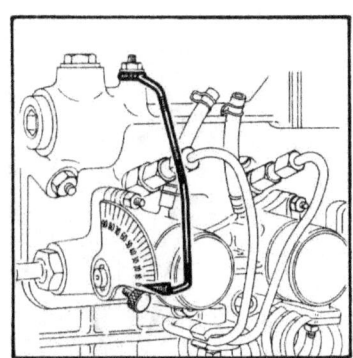

C.6.0143 Index, to fit on manifold, for throttle shaft goniometer

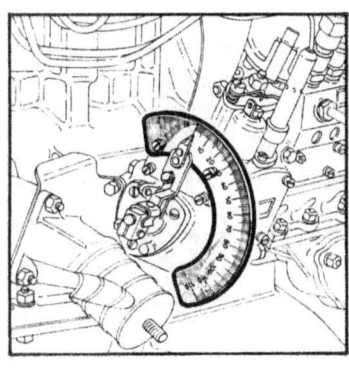

C.6.0140 Goniometer, governor control levers

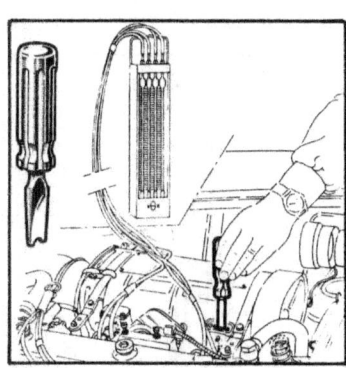

A.2.0183 Screwdriver, minimum screw adjustment

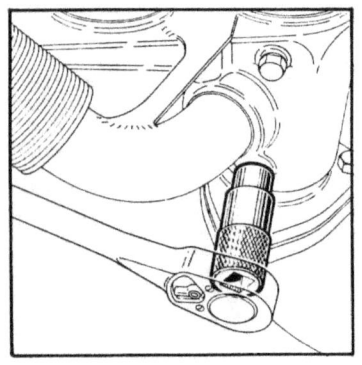

A.5.0212 Wrench, for exhaust gas intake screw on manifold

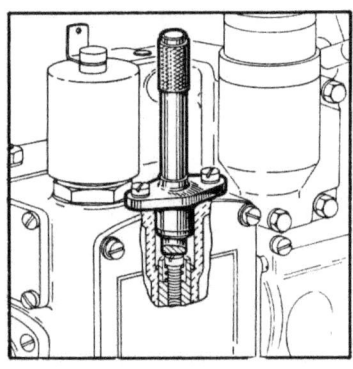

A.4.0159 Dummy thermostat, 19 mm

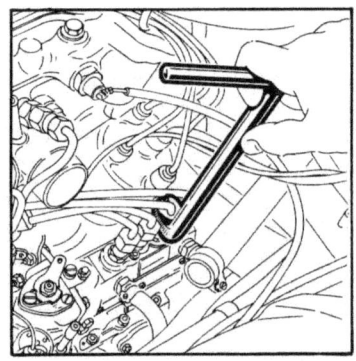

A.5.0164 Wrench, for injectors piping nuts

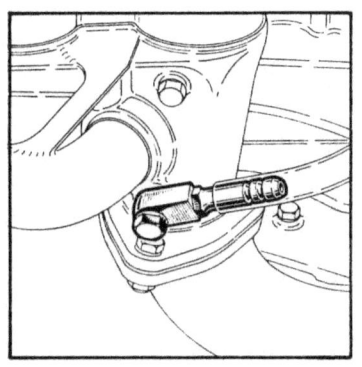

C.2.0051 Union, exhaust gas intake on manifold

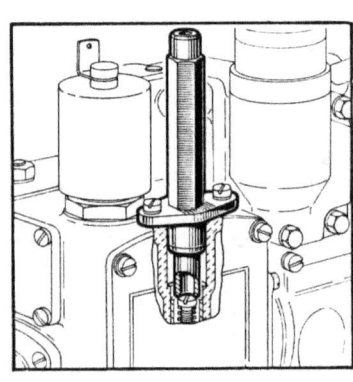

A.4.0166 Dummy thermostat, 27,8 mm

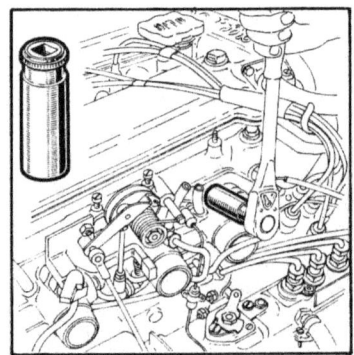

A.5.0165 Wrench, for injectors disassembling and assembling

A.5.0177 Wrench, for cut-out electromagnet ring nut

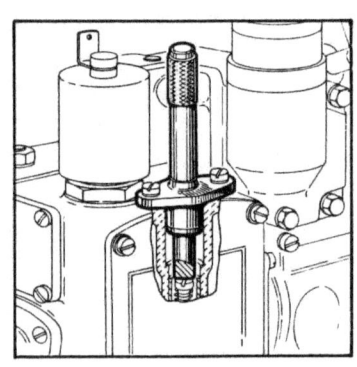

A.4.0120 Dummy thermostat, 29 mm

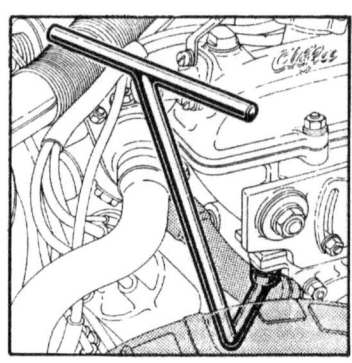

A.5.0214 Wrench, cylinder head front nuts fixing

A.5.0189 Wrench, chain stretcher screw

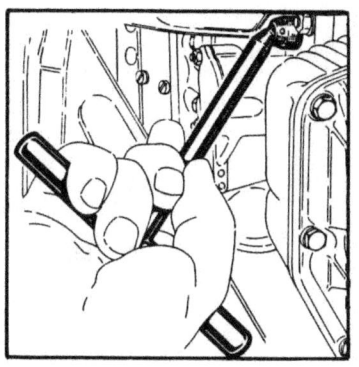

A.5.0167 Wrench, for pump nuts unlocking on crankcase

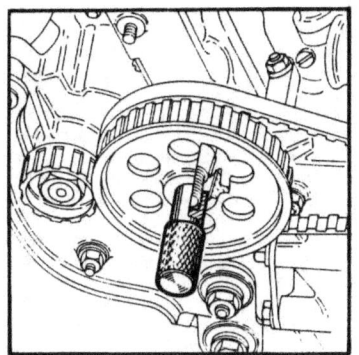

A.2.0308 Tool, injection pump pulley centering

A.5.0213 Wrench, distributor nut fixing

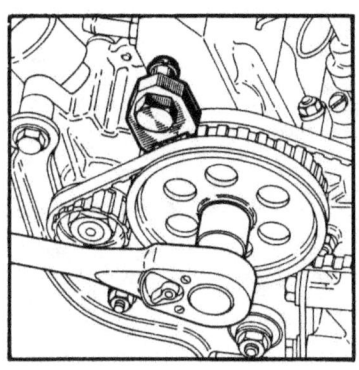

A.2.0142 Tool, injection pump pulley stop

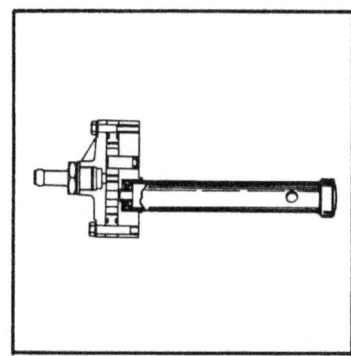

A.3.0476 Tool, oil pump seal in_serting (only for Spider cars)

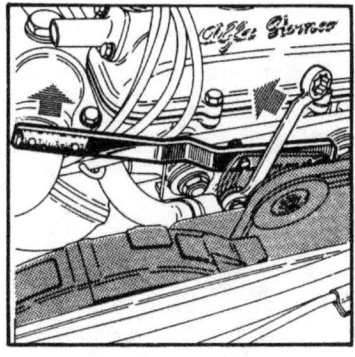

A.2.0305 Tool, air pump belt stretch adjustment

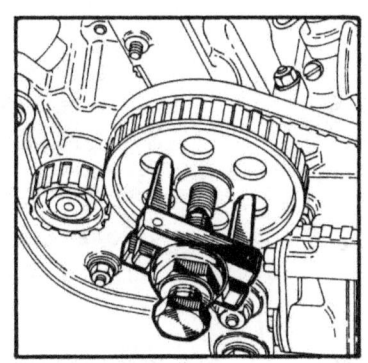

A.3.0510 Extractor, injection pump pulley

VELOCEPRESS MANUALS - MOTORCYCLE

1930'S BRITISH MOTORCYCLE CARBS & ELEC COMPONENTS (BOOK OF)
1930'S BRITISH MOTORCYCLE ENGINES (OVERHAUL & MAINTENANCE)
1930'S BRITISH MOTORCYCLE GEARBOXES & CLUTCHES (BOOK OF)
AJS 1932-1948 SINGLES & TWINS 250cc THRU 1000cc (BOOK OF)
AJS 1945-1960 SINGLES 350cc & 500cc MODELS 16 & 18 (BOOK OF)
AJS 1955-1965 SINGLES 350cc & 500cc (BOOK OF)
ARIEL 1932-1939 PREWAR MODELS (BOOK OF)
ARIEL 1933-1951 (WORKSHOP MANUAL)
ARIEL 1939-1960 4 STROKE SINGLES (BOOK OF)
ARIEL 1958-1964 LEADER & ARROW (BOOK OF)
BMW R26 R27 (1956-1967) FACTORY WORKSHOP MANUAL
BMW R50 R50S R60 R69S (1955-1969) FACTORY WORKSHOP MANUAL
BRIDGESTONE 90 SERIES FACTORY WSM & PARTS CATALOGUE
BRIDGESTONE 175 SERIES FACTORY WSM & PARTS CATALOGUE
BSA BANTAM ALL MODELS FROM 1948 ONWARDS (BOOK OF)
BSA SINGLES & V-TWINS UP TO 1927 (BOOK OF)
BSA SINGLES & V-TWINS UP TO 1935 (BOOK OF)
BSA SINGLES & V-TWINS 1936-1939 (BOOK OF)
BSA SINGLES & V-TWINS 1936-1952 (BOOK OF)
BSA OHV & SV SINGLES 250-600cc 1945-1954 (BOOK OF)
BSA OHV & SV SINGLES 250cc 1954-1970 (BOOK OF)
BSA OHV SINGLES 350 & 500cc 1955-1967 (BOOK OF)
BSA TWINS 1948-1962 (BOOK OF)
BSA TWINS 1962-1969 (SECOND BOOK OF)
CYCLEMOTOR (BOOK OF)
DOUGLAS 1929-1939 PREWAR ALL MODELS (BOOK OF)
DOUGLAS 1948-1957 POSTWAR ALL MODELS FACTORY SHOP MANUAL
DUCATI 160cc, 250cc & 350cc OHC MODELS FACTORY SHOP MANUAL
HONDA 50 ALL MODELS UP TO 1970 INC MONKEY & TRAIL (BOOK OF)
HONDA 90 ALL MODELS UP TO 1966 (BOOK OF)
HONDA 125-150cc TWINS C/CS/CB/CA FACTORY WORKSHOP MANUAL
HONDA 250-305 TWINS C/CS/CB FACTORY WORKSHOP MANUAL
HONDA C100 SUPER CUB FACTORY WORKSHOP MANUAL
HONDA C110 SPORT CUB 1962-1969 FACTORY WORKSHOP MANUAL
HONDA TWINS & SINGLES 50cc THRU 305cc 1960-1966 (BOOK OF)
HONDA TWINS ALL MODELS 125cc THRU 450cc UP TO 1968 (BOOK OF)
J.A.P. ENGINES 1927-1952 & MOTORCYCLES 1934-1952 (BOOK OF)
LAMBRETTA 1947-1957 ALL 125 & 150cc MODELS (BOOK OF)
LAMBRETTA 1957-1970 LI & TV MODELS (SECOND BOOK OF)
MATCHLESS 1931-1939 ALL MODELS 250cc THRU 990cc (BOOK OF)
MATCHLESS 1945-1956 350 & 500cc SINGLES (BOOK OF)
MATCHLESS 1955-1966 350 & 500cc SINGLES (BOOK OF)
NEW IMPERIAL ALL SV & OHV FROM 1935 ONWARDS (BOOK OF)
NORTON 1932-1939 PREWAR MODELS (BOOK OF)
NORTON 1932-1947 (BOOK OF)
NORTON 1938-1956 (BOOK OF)
NORTON 1955-1963 MODELS 19, 50 & ES2 (BOOK OF)
NORTON 1955-1965 DOMINATOR TWINS (BOOK OF)
NORTON 1957-1970 TWINS FACTORY WORKSHOP MANUAL
NSU PRIMA 1956-1964 ALL MODELS (BOOK OF)
NSU QUICKLY 1953-1963 ALL MODELS (BOOK OF)
PANTHER 1932-1958 LIGHTWEIGHT MODELS 250 & 350cc (BOOK OF)
PANTHER 1938-1966 HEAVYWEIGHT MODELS 600 & 650cc (BOOK OF)
RALEIGH MOPEDS 1960-1969 (BOOK OF)
RALEIGH MOTORCYCLES 1919-1933 (BOOK OF)
ROYAL ENFIELD 1934-1946 SINGLES & V TWINS (BOOK OF)
ROYAL ENFIELD 1937-1953 SINGLES & V TWINS (BOOK OF)
ROYAL ENFIELD 1946-1962 SINGLES (BOOK OF)
ROYAL ENFIELD 1958-1966 250cc & 350cc SINGLES (SECOND BOOK OF)
ROYAL ENFIELD 736cc INTERCEPTOR FACTORY WORKSHOP MANUAL
RUDGE 1933-1939 (BOOK OF)
SUNBEAM 1928-1939 (BOOK OF)
SUNBEAM 1946-1957 S7 & S8 (BOOK OF)
SUZUKI 50cc & 80cc UP TO 1966 (BOOK OF)
SUZUKI T10 1963-1967 FACTORY WORKSHOP MANUAL
SUZUKI T20 & T200 1965-1969 FACTORY WORKSHOP MANUAL
TRIUMPH 1935-1939 PREWAR MODELS (BOOK OF)
TRIUMPH 1935-1949 (BOOK OF)
TRIUMPH 1937-1951 (WORKSHOP MANUAL)
TRIUMPH 1945-1955 FACTORY WORKSHOP MANUAL
TRIUMPH 1945-1958 TWINS (BOOK OF)
TRIUMPH 1956-1969 TWINS (BOOK OF)
VELOCETTE 1925-1970 ALL SINGLES & TWINS (BOOK OF)
VESPA 1951-1961 (BOOK OF)
VESPA 1955-1963 125 & 150cc & GS MODELS (SECOND BOOK OF)
VESPA 1955-1968 GS & SS (BOOK OF)
VESPA 1963-1972 90, 125 & 150cc (THIRD BOOK OF)
VILLIERS ENGINE UP TO 1959 INC. 3 WHEELERS (BOOK OF)
VILLIERS ENGINE UP TO 1969 (BOOK OF)
VINCENT 1935-1955 (WORKSHOP MANUAL)

VELOCEPRESS TECHNICAL BOOKS – MOTORCYCLE

CATALOG OF BRITISH MOTORCYCLES (1951 MODELS)
INDIAN PONYBIKE, BOY RACER & PAPOOSE ILL PARTS LIST & SALES LIT
MOTORCYCLE ENGINEERING (P.E. Irving)
SPEED AND HOW TO OBTAIN IT (Motor Cycle Magazine UK)
TUNING FOR SPEED (P.E. Irving)

VELOCEPRESS MANUALS - THREE WHEELER'S

BSA THREE WHEELER (BOOK OF)
VINTAGE MORGAN THREE WHEELER (BOOK OF)

VELOCEPRESS MANUALS - AUTOMOBILE

ALFA ROMEO GIULIA WORKSHOP MANUAL 1300 TO 2000cc 1962-1975
ALFA ROMEO GIULIA TECH MANUAL CARBURETED CARS FROM 1962
ALFA ROMEO GIULIA TECH MANUAL FUEL INJECTED CARS FROM 1969
AUSTIN-HEALEY 6-CYLINDER WORKSHOP MANUAL
AUSTIN-HEALEY SPRITE & MG MIDGET WORKSHOP MANUAL 1958-1971
BMW 600 LIMOUSINE FACTORY WORKSHOP MANUAL
BMW 600 LIMOUSINE OWNERS HAND BOOK & SERVICE MANUAL
BMW 2000 & 2002 1966-1976 WORKSHOP MANUAL
BMW ISETTA FACTORY WORKSHOP MANUAL
CORVAIR 1960-1969 WORKSHOP MANUAL
CORVETTE V8 1955-1962 WORKSHOP MANUAL
FIAT 500 FACTORY WORKSHOP MANUAL 1957-1973
FIAT 600, 600D & MULTIPLA FACTORY WORKSHOP MANUAL 1955-1969
JAGUAR E-TYPE 3.8 & 4.2 SERIES 1 & 2 WORKSHOP MANUAL
JAGUAR MK 7, 8, 9 & XK120, 140, 150 WORKSHOP MANUAL 1948-1961
METROPOLITAN FACTORY WORKSHOP MANUAL
MGA & MGB OWNERS HANDBOOK & WORKSHOP MANUAL
MG MIDGET TC, TD, TF & TF1500 WORKSHOP MANUAL
PORSCHE 356 1948-1965 WORKSHOP MANUAL
PORSCHE 911 2.0, 2.2, 2.4 LITRE 1964-1973
PORSCHE 912 WORKSHOP MANUAL
TRIUMPH TR2, TR3, TR4 1953-1965 WORKSHOP MANUAL
VOLKSWAGEN TRANSPORTER, TRUCKS & WAGONS 1950-1979 WSM
VOLVO 1944-1968 ALL MODELS WORKSHOP MANUAL

VELOCEPRESS TECHNICAL BOOKS - AUTOMOBILE

FERRARI 250/GT SERVICE AND MAINTENANCE
FERRARI GUIDE TO PERFORMANCE
FERRARI OWNER'S HANDBOOK
FERRARI TUNING TIPS & MAINTENANCE TECHNIQUES
HOW TO BUILD A FIBERGLASS CAR
HOW TO BUILD A RACING CAR
HOW TO RESTORE THE MODEL 'A' FORD
MASERATI OWNER'S HANDBOOK
OBERT'S FIAT GUIDE
PERFORMANCE TUNING THE SUNBEAM TIGER
SOUPING THE VOLKSWAGEN
SOLEX CARBURETORS (EMPHASIS ON UK & EU AUTOMOBILES)
SU CARBURETORS (EMPHASIS ON UK AUTOMOBILES)
WEBER CARBURETORS (EMPHASIS ON ALFA & FIAT)

VELOCEPRESS BOOKS & GUIDES - AUTOMOBILE

ABARTH BUYERS GUIDE
COMPLETE CATALOG OF JAPANESE MOTOR VEHICLES
FERRARI 308 SERIES BUYER'S AND OWNER'S GUIDE
FERRARI BERLINETTA LUSSO
FERRARI BROCHURES AND SALES LITERATURE 1946-1967
FERRARI BROCHURES AND SALES LITERATURE 1968-1989
FERRARI OPP, MAINTENANCE & SERVICE H/BOOKS 1948-1963
FERRARI SERIAL NUMBERS PART I - ODD NUMBERS TO 21399
FERRARI SERIAL NUMBERS PART II - EVEN NUMBERS TO 1050
FERRARI SPYDER CALIFORNIA
HENRY'S FABULOUS MODEL "A" FORD
MASERATI BROCHURES AND SALES LITERATURE

VELOCEPRESS BOOKS – RACING

CARRERA PANAMERICANA - MEXICAN ROAD RACE (BOOK OF)
DIALED IN - THE JAN OPPERMAN STORY
IF HEMINGWAY HAD WRITTEN A RACING NOVEL
LE MANS 24 (THE BOOK THAT THE FILM WAS BASED ON)
VEDA ORR'S NEW REVISED HOT ROD PICTORIAL

AUTOBOOKS WORKSHOP MANUALS & BROOKLANDS ROAD TEST PORTFOLIOS

FOR A COMPLETE LISTING OF THE AUTOBOOKS & BROOKLANDS TITLES THAT WE CURRENTLY HAVE AVAILABLE, PLEASE VISIT OUR WEBSITE.

www.ingramcontent.com/pod-product-compliance
Lightning Source LLC
Chambersburg PA
CBHW060246240426
43673CB00047B/1885